# True Selves

# True Selves

## Understanding Transsexualism— For Families, Friends, Coworkers, and Helping Professionals

### Mildred L. Brown
### Chloe Ann Rounsley

Jossey-Bass Publishers • San Francisco

Substantial discounts on bulk quantities of Jossey-Bass books are available to corporations, professional associations, and other organizations. For details and discount information, contact the special sales department at Jossey-Bass Inc., Publishers.
(415) 433–1740; Fax (800) 605–2665

For sales outside the United States, please contact your local Simon & Schuster International Office.

Jossey-Bass Web address: http://www.josseybass.com

TCF Manufactured in the United States of America on Lyons Falls Turin Book. This paper is acid-free and 100 percent totally chlorine-free.

Library of Congress Cataloging-in-Publication Data

Brown, Mildred L., date.
    True selves: understanding transsexualism… : for families, friends, coworkers, and
      helping professionals / Mildred L. Brown, Chloe Ann Rounsley.—1st ed.
      p. cm.
    Includes bibliographical references and index.
    ISBN 0-7879-0271-3 (cloth : acid-free paper)
    1. Transsexualism—United States. 2. Transsexuals—United States. 3. Sex change—
United States. I. Rounsley, Chloe Ann, date. II. Title
HQ77.9.B76 1996
305.3—dc20                                                   96–10107

HB Printing           10 9 8 7 6 5 4 3

# Contents

This book is dedicated to all transsexuals everywhere and to their families, friends, and coworkers who have courageously risen to meet the challenges and rigors of first accepting and then adjusting to transsexualism

# Preface

What is life like for transsexuals? What can they do about their gender incongruity? Where do they and their families turn for help in coping with transsexualism? How do medical and mental health professionals learn more about the transsexual phenomenon in order to fulfill their role as caregivers for their transsexual patients?

These were some of the questions that came up for me eighteen years ago when I had my first personal, rather than professional, encounter with a person with gender identity problems. Until that time, as a clinical sexologist, I had planned on a career of helping individuals and couples work through sex and intimacy problems. But my direction changed after an experience that occurred while I was attending a weeklong sexuality workshop in San Francisco.

At the workshop, I became friendly with another attendee named Nick. He and I had many long conversations and really got to know each other—or so I thought.

On the last day, I got to class early, and only a few other people had arrived. One of them was an attractively dressed woman I had not seen before.

"May I help you?" I asked, puzzled, since the workshop was almost over and was closed to outsiders.

"Millie, don't you recognize me? It's me, Nick." I was amazed. What was Nick doing in a dress? Despite my professional training, seeing him that way really startled me. Suddenly, I didn't know what to say or do, and I had trouble making eye contact with him. For this to happen to me, a sexologist, was incomprehensible. The intellectual understanding I had gained at school from books, lectures, and doing term papers on gender identity didn't help when it came to handling the emotional aspects of a situation involving someone I knew personally.

I realized that it was not enough to study gender in the abstract or to understand it from a distance. It took on a different significance when someone I knew and cared about was gender conflicted. I realized that I needed to explore this subject further.

I asked Nick to meet me after class so that we could talk privately. I was ashamed about my flustered behavior and felt that I owed him an explanation. I admitted that there was much more I needed to learn about transgender issues and asked him to help me. He did. Later that week, he took me to a meeting of the only support group in the Bay Area at that time for people who had gender conflicts.

At that meeting, I saw a level of emotional pain greater than I had previously imagined possible. After listening to one individual after another share heartbreaking stories, I was overwhelmed. "My God," I said, "where do you all go for help? Who works with you?" They said they had no one. My heart went out to them. That night, I decided to dedicate myself to working with this special group of people.

I explained that I was completing my doctoral degree and clinical training in sexology and as yet had not worked with transsexuals but that I was willing to work with them if they were willing to teach me the special problems associated with their condition. They were. Three of them immediately took me under their wing, and I took them under mine. I gave them therapy, and they gave me their life experiences. They shared their anguish, their conflicts, their fears and confusion—along with their hopes and dreams for the future.

As I listened to their stories, I realized that an open mind and an open heart were prerequisites to truly understanding the transsexual phenomenon. Facts and intellectual awareness alone were not enough. The importance of the *human element*—looking at each individual as a human being who also happens to be transsexual—was one of the first important lessons I learned. I saw that one reason for my intense reaction to seeing Nick in a dress was that I had been operating primarily on the intellectual level rather than on the human level.

Now, after working with transsexuals and their families for nearly two decades, I would like to share what I have learned about transsexualism and transsexuals—not only from a clinical perspective but also from a human one.

For years, I wanted to find a way to translate the knowledge gleaned from my years of working in this field but I was not sure how to do it. I'm a therapist, not a writer. But the time was finally right in July 1994 when I met my coauthor, Chloe Rounsley, a Bay Area writer and journalist. Chloe contacted me regarding a feature article she was writing about one of my patients, a transsexual engineer who had just gone public at a large Silicon Valley corporation. After a one-month leave of absence, "he" was returning to work to begin a new life as a woman.

Awed by such courage and fascinated with the impact that such a transition would have on the transsexual, on family members, and on several thousand coworkers, Chloe began researching the subject. After interviewing transsexuals and reading all the books on the subject that she could get her hands on, she wanted to talk to experts in the field. I was one of the people she called.

When I read Chloe's sensitively written article in the *San Francisco Chronicle* a few weeks later, I felt that she had not only accurately presented the facts but had also captured the human aspect of the subject. I decided that we would make a good team and that together we could make this book a reality. I figured if Chloe could turn the facts, insights, and expertise gained from my years as a therapist into prose, we would have an effective book. We began our work.

---

The experiences described in this book are representative of transsexuals everywhere, although the transsexual journey itself is different for everyone involved. We hope that within these pages, you will find passages that speak directly to you.

We would like to thank all the patients, both current and past, for sharing their experiences and stories. Most of them emerged victorious and moved on to better lives and happier relationships.

With love, hope, and compassion, all things are possible.

We would also like to extend our heartfelt gratitude to our own families, loved ones, and friends for all their help, patience, and understanding while this book was in progress. A very special thank you goes to Bernie Brown and Chris Wisner, who not only put up with us during the sometimes seemingly endless time we were writing the book, but also helped keep us sane. Without their help, support, and encouragement, *True Selves* would not have been possible.

*San Francisco*                                          Mildred L. Brown, Ph.D.
*July 1996*                                              Chloe Ann Rounsley

# True Selves

# Introduction:
# A Question of Gender

Our own sense of being male or female is something that most of us take for granted. We don't wonder about it; we don't even consider it. If we have a male body, we feel male and think of ourselves as male. If we have a female body, we feel female and think of ourselves as female. But this is not the case for transsexuals.

Transsexuals don't take anything about their minds or bodies for granted. Something that the rest of us pay no attention to at all dominates their lives. They have a mind/body conflict; they self-identify as one sex but have the body of the opposite sex. Because this incongruity causes considerable confusion, frustration, and anguish, at some point most transsexuals feel compelled to do something to resolve their conflict so as to be able to live full and satisfying lives.

Even though transsexualism is not a recent phenomenon, it has long been a subject shrouded in mystery, myth, and misinformation. As a result, a climate of fear, negativity, and sensationalism has prevailed, and many transsexuals have chosen to live a double life rather than risk possible ridicule, rejection, and alienation from family, friends, employers, and society in general.

Although more transsexuals than ever before are revealing their condition, a serious information gap remains. Most of the literature about transsexualism to date has been autobiographical, medical, or scientific. The technical books are not readily available to laypeople, and they do not address the more human elements of transsexualism. Moreover, the pamphlets and books written by transsexuals, though useful, are not in wide circulation. For years, my patients and I searched in vain for materials that would help them communicate the transsexual experience to the people close to them.

As a clinical sexologist and therapist specializing in gender identity for more than eighteen years, I promised my patients that I would help fill this gap in the existing literature. *True Selves: Understanding Transsexualism—For Families, Friends, Coworkers, and Helping Professionals* is based on my experience working with more than four hundred transsexuals and their families.

The main purpose of this book is to provide practical information about transsexualism for laypeople, but it is also intended as a resource for physicians, counselors, and therapists. The book's primary goals are to

- Provide information to help friends, family, and helping professionals understand the transsexual experience and related personal and therapeutic issues
- Provide guidance to help family members and friends cope during the difficult adjustment period
- Separate fact from fiction regarding transsexualism

Although many dedicated professionals in the fields of medicine, science, psychology, and sexology have spent years studying and treating transsexuals, many aspects of transsexualism remain controversial. Its cause, methods of therapy, types of treatment, and the appropriateness of surgery are just a few. This book was not designed to present the full range of theories about transsexualism or to propose a single course of action or treatment. Rather, it was written to provide an overview of the transsexual experience.

Though experts believe that transsexuals make up less than 1 percent of the population, transsexualism has profound and far-reaching effects, extending well beyond a transsexual's inner circle of family and friends to the work environment, the medical and mental health professions, and society as a whole.

*True Selves* covers the vital aspects of transsexualism in this broader social context. Chapter One addresses the transsexual dilemma and provides basic background information about transsexuals and how they differ from other segments of the population. It also includes a discussion of theories of causation and provides a historical perspective. Chapters Two, Three, and Four convey the confusion and conflicts characteristic of transsexuals' childhood, teen, and adult years, respectively. Chapter Five presents the most common issues in therapy for transsexuals and covers the time period from when they first seek therapy through their journey of self-exploration, right up to the time when they come out to themselves and prepare to go public about their condition to family and friends. Chapter Six explores the psychological and physical aspects of transition, and how transsexuals go about restructuring their formal identity as the opposite gender. Chapters Seven and Eight focus on the important places where the transition takes place—in the workplace and in the family. Chapter Nine describes medical and surgical interventions that many transsexuals undergo. Chapter Ten breaks down common misconceptions about transsexualism and offers practical suggestions on what you can do to help yourself and the transsexual person in your life. In Chapter Eleven, writings and poems by transsexuals provide an intimate glimpse into the transsexual experience. The Resource Guide at the back of the book provides the names and addresses of organizations, support groups, hot lines, and computer bulletin boards.

---

The information in this book is based not only on my own experience with patients and their families over the years but also on an ongoing review of the literature and of knowledge gained from attending professional seminars and conferences on gender identity.

No simple formula can unravel the complexities of transsexualism. Every transsexual and his or her situation is different. The patients I see in my Silicon Valley–based private practice are primarily white, middle-class, educated, and employed individuals. They may differ in social and economic circumstances from the unemployed or indigent transsexual patients usually seen by therapists at social service agencies and county clinics. However, despite socioeconomic, racial, or geographic differences, most transsexuals struggle with similar inner turmoil and conflicts as they grow up, and share many common experiences, problems, and concerns.

To ensure confidentiality, the names of specific patients have been changed, but all situations and quotations have been drawn directly from patients' real-life experiences. Because common threads run through their stories, some case studies are composites of more than one patient.

Though there are many ways of handling any individual or family dilemma or crisis, the objective of this book is to take a human approach to the transsexual phenomenon. We hope it will serve you well on your path toward understanding transsexualism.

# 1

## The Transsexual Dilemma

What would you do if your daughter came to visit one day and confided her deepest, darkest secret: "All my life, I've felt like I was a boy instead of a girl."

Or imagine your reaction if your best friend, a twice-married ex–football player, announced over lunch one afternoon: "I have something to tell you. I'm planning to have sex reassignment surgery to become a woman."

And how would you respond if someone you had worked with for several years sent the following memo to everyone in the company: "Dear friends and colleagues: . . . This is to let you know that I am a transsexual."

When transsexuals summon up the courage and reveal their secret, most people are shocked by the revelation. Typically, they are caught off-guard and don't know how to react or what to say. The news is especially hard for family members and close friends to accept—they are usually profoundly confused and distressed when they find out, or may even get angry. Someone they care about and think they know intimately has dramatically changed, or so it seems. The old rules no longer apply. Long-established expectations and patterns of relating are challenged. Often they feel that their trust in the transsexual has been threatened, and the whole relationship may be viewed differently. "How could something like this happen all of a sudden?" they are likely to ask.

Coworkers are usually astonished to discover that someone they see nearly every day has managed to keep such a monumental secret. Typically, they wonder, "How could transsexuals even consider questioning, let alone changing, something so elemental, so intrinsic, so *obvious* as their sex? People change their cars, clothes, or eating habits. They change their jobs, spouses, or lifestyles—but they don't just go and change their sex. . . . Do they?"

Transsexualism is a complex and confusing phenomenon. Frequently, the general public's perception of transsexualism comes from movies or talk shows and contains only fragments of truth. People may harbor the false notion that transsexualism is a mental illness or a sexual perversion. Or they may confuse transsexuals with homosexuals, lesbians, transvestites, drag queens, she-males, female impersonators, and gender benders, even though there are significant differences among them.

Sometimes, even therapists and counselors may not have a clear understanding of the transsexual condition, especially if they have never had a transsexual patient. They may be uncertain of the best way to offer professional guidance.

The rest of this chapter will provide definitions and information to clarify the confusion.

## What Is a Transsexual?

Transsexuals are individuals who strongly feel that they are, or ought to be, the opposite sex. The body they were born with does not match their own inner conviction and mental image of who they are or want to be. Nor are they comfortable with the gender role society expects them to play based on that body. This dilemma causes them intense emotional distress and anxiety and often interferes with their day-to-day functioning.

Transsexuals frequently report that they feel trapped—destined to live out their lives "imprisoned in the wrong body" unless they correct the situation with hormones or sex reassignment surgery (SRS), formerly referred to as a "sex change operation." Most of my transsexual patients were painfully aware of their gender incongruity from early childhood, although some did not fully acknowledge it until they reached puberty or adulthood. This incongruity between mind and body is referred to in medical literature as transsexualism, gender dysphoria, and also more recently as gender identity disorder (GID).

The fourth edition of the *Diagnostic and Statistical Manual* of the American Psychiatric Association, a reference book used by psychiatrists and other mental health practitioners (often called simply DSM-IV), lists the following among the criteria for diagnosing individuals with gender identity disorders:

- A strong and persistent cross-gender identification, manifested by a repeatedly stated desire to be, live as, or be treated as the other sex or by the conviction that the person has the typical feelings or reactions of the other sex. Children may insist that they *are* the opposite sex and exhibit a strong preference for clothing, games, and pastimes that are stereotypically associated with the other sex.

- A persistent discomfort with their bodies, with boys often feeling disgust for their penis and expressing a desire for it to disappear and girls rejecting urinating in a sitting position, not wanting to grow breasts or menstruate, and asserting that they will grow a penis. Adolescents and adults exhibit a preoccupation with physically altering their bodies through hormones and surgery to simulate the other sex, usually because they believe that they were born the wrong sex.

- The disturbance causes significant distress in social, occupational, or other important areas of functioning.

It is important to keep in mind that the DSM criteria (and other criteria that mental health professionals may use) are merely diagnostic guidelines. Individuals exhibiting one or more of these characteristics are not necessarily transsexuals. An accurate diagnosis of transsexualism requires an intensive evaluation of each individual's case by a skilled and knowledgeable clinician who considers a wide range of psychological and social factors.

Although the listed criteria are frequently components of transsexualism, they are not characteristic of *every* transsexual. Most transsexuals share similar difficulties regarding their gender incongruity and often report similar life experiences as a result of their condition, but they are by no means all cut from the same cloth. *There is no such thing as a "typical" transsexual.* Transsexualism knows no boundaries; it affects people of every race, religion, and socioeconomic class and exists in every country of the world.

*Transsexual* is sometimes abbreviated TS, and transsexuals sometimes refer to themselves as "TSs" or "Ts." Individuals who were born male but self-identify as female commonly refer to themselves as male-to-female transsexuals, or "MTFs." Individuals who were born female but self-identify as male commonly refer to themselves as female-to-male transsexuals, or "FTMs."

## Prevalence of Transsexualism

It is difficult to determine the prevalence of transsexualism accurately because it is a relatively rare phenomenon, and far less research has been devoted to it than to more widespread conditions. Moreover, there are currently no reliable methods for gathering accurate statistics in the United States. Unlike some European countries, America does not have a national registry to collect information from gender clinics, mental health facilities, hospitals, and private physicians, and even if there were a central reporting system, there would still be transsexuals who would remain unreported. For example, the system would not take into account transsexuals who are confused or undiagnosed or who for whatever reasons remain "closeted" or do not seek any kind of therapy, hormone treatments, or surgery. There would also be no way to track transsexuals who go to foreign countries for sex reassignment surgery to take advantage of considerably lower surgical fees.

We do know that data from smaller countries in Europe with access to total population statistics and referrals suggest that roughly 1 per 30,000 adult males and 1 per 100,000 adult females seek sex reassignment surgery. This means that in Europe, less than 0.01 percent of the population in those countries is transsexual (using sex reassignment surgery as the sole indicator). In the United States, an estimated 6,000 to 10,000 transsexuals had undergone SRS by 1988. Taking the U.S. population in 1988 as approximately 244 million, the percentage of transsexuals who had SRS was much less than 0.01 percent.

Again, it is important to keep in mind that these figures do not include all of the transsexuals who, for whatever reasons, did not seek surgery. Experts say that it is reasonable to assume that there are scores of unoperated cases for every operated one.

## Ratio of MTFs to FTMs

Contrary to long-standing popular belief, transsexualism is not an exclusively male phenomenon. Dr. Wardell Pomeroy, a pioneer in the field of sexology, reported an MTF-to-FTM ratio as high as 50 to 1 at one time but later noted a sharp reduction to 15 to 1 and then to 4 to 1 by 1975.

Although there is currently disagreement about what the exact ratio is and why, the gap appears to have narrowed even more. Some gender clinics and therapists report the MTF-to-FTM ratio to be 3 to 2; others report seeing an equal number of male and female transsexuals; still other clinics indicate that they sometimes see even more FTMs than MTFs. The ratio appears, in some cases, to be influenced by the specialization and reputation of the gender clinic, surgeon, or therapist and to be fluid and cyclical.

My own practice bears this out. Within the past five years, the MTF-to-FTM ratio has fluctuated from as high as 20 to 1 at some times to 3 to 1 at others.

A higher ratio of male-to-female transsexuals than female-to-male transsexuals may be related to the problems associated with the female-to-male surgical sex reassignment procedures. For FTMs, at least three surgeries are required, whereas MTFs generally require only one. FTM surgeries often leave disfiguring scars, whereas MTF surgeries do not, unless skin grafts are required. The FTM surgeries are also much more expensive, and historically the results have not been as good aesthetically or functionally.

Moreover, female-to-male transsexuals may simply be underreported. Since women in the United States have far more flexibility with regard to clothing and demeanor than men do, female-to-male transsexuals are able to cross-dress (wear the clothing of the opposite gender) without attracting as much attention as their cross-dressed male-to-female counterparts. They can blend more easily into society without hormones or surgery and are sometimes mistaken for masculine-looking women or feminine-looking men.

## Gender Dysphoria: The Invisible Handicap

Many transsexuals feel that they are the victims of a handicap that clouds every aspect of their lives and causes them such severe emotional pain that it interferes with their day-to-day functioning. Yet even though they are affected in such a significant way, no one else is aware of what they are going through. Their handicap, which revolves around their gender identity, is an internal struggle that is invisible to others. Transsexuals are usually reluctant to talk about their condition because they fear they will be considered crazy. Consequently, many internalize their conflict and feelings and often become moody, withdrawn, and despondent.

Gender dysphoria (dysphoria is derived from a Greek word meaning "hard to bear") is a term often used as a synonym for transsexualism. The term also refers to the emotional anguish, dissatisfaction, and discomfort that transsexuals (and, less commonly, other transgendered individuals) experience about their gender. However, anatomical dysphoria may actually be a more appropriate term because the discomfort and anxiety that transsexuals experience is less with their gender identity and more with their physical body, especially their genitalia.

Most of my patients tell me that they hate to look at their body in the mirror, especially from the neck down. They feel detached from it; it's not the right body. It contradicts what they feel inside. Female-to-male transsexuals are usually very uncomfortable with their breasts, their curves, and the soft appearance of their body, and male-to-female transsexuals are usually very uncomfortable with their muscles, their hairiness, and their male physique in general. One patient despised his body to such a degree that he only showered at night, in the dark.

In cases where the gender dysphoria is extreme, it is not uncommon for transsexuals to turn to suicide or self-mutilation. The tendency toward both runs disproportionately high among the transsexual population. Estimates of attempted suicide by transsexuals range from 17 percent to 20 percent.

To escape their pain and to express themselves honestly as their true selves, some transsexuals cross-dress and live in the world as the gender that matches their inner identity. But for the majority, cross-dressing alone is not enough, and they turn to hormone treatment and sex reassignment surgery. Transsexuals seek to change their physical body because we have not found an effective way to alter the mind to match the body. Over the years, transsexuals have undergone all kinds of mental health treatment including daily psychoanalysis, hypnosis, aversion therapy, and even shock therapy. Yet there has been little, if any, change in their internal feelings.

For this reason, most therapists trained in treating patients with gender identity disorders now work toward helping transsexual patients realistically examine their life options and make healthy choices—which are different for everyone—rather than trying to change or "cure" a medical condition over which patients have no control. Transsexualism is not a choice—a topic that we will address in more detail later in the book.

## Confusion About Terminology

We have already defined the terms *transsexual* and *gender dysphoria*. But there is a great deal of confusion about how male-to-female transsexuals differ from *intersexed individuals, transvestites, homosexuals, drag queens, she-males, female impersonators,* and *gender benders.* Likewise, female-to-male transsexuals are often confused with *lesbians, female transvestites,* and *gender benders.* To help clear up the confusion, let us clarify these various terms and a few others that will recur throughout the book.

## Intersexed Individuals

Intersexed individuals (formerly referred to as "hermaphrodites") are born with both ovarian and testicular tissue (either fully or partially developed). Some also have some obvious physical abnormality or ambiguity at the time of birth involving the external sex organs. Parents or physicians are often placed in the difficult position of having to make an arbitrary decision as to the sex of the infant. Sometimes parents elect to have the ambiguity corrected by genital surgery. In cases where either the "assigned" sex or the surgically corrected genitalia do not match the child's gender identity, the individual will likely be gender dysphoric and, like transsexuals, will often seek sex reassignment surgery.

## Transvestites

Transvestites, or cross-dressers, are individuals who wear clothing of the opposite gender primarily for erotic arousal or sexual gratification, although some do so for emotional or psychological reasons as well, especially as they get older. Because the overwhelming majority of transvestites are men, we'll focus on them first.

Typically, transvestites are heterosexual, married, and well-educated males. Some of them may have sexual fantasies about being female (and a few may even take small doses of estrogen for feminization), but transvestites have a male gender identity, enjoy their male bodies, including their genitals, and have no desire to change their sex.

Cross-dressing typically begins at puberty and may continue throughout a transvestite's lifetime. During puberty and the teen years, cross-dressing for males has a strong sexual component. Such boys generally become sexually aroused by wearing one or more articles of women's clothing (which they usually "borrow" from their mother, a sister, or any other female who happens to live in the household) and typically masturbate while wearing these garments.

For some, the sexual component to cross-dressing remains firmly fixed throughout their lives. For others, the sexual arousal disappears as they get older or becomes secondary to a sense of comfort, relaxation, or well-being when they cross-dress. Some transvestites report that cross-dressing allows them to express a more feminine side, a "second self," or a softer, more emotional side. While some say that cross-dressing is calming and releases them from the pressures inherent in society's rigid stereotypical expectations about the male role, others report that it makes them feel exhilarated or "more alive."

The extent, frequency, and visibility of cross-dressing differs widely. Some males wear only one item of female clothing (for example, panties or hosiery) either in a fetishistic way (that is, because it brings on sexual arousal) or as a garment under their male clothes, while others dress from head to toe in female clothing, including makeup and wigs.

Transvestism can run the gamut from mere dabbling to full-time preoccupation. Whereas some transvestites cross-dress only occasionally, others do so on a daily basis and adopt a female name and persona. Many transvestites are able to compartmentalize their "female side" so successfully that they exhibit no hint of femininity while in the male role.

Some transvestites cross-dress only in the privacy of their home or a hotel room, while others enjoy a very public, exhibitionistic cross-dressing life. Transvestites are often narcissistic and revel in drawing attention to themselves, being seen, preening in front of the mirror, and having their picture taken.

Transvestism is far less prevalent among women than men—some researchers believe that there are thousands of male transvestites to every one female transvestite—but the reasons for this disparity are not entirely clear. Because of their scarce numbers, there has been far less research done on female transvestites and less information compiled about them than about their male counterparts. It has been speculated that women may have less reason to cross-dress. Because society is far less rigid about female clothing standards, women can wear masculine-looking clothes or actual male attire without attracting much attention.

Female transvestites may wear one item of male clothing (for example, undershorts) or may don an entirely male outfit. Although they enjoy wearing male attire, they have a female gender identity and, like their male counterparts, have no desire to change their sex.

The major difference between male and female transvestites is the underlying motivation for cross-dressing. Whereas male cross-dressing is generally associated with fetishism—sexual arousal elicited by an inanimate object such as lingerie or shoes—this is not the case for female cross-dressing. Experts believe that because women almost never have fetishistic tendencies, there is little or no erotic component to cross-dressing for female transvestites. Instead, according to the female cross-dressers I've worked with, their cross-dressing emanates from a desire to embrace and experience male power and status and what is perceived to be male privilege.

It is also possible that female transvestites, like female transsexuals, may be underreported. Much more research is necessary regarding female transvestism before we can draw more conclusive answers.

*Transvestite* is sometimes abbreviated TV, and transvestites sometimes refer to themselves as "TVs."

## Homosexuals and Lesbians

Homosexual men (who often refer to themselves as "gay") and lesbian women are individuals who are sexually and emotionally attracted to members of their own anatomical sex. Homosexuality, like heterosexuality, is a sexual *orientation* and should not be confused with a gender identity disorder like transsexualism. Although homosexuality has long been regarded by the general public as a sexual "preference" or "choice," more and more experts are beginning to believe that, as with transsexualism, a genetic component is involved.

Some gay males are effeminate in appearance, dress, and mannerisms. These individuals are sometimes referred to as "queens." And some lesbians who are very masculine in their appearance, dress, and mannerisms are sometimes referred to as "butch lesbians."

However, homosexual men self-identify as male, and lesbians self-identify as female. Both view their bodies as being appropriate to their gender identity and do not wish to have surgery to change their sex.

## Drag Queens

Drag queens are homosexual cross-dressers who don female clothing for their own erotic and sexual pleasure or for that of partners who are attracted to female *presentation* in a male. Drag queens don't aspire to *be* females, and their partners don't want anatomical females—both value their own and their partner's maleness. Drag queens self-identify as male, view their bodies as appropriate to their gender identity, and do not wish to have sex reassignment surgery.

Drag queens generally take a more theatrical or "camp" approach to cross-dressing than transvestites, often affecting exaggerated and pronounced female patterns of speech, movement, gestures, and attire. They cross-dress primarily for show, enjoy being seen in their role, and relish the effect their presentation has on others. Many drag queens dress androgynously during the day (or lean only slightly toward the feminine side) but enjoy the nightlife circuit dressed in full drag regalia.

Although some experts believe that drag queens make up only 5 percent of the total gay population, their flamboyance often makes them more visible than other members of the gay community, thereby precipitating the common misconception that all gay men like to wear female clothing. This is, of course, not true.

The usage of the word *drag* dates back to early theater days when women were not permitted to perform on stage because it was not considered ladylike. Consequently, all roles were played by male actors. Though precise origin of the word is unknown, *in drag* (which probably meant "in costume") evolved as a way to designate men who played female roles and donned female garb on stage. Some say that it referred to the long, flowing, feminine gowns that dragged on the floor; others believe it to be a reference to the heavy trunks of costumes that had to be dragged from place to place; and still others speculate that the word was an acronym for "dressed as a girl" (DRAG).

## She-Males

She-males are men, often involved in prostitution, pornography, or the adult entertainment industry, who have undergone breast augmentation but have retained their male genitalia. She-males may make their living based on the dual nature of their hormonally or surgically altered bodies. Typically, they are distinguished by flamboyant feminine attire, makeup, and hair styling while signaling an unmistakable male body beneath the costume. Their dramatic dress and appearance serve as advertising to potential "dates" and also as a way to feel more attractive.

Some she-males choose to alter their bodies for commercial reasons and others because the image of the duality of their bodies is sexually arousing to them. These men are less likely to pursue surgical sex reassignment than gender dysphoric men whose erotic self-image includes a vagina.

## Female Impersonators

Female impersonators are males who wear female apparel to entertain a theater audience. They take great care with makeup, hair, speech, and mannerisms in order to present as flawless an imitation of a female as possible. Often they impersonate well-known female singers, actresses, and comediennes. Song and dance are often a prominent part of the show, and female impersonators either sing or lip-sync to recorded music.

A female impersonator may be a homosexual male, a bisexual male, or a heterosexual male. Most are drag queens, some are transvestites (who may or may not cross-dress offstage), and only a few are transsexuals. Only female impersonators who are also preoperative transsexuals desire sex reassignment surgery.

This type of cross-dressing is primarily an acting job, a stage performance that dates back to the early days of theater in Greece, Rome, England, China, Japan, and other parts of the world.

There are also male impersonators. In Japan, for example, female theater stars called *otoko-yaku* sing, dance, and perform in male roles to sellout crowds. These women are said by some to be among the most beautiful, elegant, and romantic "men" in Japan, even though they are really women.

## Gender Benders

Gender benders are males or females who challenge and cross traditional gender boundaries, often in outrageous ways. They dress and behave to surprise or shock. An example is men who wear dresses but have full beards. Some male and female rock stars are gender benders, at least while they are performing.

Gender bending is usually done to entertain, for dramatic effect, to get attention, or simply to break away from the limits of traditional clothing and demeanor. Some gender benders consider cross-dressing and cross-gender behavior an act of rebellion or a political statement—their way of telling society that they refuse to be governed by stereotypical clothing, presentation, or gender roles. Gender benders do not, however, desire surgery to change their sex.

## Transgendered Individuals

There are two common definitions for the term *transgendered*. The first refers to transsexuals who choose to live in the world as the opposite gender on a full-time basis but do not wish to undergo sex reassignment surgery. The second and more general definition (the one we will use in this book) is as an umbrella term used to describe the full range of individuals who have a conflict with or question about their gender. This includes everyone from transsexuals who desire surgery, those who have no desire to have surgery, and post-operative transsexuals to male and female transvestites, drag queens, female impersonators, male impersonators, gender benders, and people who are experiencing gender confusion but don't know exactly where they fall along the gender spectrum.

## The Motivation for Cross-Dressing

You have probably noticed by now that except for cross-dressing, transsexuals have little in common with any of the other transgendered individuals. Even though transsexual men and women dress in clothing traditionally associated with the other gender, their *motivation* is distinctly different from that of the other cross-dressers.

For transsexuals, cross-dressing is *not* about playfulness, eroticism, fetishism, exhibitionism, or show business. Nor is it about power and status. Transsexuals do not cross-dress as a form of rebellion or to make a political statement, nor do they do so to get attention or attract partners or, as was assumed in the medical literature of past decades, as a form of denial of a homosexual orientation.

Transsexuals dress in the attire of the other gender solely as an outward expression of their core identity. Male-to-female transsexuals feel female and therefore find that dressing in women's garments feels natural, comfortable, and gender-appropriate. The same is true for female-to-male transsexuals who wear men's clothing.

## It's Not About Sexual Orientation

A common misconception about transsexuality is that it is one and the same as homosexuality (particularly in the case of MTFs). Perhaps confusion exists because some gay males exhibit effeminate behaviors (or wear female clothing, as in the case of drag queens), and there is a tendency to confuse effeminacy with femaleness. A similar misconception exists around FTMs and butch lesbians.

Though there may be similarities between homosexual and transsexual individuals in outward presentation, the distinguishing characteristic is that transsexuals' inner self-identification does not match their physical body, whereas gay individuals are attracted to sex partners with the same anatomy as their own. What we are dealing with here are two separate constructs: transsexuality concerns gender identity and homosexuality concerns sexual orientation.

Our *sexual orientation* is defined by the sex of the individuals to whom we are erotically and emotionally attracted. There are only three possible sexual orientations: heterosexual, homosexual, and bisexual. This is true for every human being—transsexual as well as nontranssexual. If we are attracted to members of the opposite sex, our sexual orientation is heterosexual; if we are attracted to members of the same sex, our sexual orientation is homosexual; and if we are attracted to members of both sexes, our sexual orientation is bisexual. Even individuals who are asexual or celibate have (or have had) sexual fantasies about members of the opposite sex, the same sex, or both.

It is important to distinguish further between sexual orientation, sexual behavior, and sexual fantasies. Whereas sexual orientation refers to which sex one is attracted, *sexual behavior* refers to the sexual activities or acts in which one engages. Kissing, masturbation, and oral sex are three examples in the wide range of possibilities for individuals of *all* sexual orientations. Furthermore, a person may choose a sexual partner who does not necessarily match his or her sexual fantasies. For example, a woman may be married to a man even though all of her sexual fantasies are about other women.

## It's Not About Sex

The terms *sex* and *gender* are typically used interchangeably in our culture today and in this book, but it's important to keep in mind that there are distinguishing characteristics between the two. *Sex* refers to the *biological* classification of being either male or female and is usually determined by the external genitalia. *Gender* refers to the culturally determined *behavioral, social,* and *psychological* traits that are typically associated with being male or female.

In the United States, as in most other countries, we live in a culture in which our sex—whether we are male or female—is presumed to be an absolute. When an infant is born, the doctor and parents look at the external genitalia and proclaim, "It's a boy" or "It's a girl," depending on whether they see a penis and scrotum or a vulva. From that moment on, the infant is treated in the culturally prescribed manner for a male or a female, as if genital anatomy were the sole indicator of sex. But determining an individual's sex is not that clear-cut.

From a sexological point of view, there are at least eight factors—five biological and three social and psychological—to be considered in determining sex. The biological determinants are *chromosomes, hormones, gonads (glands that produce sex hormones), internal sexual and reproductive organs*, and *external sex organs*. The social and psychological determinants are *gender of rearing, gender role*, and *gender identity*.

For most people, all eight factors are in perfect agreement. For example, someone born with male genitalia will have the chromosomal and hormonal makeup of a male and the gonads and internal sex organs that are consistent with male anatomy. Moreover, such persons will be reared as males, play the roles typical of males in our society, and self-identify as male.

For transsexuals, however, the eight factors are not in perfect agreement. The eighth, gender identity, is out of sync with the others. This is the crux of the transsexual dilemma.

## It's About Gender Identity

Transsexualism is not about sex, sexual behavior, or sexual orientation—it's about gender or, more specifically, gender identity.

## Gender

As indicated earlier, gender is a social construct used to distinguish between male and female, masculine and feminine. When we are born, our external genitalia determine whether we are male or female. As we grow up, we learn how to move, speak, dress, and behave in the way our culture deems appropriate for a male or a female (that is, we learn our gender role). Thus, when we meet a stranger we mentally attribute a gender to the person based on a variety of arbitrary bodily and behavioral cues. These things are all part of the way society defines gender, and they can vary from one culture to another.

## Gender Identity

Gender identity, or psychological self-identification, by contrast, cannot be attributed by others. It is our own deeply held conviction and deeply felt inner awareness that we belong to one gender or the other. This awareness is firmly in place by the time we are five years old.

Gender identity is private and internal. It is felt, not seen. It is the only one of the eight factors that is totally subjective. It cannot be deduced from how a person looks, moves, dresses, or behaves, nor can it be determined by medical or psychological testing. *The only way to know a person's gender identity is if he or she tells you.*

For the overwhelming majority of people, their gender identity matches their body, but transsexuals are not so fortunate. Despite all physical evidence to the contrary, they do not perceive themselves as a member of their anatomical sex. Their mind and body are in opposition; one says female, the other says male. Much of this book will focus on describing the complex ramifications this vast incongruity has on the lives of transsexuals and the people around them.

## Theories About Causation

Naturally, there has been much speculation about what causes transsexualism. Are transsexuals born that way? Does the answer lie with biology—chromosomes, hormones, physiology—or do social and cultural factors play the dominant role?

We don't really know for sure. Transsexualism is a complex phenomenon, and many different theories of causation have been proposed over the years. Though some may be applicable in certain cases, there is no agreement on any single determinant or trigger for transsexualism. Nonetheless, let's take a brief look at a few of the theories.

When scientists look at any human developmental or behavioral disorder, their arguments regarding causation usually come down to nature (heredity) versus nurture (environment) or some combination of the two. Theories about the underlying causes of transsexualism are no exception. There are well-respected proponents of all three schools of thought.

## Nature

Early researchers investigating the etiology (that is, origin) of transsexualism looked for biological causes. They found that while some transsexuals did have chromosomal, hormonal, and genital or reproductive organ irregularities, these were the exception rather than the rule, and that the average transsexual was remarkably similar to the average nontranssexual in these areas. This led investigators of the nature school to turn to other areas of human anatomy or physiology, especially the brain.

Many medical researchers favor a prenatal neurohormonal explanation for gender identity disorders and believe that gender is determined long before we are born. They look to the hypothalamus, the endocrine control or "gender identity control center" of the brain, for answers. They propose "a disturbed interaction between the developing brain and sex hormones." It is an established medical fact that it is not until the twelfth week in the prenatal cycle that the genitalia of the human embryo differentiate as either male or female. However, it is not until approximately the sixteenth week that the gender identity portion of the brain differentiates in the unborn child. Some researchers believe, therefore, that if certain hormones are not present or if there is a hormonal imbalance during this critical four-week period, gender identity may not develop or differentiate along the same lines as the genitalia. In those cases, the child may be more likely to be born gender dysphoric.

There are also theorists who believe that the mother's overall physical and mental health during pregnancy could have an effect on the unborn child's gender identity. For example, certain prescription drugs taken during pregnancy could interfere with fetal brain chemistry in unknown ways. Severe emotional trauma or extremely high stress levels could also be significant. Obviously, identifying such factors at a later date, determining if they occurred during the critical period, and establishing their effect on gender identity are difficult to do in a scientific manner.

Scientists have conducted electroencephalogram (EEG) tests on transsexuals and nontranssexuals to monitor brain wave activity to determine whether the results differ and, if so, how. Medical researchers have checked for lesions and irregularities in the brain. Currently, a northern California research team is employing magnetic resonance imaging (MRI) scans to investigate size differences of the midline white-matter structures connecting the cerebral hemispheres of the brain, with promising initial results. It is postulated that these differences could be related to differences in gender identity and cognition. In late 1995, a team of scientists from the Netherlands performed autopsies on six male-to-female transsexuals and found evidence that they had brain structures that were strikingly different from those of other men. In one key area of the hypothalamus called the BSTc, which is generally 44 percent larger in men than in women, all subjects had BSTc regions that were the size of women's. Although these results hold promise for finding a biological cause for transsexualism, it is important to note that these are just preliminary results based on a very small sample. Moreover, it is possible that these results could have been produced by the estrogen that these MTFs had been taking. Further research is necessary.

## Nurture

On the nurture side, theorists claim that gender identity is taught or is a product of early social learning rather than being established prenatally. They believe that the home environment and patterns of rearing have a powerful impact on early childhood developmental disorders, including those involving gender.

There are children who, in rare instances, are not raised according to their sex of assignment at birth. Whether their parents dress them in clothes of the opposite gender because they want a child of that gender or they treat the child that way as a form of punishment or humiliation, the outcome can be the same. If a young boy is repeatedly dressed in girls' clothing, is positively reinforced for all feminine behaviors, or is rejected or punished for all behaviors that are considered to be typically male, chances are very good that eventually he will learn to behave in a feminine manner. It is all part of the social learning process that occurs during early childhood. The same is true for young girls who are reinforced for male behaviors. However, although this kind of potentially damaging child rearing does occur, it is not the case for the average transsexual.

Some proponents believe that gender identity disorders may occur (or may be more likely to occur) when one or both of the parents are physically or emotionally absent from the home during the child's formative years. They cite cases where one parent had been abandoned, abused, or physically ill and called on the child to act as a substitute "wife" or "husband." Long-term depression and mental or emotional illness on the part of a parent may also have an effect on a child's development in a variety of areas, including gender identity.

Likewise, some psychoanalytical theories propose the classic "smothering, overbearing mother and weak, distant, or absent father" syndrome as an underlying cause for gender dysphoria. They suggest that when a mother is overprotective or engages in excessive physical contact with her young son, the child may begin to overidentify with her. Lack of a strong male role model may also have a negative effect on the development of normal gender identity. Thus, if the father is made to appear weak or powerless by his wife, eventually a male child may no longer wish to identify with his father. A female child may assume a protective "caretaker" role toward her mother in an attempt to compensate for the failures or weaknesses of her father.

As important as environmental factors may be, to date they have not given us any more conclusive answers for causation than hereditary influences have. While some transsexuals report coming from seriously dysfunctional families, many do not. With regard to child rearing, transsexuals report a wide range of experiences, from hideously abusive to extremely loving and supportive.

Though we know that biological as well as environmental factors have at least some effect on a child's development, when we look at a specific aspect of development, such as gender identity, it is very difficult to draw conclusions about whether nature or nurture is at work. How does one look back and objectively separate one from the other when looking for causation?

## Nature and Nurture

Many gender identity experts today believe that neither nature nor nurture alone is the cause but rather that transsexualism is most likely the result of an interaction of the two. Some propose that nature may in certain instances provide a *genetic predisposition* toward incongruous gender. Then, if certain family dynamics or socialization factors (such as those described previously) do occur for a person with a biological predisposition, gender dysphoria may develop.

## Historical Perspective

It is becoming clear that gender dysphoria is far more complex than previously thought. And even though there is still no scientific agreement about a single developmental pathway that leads to gender dysphoria, one indisputable fact remains: transsexualism exists and has always existed.

Indeed, transgendered individuals have existed throughout recorded history. Whether these men and women were ridiculed, feared, or persecuted—or whether they were accepted, respected, even honored or revered— depended on the culture and the era in which they lived.

Shamans and medicine men were thought to hold special powers and were considered "twin-souled," with knowledge of both male and female secrets. As such, they typically played prominent roles in ancient rituals, fertility rites, religious festivals, medieval folk ceremonies, and seasonal celebrations. These individuals were typically men who dressed in elaborate skirts, feathers, makeup, and ornamentation. Most cultures had at least one such individual, who held a unique position within the group.

Native American folklore, like the folklore in many other parts of the world, includes reference to individuals who cross-dressed and engaged in cross-gender behavior. Early European explorers were aware of this phenomenon and referred to these transgendered individuals as *berdache*. Today, the tradition of the berdache still exists in various parts of the world, including Central and South Asia, Amazon regions, Australia, Tahiti (where they are called the *mahu*), and India (where they are called the *hijras* and officiate over important ceremonial events).

Similarly, we know of prominent men throughout history who frequently or occasionally dressed as women. The Roman Caesars, Nero, and Caligula reportedly did so. The French writer François Timoléon de Choisy, also known as the Abbé de Choisy, wore petticoats, corsets, and dresses for most of his life. The same is true of Charles de Beaumont, known as the Chevalier d'Éon, a French diplomat born in 1728 who is perhaps the most famous cross-dresser in European history. During his extraordinary and controversial life, he lived as female for much of the time, even when serving as a French ambassador abroad.

In North America cross-dressing was not limited solely to tribal people. For example, Edward Hyde, governor of New York and New Jersey from 1702 to 1708, was notorious for walking through the streets of New York City dressed in flowing gowns like those worn by his cousin Queen Anne, to whom he was said to bear a strong resemblance.

History also includes accounts of women who served in the military, became monks, pursued what was considered to be male-only occupations, or lived as hermits. Many of them adopted male clothing and passed as men for much of their lives. One of the most famous of these women was James Barry, a well-respected army surgeon who served in posts all over the world.

Christina Davis, born in 1667, enlisted in the army under the name Christopher Welsh. Another woman, Mary Anne Talbot, born in 1778, was a sailor who was known as James Taylor. There were even female pirates such as Ann Bonny and Mary Read who lived as male crew members on Captain "Calico Jack" Rackham's buccaneer vessel. Both were convicted of piracy in 1720. Some historians believe that Joan of Arc, perhaps the most famous female warrior and martyr of all time, was executed in 1431 primarily because she refused to wear female clothing and adopt the traditional female role.

Of course, we have no way of knowing with certainty where these individuals fell on the transgender spectrum. However, their cross-dressing and cross-gender behaviors are indicators that they had gender identity issues of some sort. We also have no way of knowing about the countless other transgendered people about whom nothing was written and no records were kept. As we have discussed, in some cultures, cross-gender behavior may have gone virtually unnoticed because it was viewed as an accepted human variation that affected a small percentage of individuals in a given group.

## Recent Well-Known Transsexuals

In the United States, however, transsexualism was not something that most people acknowledged, talked about, or necessarily even knew existed until the 1950s, when the Christine Jorgensen story made headlines around the world and both shocked and fascinated the American public.

In 1952, an American GI named George Jorgensen traveled to Denmark to have a "sex change operation," as the procedure (crude by today's surgical standards) was called at that time. Although Jorgensen, who took the name Christine, was not the first male-to-female transsexual to undergo such surgery, her case was the first highly publicized one. Others soon followed. Some of the best-known cases include male doctor–turned–tennis player Renee Richards, nonoperative female-to-male musician Billy Tipton, male-to-female composer Wendy Carlos, and transsexual writers such as male-to-female Jan Morris, male-to-female Nancy Hunt, and female-to-male Mario Martino.

## The "Grandfather" of Transsexualism

In 1966, when Dr. Harry Benjamin's book *The Transsexual Phenomenon* was published, transsexualism was still widely viewed as an aberration or an illness—a misconception that has been difficult to dispel to this day. Part of the problem was that the medical community had extremely limited experience with transsexuals, and the general public had little or no access to factual information about the condition.

Benjamin's book was the first serious work on transsexualism to appear in this country and as such was instrumental in demystifying and depathologizing the condition. Until that time, the tendency in the medical community was to group anyone who cross-dressed or exhibited cross-gender behaviors under the category of "transvestism." Benjamin, however, a New York endocrinologist and sexologist, saw hundreds of transgendered people in his private practice, and over the years it became apparent to him that there was a wide range of variation among his patients. Not all patients who cross-dressed had the same motive for doing so, nor did they all share the same degree of gender confusion or discomfort. Adopting and popularizing the word *transsexualism* (first used by Dr. D. O. Cauldwell in 1949), Benjamin and his colleague Wardell Pomeroy split cross-dressers into two separate diagnostic categories—transvestites and transsexuals. Benjamin also heightened public awareness that transsexualism was a female as well as a male phenomenon.

Although sex reassignment surgery was not available in the United States during the first forty years of Benjamin's practice, he grasped the essence of the transsexual dilemma and was able to help his patients bring their bodies more in line with their gender identity through hormone treatments.

Benjamin viewed transsexualism as just another facet of the human condition and was instrumental in introducing a more compassionate approach to its treatment. Through his research, published works, and lectures to physicians about the condition, he greatly enhanced professional awareness and understanding of the transsexual phenomenon among his colleagues. The publication of his groundbreaking book in 1966 had an enormous impact in increasing public awareness and understanding as well.

Recognized as the "grandfather of transsexualism," Benjamin was honored for his work in the gender field in 1969 when the international professional organization for gender specialists named itself the Harry Benjamin International Gender Dysphoria Association (HBIGDA).

---

In the next two chapters, we look at what it means to grow up with gender dysphoia.

# 2

## The Childhood Years

Childhood, for many youngsters, is the happiest and most care-free period of their lives. With their young minds filled with wonder and curiosity about the world, children explore their surroundings, learn new things, play games, go to school, and make friends. Ideally, their physical and emotional needs are taken care of by loving parents until they venture forth into the world on their own.

Of course, we don't live in a perfect world. Some children seem to have more than their share of problems—whether they are family, health, economic, or social problems. But for most children, despite the challenges that come up for them over the years, one thing they don't have to worry about is what sex they are. They are boys, or they are girls, period.

For gender-identity-conflicted children, however, this is not the case. Along with the ordinary problems typical of childhood, their daily existence is plagued by nagging doubts and confusions because, in spite of anatomy that says otherwise, they self-identify as the other gender. As a result, their childhood is often a nightmare. The overwhelming majority of my patients—approximately 85 percent—recognized their gender dysphoria by the time they began grade school. They all report that their childhood years were a torturous experience as they struggled with the constant burden of trying to live up to the expectations of their family and society about the gender role they were *supposed* to play.

One of my patients, Tommy, struggled with this every day of his childhood. He was a serious boy who didn't show an interest in any of the activities his older brothers had enjoyed. His parents told him he was a boy; he had a boy's name, was dressed as a boy, and was given toys that boys typically enjoy. Yet none of it felt right to him. He didn't feel like a boy. He preferred playing with girls and yearned to be just like them. Although Tommy's parents encouraged him to engage in male-oriented activities and positively reinforced any boylike behaviors in him, he was unable to live up to their expectations. They couldn't figure out what was wrong with him. Neither could Tommy, and he was miserable about it.

Greg had similar experiences when he was young, but his mother was much more emphatic in her disapproval of behaviors that she considered feminine and therefore strictly off-limits. "My mother," Greg recalled, "knew that I was transgendered from age four on, and she was bound and determined to crush that and to make a male out of me." His mother was frequently angry and embarrassed by her fragile-looking son's behaviors. He got the message loud and clear that he was a disappointment to her. He explains:

Even at such an early age, I was very conscious of how different I was and how much more feminine I looked and acted than the other boys. I was always being told by my mother to do things differently. "Don't hold your books like that; girls hold their books like that. Don't walk like that; girls walk like that. Don't cross your legs; only girls cross their legs like that." Eventually I began to feel like I was a total failure. About that time, I began to wonder if my feminine behavior was the reason my father left my mother and me. I felt like it must have been my fault.

These types of experiences cause intense conflict and confusion in children because they are eager to please their parents and want their parents' attention, approval, and affection. Children listen and pay attention to what is happening in the world around them and

learn from their experiences. They get input from their parents—
their primary role models—and they also observe their brothers
and sisters, watch television, and interact with other children and
adults in day-care and school settings. By age five, most children are
fully aware of what sex they are and of the socially acceptable gender roles for that sex.

Typically, children are positively reinforced for behaviors that
are considered gender-appropriate, and come into conflict with their
family over or are discouraged from those that are not. That is why
life is so hard for transgendered children. What they are told they
should do doesn't feel right and is distressing to them. They have
difficulty integrating their emotions and cross-gender inclinations
into the narrow parameters of our culture's rigid two-gender system.
It requires great effort on their part to play out the role expected of
them. Although these children don't understand their gender
incongruity and usually wouldn't have the language to express it
even if they did, some do try to verbalize their confusion.

Cindy remembers tugging on her mother's hand when she was
seven years old and saying, "Mommy, why does everyone think I'm a
girl? Tim and Joe are boys, and I know I am too." Her mom, although
momentarily at a loss for words, said, "That's just the way it is. You
were born that way. Your brothers are boys and you're a girl." The
youngster concluded that if her mother was right, something must be
very *wrong* with her. Yet she, like most gender-conflicted children,
didn't know what to do about the way she felt inside.

## "Who Am I, and Why Am I Different?"

Nearly all transgendered children have strong feelings of being different and not fitting in. However, they don't all experience their
dysphoria in the same way. Some believe that they should have
been born the opposite sex. Many think that they will become the
opposite sex (the sex they want to be) when they reach puberty or
when they "grow up." Others are convinced that they really *are* the
opposite sex despite all appearances to the contrary. A few feel, like

Rachel, as though they are a member of a third sex. "It was not that I felt like I was a boy," she said. "I just didn't feel like a girl. I didn't seem to fit anywhere."

Some gender-confused children assume that everyone else is experiencing the same kind of gender conflicts. One patient recalls asking one of his friends in kindergarten about whether he "sometimes wished he was a girl." He was amazed when his friend said that he never had those feelings.

Janet was another child who experienced early gender confusion but assumed that other children did too. She wasn't comfortable being a girl, but she didn't know how else it could be. "You can't tell fish about water because they live it in," she said. "I couldn't even imagine that other kids didn't feel the same way. I figured everyone had this stuff going on."

## Finding Their Place

Some transgendered children don't have any idea what is wrong—they just know that something isn't right. What these children usually have in common is an overwhelming feeling of not fitting in. Robert Fulghum's story "Giants, Wizards, and Dwarfs" from his book *All I Really Need to Know I Learned in Kindergarten*, eloquently addresses those children who are different, who do not fit the norm and do not accept the available boxes and pigeonholes. He describes a game he organized for a large group of youngsters. They were all required to decide which they were—a giant, a wizard, or a dwarf. While all the others huddled in frenzied, whispered consultation, one child tugged at his pants leg and asked in a small, concerned voice, "Where do the mermaids stand? You see, I am a mermaid." When he told her, "There are no such things," she persisted. "Oh, yes, I am one."

Here was a child who did not relate to being a giant, a wizard, or a dwarf. She knew her category: mermaid. And she intended to participate wherever mermaids fit into the scheme of things and without giving up her dignity or identity. She took it for granted that there was a place for mermaids and that Fulghum, as an adult, would know just where that was.

Parents, however, when faced with perplexing questions about gender or about their own child's obvious cross-gender preferences, are usually very uncomfortable. They don't know how to deal with their child's situation or where to turn for advice. Some parents rush their transgendered kids to the nearest psychologist or psychiatrist, but usually with limited success because these kids are generally too afraid to express their true feelings. In some cases, the therapist may downplay the significance of cross-gender behaviors or suggest that eventually the child will "outgrow it."

Randall, whose concerned parents took him to three different therapists by the time he was ten, described his early gender dysphoria in this way: "I didn't have a word for it. I just knew that I was different, and I did what people tend to do: I looked for reasons. I figured, I'm bright, smarter than most kids, that must be it. Or my father makes us wear crew cuts, that must be it. I tried to figure out why people said things to me that didn't make sense." Looking back on his early years, he remembers having a great deal of difficulty relating to people because his perceptions were so different. As he put it, "My map of things didn't match other people's map of things. Consequently, I was left out much of the time. The girls didn't really want to have a boy in their space, and the boys wanted to have nothing to do with me at all. So I spent a lot of time alone."

This is the case for many children with gender conflicts. Since they don't fit in, they become loners and end up spending much of their childhood in isolation. Often these children sense that their family and the other kids think they are strange. And, sadly, they may begin to believe it themselves after a while. Some are so consumed with shame that they feel like freaks or monsters. While other youngsters talked about what they wanted to be when they grew up, Renee, a withdrawn, troubled little girl, felt so lost and alienated that the only place she could imagine ending up was "locked away in a cage in a circus sideshow." She assumed that people would line up and buy tickets just to gawk at her.

## Living Under a Cloud

Gender dysphoric children often feel as if they have a monstrous dark cloud hanging over them—an invisible handicap—and in a way, they're right. Gender dysphoria is not something that can be seen, nor is it easily explained. Imagine how confusing it must be for these children to be constantly receiving information that doesn't correlate. Daydreaming is sometimes their only escape. They dream about magically and mysteriously becoming their "true selves." After all, their parents read them fairy tales about frogs that turn into princes, ugly ducklings that wondrously emerge as beautiful swans, and "good little children" who end up living happily ever after. Even though older children recognize these as fables, most transgendered kids still like to believe that transformation does lie within the realm of possibility.

Many of these kids fall asleep at night praying, hoping, and dreaming about waking up in the morning as the "right" sex. Some said they ran to the mirror nearly every morning to see if their prayers had been answered and the much-wished-for transformation had occurred.

These children pray and wish and wait and wait some more. Ultimately, of course, they are sorely frustrated and disappointed. Many get to the point where it becomes increasingly difficult to function on a daily basis. So much of their energy is focused on their gender confusion that their performance in school is often significantly affected. Alan was such a boy. He described himself as constantly exhausted and unable to concentrate. "I was so upset about my unanswered prayers," he said, "that I began to feel anger at a God who didn't listen. I woke up tired and angry every single morning and was never in a good mood."

Nancy, a large girl even at age six, tried to ease her gender dysphoria by living in a world of fantasy. She watched her favorite cartoon show, *Popeye*, with rapt attention and even recalls admiring Brutus, Popeye's burly nemesis. Their muscular bodies, macho attitudes, and action-packed adventures held a strong appeal for her.

Although she didn't believe that tossing down tins of spinach would instantly make her strong and ferocious, she did secretly hope that her body would transform into a muscular male body when she reached puberty. Her daydreams were never about being Olive Oyl, the helpless heroine whom Popeye routinely saved from fates worse than death. Instead, Nancy wanted to be like Popeye. She spent many hours engrossed in fantasies about assuming male roles and living life as a male.

Other children verbalize their wishes, sometimes much to their parents' dismay. Lily will never forget her seventh birthday party. The entire family gathered around to watch her blow out the candles. "Make a wish," her mother urged her. In her excitement, Lily blurted out, "My wish is to grow a penis before my next birthday!" There were gasps of astonishment followed by complete silence. Then her brothers began to hoot with laughter, and her father stomped out of the room. This was just one more in a long series of incidents in which Lily had expressed cross-gender preferences.

## Cross-Dressing

Young children are naturally curious. Most of them enjoy playing dress-up and putting on not only Mommy's dresses but Daddy's shoes to play house or other games that imitate their parents or other people they know or see on television. But transsexual children cross-dress for an entirely different reason: cross-dressing allows them to transform themselves temporarily into an entity that more closely matches their own identity and helps them to achieve a wholeness that is rare in their daily lives.

Many male-to-female transsexuals recall rushing to their mother's or sister's closets whenever they were left alone in the house to select lovely feminine articles of clothing to wear. Trevor was just such a boy. He adored his mother's closet. "I used to try on my mother's clothes when I was about six years old," he said, "by standing under the hanger of her dresses in the closet. The sensation was one of peacefulness and integration."

When Trevor was nine, his mother took a full-time job, and he then had two precious hours after school before she would return home from work. This meant he could take garments off the hangers and actually wear them, but he was always extremely careful to make sure every item was returned to the exact spot where he had found it. He was equally meticulous about returning garments to his mother's drawers; he drew detailed little diagrams to help him remember how to fold and arrange everything just right. He was determined not to get caught. The thought of being deprived of these opportunities to cross-dress was unthinkable to him.

Some gender-conflicted girls throw tantrums every time they have to put on a dress or else flatly refuse to wear them. Dresses just don't fit their image of who they are. Bernice remembers how frustrated she used to get every time her mother tried to dress her in frilly clothes or put ribbons in her long, curly hair. She wanted nothing to do with anything even remotely feminine. She wanted to wear jeans and T-shirts like the "other guys." Her mother hoped that this was simply a phase, but it wasn't. Whenever her mom insisted that she wear a dress, young Bernice would usually come home with it "accidentally" ripped or stained. Once Bernice even took scissors to her long hair and hacked it off because it was so incongruous with the boy she knew she was. "My mom was so upset," she recalls, "that she burst into tears as soon as she opened the bathroom door and discovered what I had done." Her mother had to take her to the beauty salon, where the remaining hair had to be cut shorter still to even it out. Bernice was secretly thrilled because it made her look even more like a boy. It was about that time that she began to stand up to urinate on a regular basis and insisted that people call her "Bernie" instead of Bernice.

Even though gender dysphoric children feel compelled to cross-dress, they usually worry about the possibility of getting caught. Some youngsters will lock themselves in the bathroom for extended periods of time so that they can pull clothes out of the hamper and wear them in relative privacy from the rest of the family. Others will hide garments in various places (under their mattress or in the attic, garage, or backyard) where they hope they won't be found. Some do get caught if their parents walk in on them when they are cross-dressed or find their secret stash of clothes. Getting caught, however, is seldom a deterrent. It simply makes them more careful in the future.

For some gender-conflicted children, the need to cross-dress is so strong that if they do not have access to the clothing they need, they get creative and use whatever they can get their hands on. Some drape T-shirts, towels, or sheets around themselves to resemble dresses or robes. Some boys go so far as to a stuff a teddy bear or pillow down the front of their clothes or pajamas so they can look pregnant like their mothers.

Other gender dysphoric children are far too terrified of punishment to risk cross-dressing. Instead, like eleven-year-old Doug, they settle for cross-dressing fantasies. Doug had a recurring fantasy about running through a beautiful meadow in a simple white dress. "I still remember the freedom I felt," he said, "the lightness of heart and spirit. I used to concentrate really hard about the fantasy before I fell asleep, hoping that I might dream about it, and sometimes I did." He also remembers waking up crying on several occasions. He knew that he would never feel the same as in the dream, even if he could wear a dress, because his body was not right.

## Games Children Play

Traditionally, little girls are expected to enjoy female-oriented toys like dolls and dishes, to dress up in mother's clothes and jewelry, to play house, and to mimic the behaviors that are considered part of the feminine experience. Boys are expected to prefer stereotypically male toys such as cars and trucks, model airplanes, building blocks, toolboxes, and toy soldiers and guns. They tend to emulate behaviors considered part of the masculine experience. Although gender-specific activities are not as rigidly encouraged today as in the past, cultural attitudes of this type are very slow to change.

Most girls, nonetheless, *do* enjoy the toys, games, and activities that typically interest female children, just as most boys are usually drawn to the toys, games, and activities that typically interest male children. But transgendered girls are usually far more interested in male-oriented pastimes. Given the choice, they'd much rather do things like crawl around with a wrench and help dad fix the car or play baseball with their older brother or neighborhood friends. Transgendered boys are much more interested in female-oriented pastimes. They recall many happy hours spent baking cookies, doing indoor projects, and hanging out with their mothers and sisters.

Jason's favorite games involved dolls that he would sneak from his sister's room whenever she was playing outdoors. More than anything, he wanted a doll of his own, and he finally had his chance when he was eight years old. He had been wetting his bed on a regular basis, and his mother had tried everything she could think of to help him overcome the problem. She promised him anything he wanted if he could keep his bed dry for two weeks. "I want a dancing doll," he said. His mother was surprised but agreed to his terms. Within three days, he stopped wetting the bed, and two weeks later, his bed was still dry. He got his dancing doll and kept it under his pillow every night when he went to sleep. And he never wet the bed again.

## Cross-Gender Play

Although most gender-confused children are discouraged from playing with certain toys or engaging in certain behaviors, they often find clever ways to integrate cross-gender behavior into childhood role-playing and games. For example, whenever Amy played "house" or make-believe games with the other little girls, the fantasy nearly always called for a boyfriend, a husband, or—her favorite role of all—a villain. This provided her with a perfect opportunity to stuff her hair into a cap or hat and to dress in oversize male garments. Sometimes she drew a mustache on her upper lip with her mother's eyebrow pencil and on occasion enlisted her mother's help in assembling her costumes and such props as eye patches, swords, or masks.

She still remembers her mother's protests. "But honey, don't you ever want to be the princess, the cowgirl, or the maiden in distress?" Amy always had a quick response ready, such as, "Someone's got to be the boy. It might as well be me," or "I make a far better bad guy than any of the other girls." Her mother had to admit that her daughter certainly was successful in assuming those roles.

Nathan, like many youngsters raised on television, enjoyed playing games loosely based on his favorite shows, especially Westerns. The highlights, for him, were always the rescue scenes. He loved to watch the cowboy hero toss his hat aside, draw his gun, and save the frightened saloon girl from the advances of drunken cowpokes (or some other impending catastrophe). Yet Nathan didn't identify with the cowboy. When he watched the cowboy put his arms around the girl and pull her to safety, Nathan desperately wanted to be that girl. But when he played cowboy games with his friends, he learned the hard way that he could never play a female role without being subjected to their scorn and taunts.

For many gender dysphoric children, especially the boys, Halloween offers a perfect opportunity to cross-dress publicly with the full approval of parents and society. Even as adults, many of my male-to-female patients remember the delight they felt when they were able to convince their mothers to let them dress up as princesses, fairies, or ballerinas for one glorious night.

"Doctor" is a make-believe game that many children play at some time or another. But the disrobing that is often part of the game can be upsetting for children with gender conflicts. For Rick, it was a turning point. He explains:

> When I was about four years old, I was playing doctor with a girl named Cheryl who I played with on a regular basis. She insisted that I should be the doctor, and she got undressed to be "examined." I was totally confused and shocked when I looked down and saw something different on her than I saw on myself. I didn't understand how I could have such a sense of oneness with her when we were so physically different. It

was about that time that I started to hate my penis. I would tuck it under so I would look like her down there. And I started having fantasies that someone would sneak into the house and cut it off me and take it over and make Cheryl be the boy. I would dream constantly about being Cheryl.

Some boys with gender identity disorder (GID) pretend that their penis isn't there. Others have a disproportionate number of accidents or injuries involving their penis. One patient remembers having the lid of his toy box fall down on it. Another time, he closed the top of the laundry hamper on his genitals. He recalls, "It was almost as if my desire was so strong to not have a penis that I subconsciously wished to injure myself there. I was always banging into things."

Many transgendered boys long for the opportunity to spend time playing, talking, and enjoying the company of girls and women. The dolls, playhouses, books, and board games that their sisters enjoy seem far more interesting than the "boy stuff" they are expected to play with. Christmastime for such youngsters is always a disappointment. They are frustrated because they don't have access to the toys toward which they naturally gravitate. Those toys are withheld from them, and the ones they do get hold little interest for them. One child used to sign his wish list to Santa Claus with a feminized version of his name. His hope was that he could somehow fool Santa Claus into bringing him the Barbie doll he so desperately wanted. Other boys beg or bribe their sisters into asking for the toys they want, since they know they can't ask for these toys themselves without eliciting their parents' disapproval.

## Tomboys and Sissies

Children can be tough on each other during the growing-up years. Any child who is perceived as different from the rest may be teased or bullied by other children. Since gender dysphoric youngsters have an affinity for activities, games, and mannerisms more typical of the opposite gender, they are natural targets for abuse and the unkind labels kids fling at each other. Unfortunately, these labels have withstood decades of use.

Boys seem to take the brunt of this kind of bullying. Our society tends to look more kindly on masculine-oriented girls than on feminine-oriented boys, and the "tomboy" label carries far less stigma than the "sissy" label. To many kids, being called a sissy is considered the ultimate insult. Tomboyism, on the other hand, is not only tolerated but is sometimes even grudgingly admired. It is typically viewed as simply a phase or a stage that some girls go through and will eventually outgrow. But this does not happen with transsexual girls; for them, it is not a temporary phase. They are masculine-oriented as an expression of the boy they feel they are.

Lisa was called a tomboy from as early as she could remember, and she strongly objected to the term. To her it seemed ridiculous and distasteful because she knew that she was a "real" boy. She recalls that when she was seven or eight years old, she used to visualize herself growing up to be a man. She came from a big family, and frequently her relatives would ask her, "Lisa, what do you want to be when you grow up?" They expected her to say "a ballerina," "a teacher," "a nurse," or something like that. Instead she would reply as honestly as she could: "I want to be a cowboy. Or maybe a football player. Or perhaps a priest." The relatives thought it was cute at first, but when it persisted, it was a different story. For a while they tried to steer her toward female-oriented professions. When that didn't work, they simply avoided the subject altogether.

Like many transgendered youngsters, Lisa felt that her whole childhood was dominated by family members trying to make her change her clothes, her manner, her way of speaking. She still remembers how her mother once reprimanded her about the way she walked. "For heaven's sake, Lisa, you walk like John Wayne!" To Lisa, this was the greatest compliment she could have gotten, although that was not at all what her mother had intended. Lisa was always masculine, and it took her parents years to realize that their daughter was never going to become a gentle, ladylike young woman—a fact that was a constant source of disappointment to them, for she was the only girl in a family of six boys.

## Taunting, Teasing, and Bullying

The school environment often poses formidable challenges for transgendered children. Not only do they frequently feel like outcasts in the classroom, but they also often dread recess periods and lunch breaks. As Ben said, "I didn't even fit in on the playground. I didn't care for those little dominance games the boys played. Nor did I like basketball or baseball or football or running fast or being better or stronger or smarter. I just wanted out of everything. I just wanted freedom. I didn't know at the time exactly how to put it in words, but I knew that I just wanted to be me, not something that society and biology wanted to program me to be."

Carlos found himself so inept at sports that he was told on several occasions, "Why don't you go jump rope with all the other girls?" Though these episodes were painful, he was plagued with conflicting emotions. "The pain was indescribable, but so was the desire to be able to do exactly that. I longed to be able to go jump rope and play jacks and hopscotch with all the 'other' girls.

"Looking back on my grade school experiences," he continued, "I am amazed at how cruel young boys can be. Being surrounded by them, and being expected to survive among them as one when you are not one, was tantamount to putting a lamb in the skin of a wolf and placing it in among a pack of wolves with no means of escape. Sooner or later, the 'other' wolves sense what's going on, and the result is inevitable."

Little boys who are not interested in rough-and-tumble games and competitive sports are often teased mercilessly. Eventually, the teasing, bullying, and taunting they endure may escalate into physical violence. Many report that they got beaten up on a regular basis.

This was the case with Bert. "All through my elementary school years," he says, "I was picked on by the other boys and called names like 'wimp,' 'fairy,' or 'Little Lord Fauntleroy.' Even though I was bright and had a high IQ, I didn't know what those words meant, much less why they were calling me that." He much preferred the company of girls and did not like the aggressiveness and fighting that always seemed to be a part of the boys' games. "I dreamed constantly of what my life would be like as a girl."

All the violence that became such a prominent part of his life was utterly bewildering to Bert. "I was running home from school almost daily to avoid being beaten up by my schoolmates. And then I was getting into trouble with the school authorities because I was running across streets to avoid fights." When he got home, he would get in trouble again for being involved in fights, even though he was always at the losing end. "I could not understand the cruelty shown by other boys toward me. I was not socially adept at that age, but I also did not provoke anyone's wrath intentionally. I guess I was just different in their eyes and represented a threat or challenge to them in some way."

Though not all transgendered boys look or behave effeminately, some do. Michael was one. He was pushed and shoved while he waited for the bus, had his lunch money and school supplies taken from him, and was picked on in class. The recess breaks in the schoolyard were the worst times of all because he was completely vulnerable to attacks in that environment. Perhaps most upsetting to him was the way the other boys would pretend to include him in a game, only to seize the first opportunity to ridicule him or knock him around. "I was never able to defend myself very well," he said, "and my dad would get so mad because I'd come home from school bleeding on an average of once a week. He used to say, 'Why can't you be a man and stand up to them?' It was inconceivable to him that I didn't do something to deserve whatever treatment I got. A few times I even considered telling him that the blood on me belonged to one of the boys *I* had beaten up. But of course, I knew he'd never believe that."

Some gender dysphoric children just want to escape or hide from their tormentors and the world in general. They spend every free moment at home with the door locked or at the library with their head buried in a book. The latter may result in very good grades, for scholastic endeavors are the one area in which they feel they can excel.

Some boys, like John, devised other ways to insulate themselves to some extent from the brunt of the seemingly endless physical attacks. He recalls:

> Until the time I was nine, they would chase me, call me names like "queer," throw rocks at me, or beat me up. Once I even had a brick thrown at me. They attacked me so often that I began to feel like I had a bull's-eye painted on my back. But then I got smart and started hanging out with the largest bullies I could find. Even though I still got beaten up, at least I had protectors of sorts. It's true I was their personal punching bag, but at least I knew only they would be hitting me and no one else would.

Another patient described a traumatic experience that occurred at summer camp when he was ten years old. On the very first day, several of the boys caught him in the bathroom sitting down to urinate, as he always did. They yanked him up, roughly pushed him around, and wouldn't let him pull up his pants. Then, as a final humiliation, they dunked his head in the toilet.

After that, every time they saw him, they taunted him and called him "little faggot" or "mama's boy." The names not only persisted throughout summer camp but also stuck with him back in school the following September.

Although even masculine-acting boys are sometimes called disparaging names as a put-down, to a boy who really is more feminine, such taunts are particularly hurtful. Because a transsexual boy feels that he is in fact a girl, he is being mocked for simply being who he is. Similarly, transsexual girls are being mocked for who they are. Thus transsexual boys and girls often begin to try to cover up their true selves and their true feelings in order to gain acceptance and approval. They learn to pretend.

## Young Actors, Chameleons, and Impostors

Children who are gender dysphoric have a formidable secret. They learn at a very early age that what they really feel about their gender must be kept locked inside if they want to fit in and to belong. They often put all of their energy into trying to become what their parents and society want them to be. They become skilled little actors and chameleons, readily able to change at will to suit the circumstances. They do this by trying to determine what other people want and expect from them and then acting accordingly. They often become adept at their roles and at pleasing others. They want to convince the world that they are "normal."

They typically seek to play their parts to perfection as the "good son" or the "perfect daughter." It doesn't take them long to figure out that as long as they pretend to be what they are expected to be, they may be able to fool the world and won't get hassled. Now and then they may even be able to fool themselves. They sometimes believe that eventually they'll "get it right." After all, they receive lots of prompts and cues from their parents, their teachers, their friends, and the media. Some are more successful than others in maintaining a facade. But it takes a great deal of effort and vigilance for these children to make sure nothing slips out.

As one transsexual named Sue said looking back on her childhood, "Every day, I felt like I was walking on a tightrope without a safety net." She didn't ever let people get close to her and found it easier just to remain silent. "I didn't want to talk. I was afraid the truth would come out. So I led a life of omission. I learned that if I kept my mouth shut, it would keep me out of trouble."

However, such rigidly controlled behavior takes an emotional toll. As Tom poignantly stated, "I learned to become a chameleon, to fabricate little masculine selves that had nothing to do with me but that I could send out into the world. And these poor little people went out, and I was locked away in there. As a result, I ended up being very sad and very isolated."

Some children have trouble acting or playing a role because they are less sure about what behaviors to simulate. Because they

see only two gender roles to pick from, they will instinctively identify with the role that most closely matches their emotional temperament. Jeff was one such child. He found himself crying day and
night. His parents were very upset by his behavior and by the fact
that he had no friends.

"I wasn't liked for who I was," Jeff said. "I would walk out in the
street and express myself in the only way I knew how, with a very
childlike innocence. Just being alive seemed to be enough to draw
taunts. It was obvious that something about me was so strange that
the other kids found me repulsive. I didn't know what they were
seeing, but whatever it was, it was me, and they weren't liking me.
And so I ended up not liking me." His feelings of shame and self-
loathing were but the precursors to an even worse puberty.

Still others, like Duncan, have trouble adapting, despite parental
prodding. He remembers having serious behavioral problems at home
and school. "I went to four different grade schools and seemed to be
in trouble all the time. I demonstrated feminine characteristics, and
one by one they were removed from my behavioral and physical pat-
terning by my parents and my teachers. Sometimes it was through
coercion, other times through beatings or humiliation."

---

Many of the experiences of the gender dysphoric children
described in this chapter are heartbreaking. Unfortunately, such
experiences are the rule rather than the exception. Children who
grow up with gender confusion almost always have serious self-
image and self-esteem problems because they don't feel comfortable
with their bodies and don't fit in with their peer group. For many,
the degree of gender dysphoria is extreme.

It is important, however, to remember that transsexualism is a
disorder of gender identity. It should not be confused with isolated
instances of children engaging in cross-gender behavior or verbally
musing about what it would be like to be the other sex. Often, *non-
transgendered* children of both sexes express curiosity about clothes,
toys, and activities that are generally the domain of the opposite

sex. This is natural and part of a child's normal curiosity. An older sister, for instance, may envy her younger brother because she sees him getting more attention. That doesn't mean she wants to be a boy. Or a boy might say, "Gee, I wish I were a girl so I wouldn't have to mow the lawn." Such words or wishes are the result of what are perceived to be familial or cultural advantages of being the other gender—nothing more.

By contrast, the strong, persistent cross-gender identification discussed in this chapter is something that only transsexuals experience during their childhood years. And their cross-gender tendencies, behaviors, and desires do not subside as they enter adolescence. If anything, at that time they become even more conflicted about the disparity between their bodies and their minds.

# 3

## The Teen Years

Puberty is often an extremely difficult time for young people. Peer pressure to conform to highly specific and often inexplicable standards of behavior becomes stronger than ever. Moreover, body image becomes of paramount concern right at the time when raging hormones are producing major physical and psychological changes. Adjusting to all of these changes can be confusing and distressing for teenagers.

Puberty is a time for young people to test their limits. A whole new world—an adult world—lies ahead, and the possibilities seem endless. Fueled with bravado and excitement about the future, teens typically experience a new sense of power, but that power is tempered with equal doses of self-doubt and self-consciousness. Most teenagers find the teen years exhilarating but often unsettling at the same time.

### Nature's Cruel Trick

Gender dysphoric teens, however, rarely report feelings of exhilaration. Instead of excitement and anticipation, they experience profound disappointment, panic, and confusion. Patients often refer to puberty as "a curse" or "hell for transsexuals."

As children, they may have been able to delude themselves into thinking that a transformation to the opposite sex might still occur.

But all hope is lost with the emergence of their secondary sex characteristics. For males, these include deepening of the voice, development of the Adam's apple, growth of body hair, development of a more masculine physique, and maturation of the genitals. For females, they include development of breasts, hips, and a softer, more feminine shape; maturation of the genitals; and the beginning of menstruation. With the arrival of puberty, transsexual teens must face the harsh reality of nature's cruel trick—that their bodies are finally changing but the changes are all the wrong ones.

## A Time of Betrayal

Transsexual teens typically feel shame, despair, and anger because they are developing the adult body of the wrong sex. Puberty, to them, feels like the "end of the line" because it provides the indisputable evidence that their bodies are never going to match their gender identity.

While the average teenage boy eagerly waits for the first glimpse of "peach fuzz" on his face so that he can begin the time-honored male ritual of shaving, the transsexual male finds such facial hair repulsive. More than anything, he wants his body and face to remain soft and to become more feminine. Young girls who had hoped eventually to grow into men find their dreams shattered when they realize that the passage into manhood they had eagerly anticipated is not going to happen. Their bodies have betrayed them by becoming more feminine instead of more masculine. They are appalled as they watch their breasts begin to swell and they began to menstruate. There is an interesting difference, however, between male and female expectations about puberty. While only a small percentage of my male patients thought they would actually become female at puberty (despite their male bodies), almost all of my female patients reported that they believed they would develop male bodies at puberty.

This was the case with Lydia. She fully expected that her body would magically straighten out when she "grew up." From an early age her perception had been that "eventually you either got your period or got a penis."

For Malcolm, the unhappiness grew incrementally with the development of each new secondary sex characteristic. "While I was growing up," he said, "I prayed that it wouldn't happen to me. All that hair and the voice and getting tall and everything. And one by one, they all happened. Each one was like a hammer blow to my head, spread out from when I was fifteen until my first year in college, when I started growing facial hair, as well as hair in other places."

Worst of all, there is absolutely nothing that these teenagers feel they can do about their plight. The mysteries of puberty have finally unfolded only to fail them. Many patients said that their visibly maturing bodies were a daily reminder of "nature's cruel trick."

As Rhonda put it, "Puberty was simply awful, especially when I developed breasts and began to menstruate. Both were so unwanted. I was horrified and embarrassed." Like her transsexual male counterparts, Rhonda felt like a "freak of nature." "It seemed bad enough to me," she said, "that I had been born with the wrong body, but at puberty I felt as though my body was betraying me all over again."

This sense of betrayal is a common theme among these teenagers. Betty was a patient who felt it so strongly that she described herself as feeling disassociated from her body. She began consciously to avoid mirrors and other reflective surfaces that would show her newly maturing body from the neck down. "I simply could not reconcile the physical image with my mental image of myself," she explains. "Although childhood was tough, it was far worse when I became a teenager. Even simple activities like bathing became traumatic. Not only did I have trouble facing myself, but I also found it hard facing my family and the kids at school. I quickly learned to disengage my mind from my body in order to get through."

## Negative Body Images

A strongly negative body image is typical for transgendered teens. It is difficult, if not impossible, for them to value a body that is so blatantly different from the one they want or think they should have. Natalie felt that way.

"I was always very uncomfortable as a teenager," she said, "whenever my family or friends complimented me on my appearance. I didn't want to look good as a female. Even though my parents bought me nice clothes, I knew that clothes would never make a woman out of me." Her parents pressured her to pierce her ears and to wear makeup because she was so frequently mistaken for a male. "I hated to shop for bras and dresses," Natalie recalls. "I just couldn't understand why other girls got so excited about shopping and buying lingerie and clothes. It seemed so silly and distasteful to me. I did everything I could to de-emphasize my femininity and the fact that I was female."

Gender dysphoric boys, by contrast, want desperately to be female. They crave femininity. When Matthew was growing up, he looked up to his teenage sister and her friends and wanted to be just like them. Everything they said and did was of vital interest to him. In his innocence, he associated their femaleness with their chronological age. He was able to endure his frustration with the male-oriented toys and clothing that were constantly being thrust at him only because he was sure that he was just "biding his time" until he too became a female teenager.

He was one of the males who believed he would become female upon "coming of age." When he didn't, he fell into a deep depression. His black moods were compounded by feelings of self-contempt because he felt so "completely ignorant" and naive about his assumptions.

Others are less naive. They know they won't magically turn into the opposite sex at puberty, and they worry a great deal about exactly how puberty will manifest itself. As one patient put it, "Puberty came, and I was scared and anxiety-ridden. Was I going to get large and hairy and ugly like all the other boys?"

One of the frustrations of puberty for these teenagers is that the distressing physical changes are so obvious and hard to hide. They imagine that everyone around them can readily witness their "inappropriately" developing female figures or male physiques. As a result, some try to conceal their bodies. Girls will cover their burgeoning breasts and hips under bulky, oversize, loose garments or multiple layers of clothing. One patient said that she wore a jacket every single day no matter how hot it was in order to hide her figure. Some girls wear tight T-shirts or leotards under their clothes to try to flatten their breasts. A few even bind them with tape.

Males also sometimes bind themselves to hide any bulge in their trousers. Larson was one teenager who did so. He considered his penis an unwanted ugly growth. While the other boys in gym class were proudly purchasing and wearing jock straps or athletic cups to protect themselves during sports, Larson was buying rolls of white surgical tape so that he could tape his penis down so it wouldn't show. Some males even learn to hide their testicles by pushing them back up into the inguinal canals through which they originally descended.

While some experience feelings of disgust about their penis, others are merely indifferent to it. They may use it because they have no choice but would be happy to be rid of it. Some try to avoid handling their penis for any reason. They don't like to hold it to urinate or touch it to masturbate. Generally, these teens will instead rub against the mattress to masturbate.

Some of these male teenagers report that their body feels so alien to them that their penis seems like a foreign appendage or tumor. Many, like Sid, used to tuck it out of sight. "My genitals never felt like a part of me. Even as a child, my dislike for them made me feel like they were implanted at birth or something. I assumed this probably happened because my parents wanted a boy and I was not one. I used to hide myself between my crossed legs and look in the mirror just to admire how it would be if my body were really like that."

Others dream or fantasize about accidents where their penis would be ripped off, hunting accidents where it would be shot off, or a fire where it would be burned. However, in fantasies of this type, no other part of their body is damaged.

## Social Interactions

The lack of privacy in the school locker room is embarrassing for most teenagers but agonizing for those who are gender dysphoric.

They cringe under the gaze of their classmates, who see their excru-
ciatingly "wrong bodies" while they are changing clothes. Navigat-
ing the humiliating shower experience as invisibly as possible is
even worse. Some get notes from their doctor in order to be excused
from gym class or try to schedule gym for the last class of the day so
they don't have to shower. Others dawdle in order to be the last one
into the shower. The fewer people who see them undressed, the better. They're afraid that their naked body will give them away and
that surely some telltale sign or aura will reveal to others that they
actually are the opposite sex.

Ron dreaded gym class. He was deeply ashamed of his tall, gan-
gly body and was never comfortable showering with the other boys.
He longed for privacy. "It was embarrassing for me to be with the
guys," he said. "I thought I was a girl. Even though I had the same
equipment, they were boys and I was a girl. Unfortunately, a tall,
skinny girl, but a girl nevertheless, and there I was, naked in front
of thirty boys!"

Social interactions with peers are difficult for transgendered
teenagers. They may have been able to get away with some of their
cross-gender behaviors during childhood, but as teenagers, they
quickly discover that the rules are far more complex and confusing.
The peer pressure to conform that they experienced during childhood, however painful it may have been, is minimal compared to
the formidable social ostracism that can occur in the school setting
for the teen who doesn't fit in.

Gender roles during the teen years become increasingly difficult
to sustain, even for the more talented young "actors." Now that
nature has played its final hand, they find themselves having to
become even greater chameleons and impostors than ever before.

Gordon found his self-identity as female a never-ending struggle because it was so difficult for him to modify his feminine behaviors. He was always nervous and frustrated. "Even my mother would
notice. She'd tell me to keep my hands still. I remember she said
that I ought not swish my rear end when I walked, that men didn't
do that sort of thing. The truth is, in the male role I felt myself for-

ever on guard, forever monitoring the way I moved my hands and spoke my phrases."

Jennifer recalls that after a while, deception became a way of life for her. "My whole life was a lie," she said, "because I was always hiding my true gender. It wasn't until sometime in high school or the beginning of college that I realized that I was lying to myself more than anyone. I know now that I had a really good reason for doing this—there were truths I never wanted to face. And so I had to lie to myself and make up a personality I could live with."

Some gender dysphoric teenagers are more adept at keeping up their deception and may function fairly well. Others feel inept and miserable about faking what they consider an inappropriate role. Certain transsexual teens will rebel altogether and refuse to play a role. To distract themselves from the dysphoria, some find diversions such as sports, computers, hobbies, or schoolwork on which to focus their attention. For others, nothing can distract them for long, and their inability to concentrate may cause them to drop out of school altogether.

## Nowhere to Turn

Some GID teenagers feel so isolated and out of step with the rest of the world that they become desperate. They feel as though they have nowhere to turn. This desperation may manifest itself in rebellious or inappropriate acts resulting in social problems at home or at school and in self-destructive, abusive, or criminal behaviors. Others become the victims of abuse and violence themselves.

Transgendered teens who were beaten up as children for being different often find that the only difference between their childhood and their teen years is that the teenage bullies are bigger and stronger. Male-to-female transsexuals continue to be the objects of physical abuse, while the female-to-males are often the victims of verbal abuse. Avoidance or withdrawal generally seems to be the safest route. One of my patients named Lydia recalls the pain of adolescence because of the ridicule she often faced in class. She still remembers a specific incident that occurred during a high school psychology class discussion on Freudian theory. When the teacher mentioned "penis envy" in her lecture, one of the guys yelled out, "Yeah, penis envy—that's what Lydia has." When the class roared with laughter, Lydia remembers feeling more angry and frustrated than embarrassed. She was used to being the butt of cruel jokes because of her masculine-looking clothes and haircut, but that particular remark upset her for a different reason. As Lydia put it, "I didn't envy boys. I *was* one. I didn't know until puberty that I wasn't, and that bothered me all through high school. While I knew inside that I was a boy, all the evidence was against me on that. My breasts. My periods. I had nothing tangible to prove that I was male."

Another patient, Tina, remembers the concentration she had to summon each day to perform even the most routine activities, such as using the rest room. "I'd always automatically head right for the men's room instead of the ladies' room," she said. "It took mental gymnastics every time to force myself to veer away and enter the 'proper' rest room."

She recalls with particular clarity how strange she felt on the evening of her high school prom. She had not looked forward to attending the event, at least not as a female. Instead her fantasy revolved around wearing a tuxedo and having a beautiful girl as a date. However, after being pressured by her mother and several classmates, Tina grudgingly agreed to go. Her mother had gone out and bought her an elegant gown for the occasion, much to Tina's dismay. As soon as she put it on and saw her image in the mirror, her first words were, "Jesus, I'm in drag." She couldn't help thinking how great her gown would have looked on a "real" girl.

Another patient, Brenda, experienced similar feelings, especially with regard to intimate garments that symbolized her progression into unwanted womanhood. "Puberty was a horrible experience for me," Brenda said. "First of all, I didn't want to wear a training bra. The whole concept seemed absurd to me. What on earth was I in training for? And I hated the bodily changes and monthly menstrual cycle. Even though I loved my mom and was very close to my sisters, I still feared the prospect of having my body change to resemble theirs."

## "Nobody Understands—I'm All Alone"

Most transgendered teenagers can't imagine telling anyone about their gender dysphoria. They feel so alien that it seems inconceivable to them that anyone could understand their formidable secret. They barely understand it themselves. And even if they feel safe enough to confide their long-held anguish to someone else, they usually don't have any idea how to explain it. Most of them have never heard of transsexualism. They are unaware that other individuals like themselves exist, and they usually assume that nobody else could possibly be experiencing the same gender confusion. Many of my patients report, "I thought that I was the only person in the whole world who felt this way."

Gender-conflicted teens don't seem to fit in with either the boys or the girls in school. They frequently describe themselves as outcasts or misfits. They report feeling as if they are in limbo or straddling a gender border—they are neither male nor female but something in between.

Many are reluctant to draw more attention to themselves than is absolutely necessary because they get so many signals, both subtle and overt, that something about their behavior, manner, or appearance is not quite right. Thus they often decide that being alone is their safest bet. That way there is less chance that their secret will be discovered. But withdrawing into a shell leads to loneliness. And loneliness can become a dark abyss of depression.

As Laura described it, "At least when I was little, even though I felt odd and 'out of the groove,' so to speak, I still felt like there were people who cared about me. But that changed dramatically when I became a teenager. I began to feel totally trapped, almost as if I was in a prison cell, because I realized that I would be stuck in my body forever. It was a solitary confinement cell that no one else could enter to give me solace or to keep me company. I felt so utterly, totally alone."

A transsexual named Jill vividly recalls her dysphoria and feelings of isolation and inferiority:

> My teen years were the worst part of my life. I became very shy and introverted. I felt like a "nothing." I was out of touch with every part of myself. Even going into a store to buy a candy bar was almost more than I could handle because I was so sure that everyone would see how different and inferior I was. I never dated and had very few friends, and those I had were on the social fringe, just like me. I felt as though I had no one to really talk to about the important things, the troubling things. I could not talk to my family, and there was very little information about all the questions I had, especially about what was wrong with me. As I began going through puberty, I had all kinds of fears. But my greatest concern was that someone could actually force me to marry "another man" when I grew up.

## Problems with Self-Esteem

It is difficult for many teenagers to develop self-esteem and a positive self-image. But for gender dysphoric teens, the difficulties can increase enormously because there is so little about themselves that they can take pride in. It's hard to like and feel confident about a self that is phony. Not surprisingly, insecurity and poor self-esteem run rampant among these teenagers.

"I hated being me," a patient named Bill said, looking back on his adolescence. "It was hard for me to come up with one redeeming quality about myself. When I was alone, I could escape from my problems and lose myself in fantasy. I could be the wind making dust devils in the dry autumn leaves, or the snow, or the rain, or a tree—any tree or all of them. I could be anything I wanted, but never me."

Kent described his feelings this way:

> I felt so ashamed during my teen years, so cut off, so alone.
> Everyone else seemed to have so much going for them and to
> be having the time of their life dating, partying, or just hang-
> ing out. But it was entirely different for me because I felt like
> I was damaged goods. Even though I played a charade and
> walked around with a big smile on my face, it was just to hide
> what I felt inside. Most of the time I felt totally alone and mis-
> understood. My pain was so intense that I felt like the walking
> wounded.

Many transgendered teenagers, just like their nontransgendered
counterparts, find that their relationships with their parents and
family members deteriorate during the teen years. And because gender dysphoric teens feel increasingly lost and distressed about their
bodily changes, they are often reluctant to share those concerns
with their parents. When they were younger, although their gender
problems were confusing and upsetting, they could sometimes seek
solace and reassurance from their parents. However, as teens, they
often feel that this is no longer an option.

In many cases, parental pressures and expectations intensify
during the teen years, and this causes further alienation. As George
put it:

> I could not talk to my parents. Our relationship was especially
> strained during my teens. I knew they would not understand
> that I felt I was a girl trapped in the body of a boy. How could
> I explain that to my dad, or to my mom for that matter? It was
> one thing when I was a cute little kid, quirky, perhaps, but not
> yet a loathsome thing to them. But in my teens, it was a differ-
> ent situation altogether. How could they possibly understand
> what I was going through? By age sixteen I was over six feet
> tall and overweight, had acne, and wanted to be a girl. I could
> just imagine how that would go over!

Many patients report that their parents would not or could not take their gender conflict seriously. As Todd said, "My parents didn't see anything they didn't want to see. They laid down the rules about how a 'young man' was supposed to behave, and I was expected to toe the line."

For these teenagers, the frustration builds up over time as their families push them toward rigid gender roles or, in some cases, pretend that nothing is wrong. Eventually, this frustration can manifest itself in angry outbursts and confrontations. This was the case with Bonnie. "I felt like an idiot," she said, "because I was doing all the 'girl things' that my parents wanted me to do. I tried to zero in on things that would make everyone accept me. But they didn't understand me, and I felt they never would."

Bonnie found that the only way she could deal with the pain her gender dysphoria caused her was through excessive physical exercise. She would go off by herself and jog for hours on end or go lift weights at the gym. At times, this provided an outlet through which she could defuse some of her undirected anger, although her family sometimes got the brunt of it. "There were times when I got so mad, I would scream and put my fists through the wall. My parents were completely freaked out by my behavior."

Because gender-conflicted teenagers continually play a role that demands great effort on their part, inevitably the mask slips from time to time, and upsetting episodes or confrontations occur. Even transsexual teens who are able to stay "in character" and play the expected role frequently experience guilt about the fact that they must be deceptive with the people they care about most.

One patient summed it up this way: "I wasn't brave enough to be honest. I felt angry at myself and guilty for perpetuating a lie. And that, combined with the shame I felt because I was so different, made my teen years one of the loneliest and darkest periods of my life."

Feelings of isolation and alienation are common for gender dysphoric teenagers, and they often describe them in strikingly similar terms. "I felt like I was wearing an outer male shell and was much more of an observer than a participant in my own life," was how one patient phrased it. Another said, "I felt shut off completely. It was as though my teen years were a long, dark tunnel without any glimpse of light at all." Another patient described feeling "like a satellite circling out in space. I had a sense of looking in and watching everything that was going on but not being a part of it."

## Cross-Dressing During Adolescence

Cross-dressing takes on a whole new dimension for transsexuals when they reach their teen years. Although many transsexual kids cross-dress from time to time, as teenagers they cross-dress more frequently. This is primarily due to opportunity. Teens have more freedom of movement, more money to buy clothes, and more privacy than they had as kids. Male-to-female teenagers, who as children had to sneak clothing from the laundry hamper or their mother's or sister's closets, can now afford to shop for female garments for themselves. And since their privacy is more respected, they can lock themselves in their rooms with far less risk of parental or sibling intrusion. They are also more likely to have the house to themselves for longer periods of time.

To a much greater extent than in childhood, they are aware of their gender identity conflict and cross-gender identities. Cross-dressing allows them an outlet, a way to externalize and express more of their true selves.

"I was sixteen when I started cross-dressing," one patient explained. "I'd just reached mom's height, and she had a couple of wigs back then. So I'd wait until everyone was gone—I'd make excuses to be home alone—and then dress up and put on a wig. Then I'd just sit around and read. It was not stimulating, but it made me feel wonderful in so many ways. There was an overwhelming sense of everything finally being right. I remember being dizzy with exultation. In fact, I was always happy when I cross-dressed."

Another patient, Scott, described how cross-dressing helped him cope with what he considered an otherwise "totally bogus" existence:

It was during my late teens that I fully realized that I related experientially and emotionally as a woman. While I had some serious problems during my childhood, I didn't relate them specifically to my gender, even though I cross-dressed whenever I could get away with it. But in my teens, after finding no outlet for communication and emotional discussion among my family or any male friends, I began to cross-dress whenever I had the chance. This gave me an immediate sense of comfort and satisfaction that seemed to help hold me over until the next time.

Despite fear of discovery and the consequences that might ensue, transsexual teenagers typically feel compelled to cross-dress. Mickey remembers when his parents came home unexpectedly once and caught him wearing his sister's clothes. "My father started ranting and raving and accusing me of being everything from 'on drugs' to 'obviously homosexual' to 'retarded.' My mother cried for days. I waited a few weeks until things cooled off and then started cross-dressing again, but I was much more careful after that."

## Parental Conflict over Cross-Dressing

Harry, a fifteen-year-old teenager, also got caught and faced the ridicule and disapproval of family members. His relationship with his strict father was strained, especially after he was caught wearing his sister's dress. He explains:

My father was very traditional, especially about me, his number one son. He kept me in dark clothes and crew cuts all through my school years. Since respect for my parents was such a focal point of my upbringing, I tried to live by their standards, but I knew I was a disappointment to them in so many ways. Even before catching me, they were aware of my "feminine strangeness," as they called it. Even though I felt great shame every time I tried to be real, I had to go against tradition in order to go forward. There was no way I could explain why I cross-dressed or how I felt. It was a very difficult and painful period for all concerned.

If teens absolutely don't have the leeway to dress in cross-gender clothing, they sometimes find places away from home to do so, as in the case of Mary. Mary's parents were very strict and insisted that she wear skirts and dresses to school every day. She was so miserable about this that she would stash men's shirts, trousers, jeans, and shoes in her locker at school and at her best friend's house so that she could change into them. And change she did, every single day. She considered the time, hassle, and deception well worth the effort because she felt so horrible in feminine attire.

Ed similarly remembers being caught by his parents on one occasion when he was wearing a comfortable skirt and blouse that he particularly liked to relax in. "They made a really big deal out of it," he said, "and demanded to know if I had ever done this before. I lied and said no, and they bought it, probably only because they wanted to. But they still forced me into a cold bathtub as punishment, to 'cool me down,' as they put it. After that, it was never mentioned again, although I noticed that I was less frequently left alone in the house."

Perhaps the most dramatic example of family upheaval as a result of cross-gender behaviors is David's case. David had a particularly stormy relationship with his family, and much of the animosity seemed to center around his cross-dressing. "I openly cross-dressed at home from my teens on," he said, "and although my mother grudgingly tolerated it, she was adamant about not letting the neighbors find out."

He vividly recalls one occasion when he cut his hand on a sharp kitchen knife while doing dishes and bled so profusely that he had to be rushed to the hospital for stitches. Even under those emergency circumstances, his mother insisted that he wait until she pulled the car into the garage so that he could enter from the interior door. She didn't want the neighbors to see him running down the driveway in the dress he habitually wore around the house.

"My mere presence was an embarrassment to her, and she didn't want to be seen with me, although at the hospital she had no choice.

But on the way home from the hospital, as soon as we got to our street, where people knew us, she insisted that I scoot down on the seat until she pulled back inside the garage."

David was devastated. "I became so nauseous with self-loathing," he said, "that I collapsed on the kitchen floor in a fetal position and couldn't move. I remember sobbing over and over, 'I am a person, not a thing. I have value and worth.'"

As these teens get older, problems related to cross-dressing may diminish as they acquire more freedom to dress as they wish. When parents no longer dictate what to wear, a female-to-male teen, for example, can stop wearing dresses. Furthermore, older transsexual teens have more mobility and freedom of movement. They may have access to a car and can go out of town to cross-dress or visit friends or relatives around whom they feel comfortable enough to cross-dress. Some teens move out of their parents' homes and get places of their own or share an apartment with an understanding friend and thus have ample opportunities to cross-dress.

Female-to-male transsexuals have fewer problems with cross-dressing. Females can appear in public in masculine clothes if they choose and most people won't notice or object, whereas males wearing feminine clothes are likely to be ridiculed.

Although most gender dysphoric teens cross-dress at least on occasion, some don't. They may have no opportunity, be too afraid of being caught and confronted, or be too riddled with guilt, shame, and anxiety to do so.

## Longing to Belong

Human beings are social creatures, and everyone wants to be liked and accepted by other people. Acceptance is especially important to teenagers. As they develop a more adult sense of self, they need affirmation from others to validate their own worth. Often teens try to do this by getting involved in social groups and conforming to whatever the current trend happens to be. This applies to the things they are interested in, the music they listen to, and the cloth-ing, hairstyles, attitudes, and demeanor considered socially acceptable within their chosen group. Although some teenagers are staunch individualists, most do not want to stand out or be different. They want to be popular and tend to do whatever it takes to be "just like everyone else."

Gender dysphoric teens are just like any other teens in this regard. However, it takes special effort for them to do the things necessary to blend in with their peers. If they find they can't fit into the mainstream, they often look for other places where they might be more successful.

One male patient said that he found a group of outcasts and hung out with them. But he still felt out of place. Another transsexual, Larry, described his experiences this way: "I had a couple of friends who were loners too, who liked hiking in the woods and playing long games of Monopoly and chess instead of more traditionally male-oriented things. And a couple of them were just plain nerds, which seemed easy enough, so I became one too. I thought I'd finally found my group, the people who were like me. But they weren't. Even though they were not popular guys, they were nevertheless guys, while I felt like a girl."

Larry was constantly taunted and beaten as a teenager. "I guess my crime was that I never picked up on the more typically male aggressive behaviors," he said. "It hurt me to be so excluded by my classmates, and that probably made me an easy target. Although I tried to figure out how other teenagers acted by observing them closely and by watching television shows, that didn't work. Nothing came naturally to me, even defending myself. I mean, even the other nerdy kids knew enough to fight back when someone was beating them up."

## Seeking Group Affiliations

Some transgendered teens seek friendship and group affiliation by joining an organization or a club. They may find an entree into such a group based on a shared hobby such as photography, chess, or computers. For others, motorcycles, sports, or cars have more appeal. Tom sought identity by joining a motorcycle gang. He found that he was accepted to some degree within this group. Like many of the other members, he grew his hair long, sported a mustache and beard, and got several tattoos. "I did what I thought I had to do to belong. And I got all the support in the world for being male," he said, "and none for being female. Joining a motorcycle gang seemed like taking the path of least resistance. And even though I had something of a group identity to lean on, I still felt like a freak. At times I couldn't decide whether I was suicidal or homicidal. I had so many intense, conflicting emotions going on, and so much anger."

Military training is a popular choice for both male and female transsexuals because it gives them not only a place to belong but also a strong sense of group affiliation. For transgendered females, it is one setting in which they are not only allowed to express a tougher, more masculine side of their nature but *expected* to do so. Many transgendered males join the military because they think it might make them more masculine. Sean was such an individual. "When I was eighteen," he recalled, "I moved in with my cousin, who was kind of macho, and I tried to emulate his behavior. He thought that joining the military would be a way of making me a man. I hoped he might be right, so I went along with that and enlisted in the Marines. I somehow managed to get through it, but it didn't cure my gender problems. The transsexualism was always there; I just worked like the devil to repress it."

Needless to say, these teens find themselves experiencing extreme longing to belong to the most obvious group given their gender conflict—the opposite sex. "All through junior high," a patient named Paul said, "there was always at least one girl in class who I would envy. I would spend a great deal of my time sitting there thinking, 'I wish I were her instead of me.'"

This is a common theme among transsexuals. Most report feeling that their gender identity disorder has cheated them out of the life and experiences that should have rightfully been theirs. This leaves them with a profound sense of sadness and loss.

Some report feeling more frustration than sadness during their teens because they tried so hard, but without success, to deny, resist, or change their cross-gender preferences. They desperately wanted to believe that conforming to societal norms might somehow "cure" them. They hoped that if they dated enough, became popular enough, or achieved enough, they might somehow be able to eliminate their gender identity conflict.

Some transgendered teens are, to all outward appearances, happy, well-adjusted, popular teens. They often become so skilled at "going with the flow" that no one senses their inner turmoil. One mother of a male transsexual described her son's teen years this way: "Noah was always an outgoing, popular kid with lots of friends. He was always rushing out with one group or another to do things. He also had a couple of girlfriends. His father and I sensed that he had some problems, but he didn't share them with us. For all those years, I never realized what he was struggling with inside. He hid it all so well for so long."

## Dating

During the teen years, as hormones begin surging, many heterosexual males and females begin to show an increased awareness and interest in the opposite sex that may lead to crushes, "puppy love," dating, full-blown romance, and even marriage. Although teen dating can be rather like a ride on an emotional roller coaster, many adults look back on their dating years as not just a natural part of their teen experience but one of the high points.

For transsexual teens, however, dating is generally extremely stressful and complicated. Like other teenagers, they want to date and be part of a couple. But they don't want to date someone of the "opposite sex" as their family, friends, and society expect them to do. Since a male-to-female (MTF) transsexual self-identifies as female, he doesn't want to date a female—it feels like lesbian dating to him (and inappropriate if his sexual orientation is heterosexual). What he really wants is for a male to court him, if only he had the female anatomy to make this appropriate.

Similarly, FTMs don't want a male asking them out because they self-identify as male. Going out with "another male" would feel like homosexual dating to them. Instead, they want to ask girls out themselves. They typically report that they don't know how to behave romantically as a female; it doesn't come naturally to them.

Some GID teenagers date because they feel they are supposed to, but it is just one more act. It pushes their role-playing skills to an extreme. Others never go out on a single date during their teen years. They just can't bring themselves to do so. Some gain an enormous amount of weight in a subconscious (or in some cases conscious) effort to make people less likely to want to date them.

A poignant part of the dating dilemma for transsexual teens is that they watch other teenagers live the kind of life they want for themselves—if only they had the right body. They fully recognize that dating is frequently the first step in selecting a mate. Thus the dating ritual serves as a constant reminder that they will never have the types of relationships and life experiences they desperately want.

This leaves them in a quandary. Whom do they date? They have three options, all of which are unsatisfactory. They can date members of the opposite sex (which to them would be homosexual relationships); they can experiment with same-sex relationships, which is what they really want but would be perceived by society as gay relationships; or they can avoid dating altogether.

The irony of the dating dilemma for these teens is that it is their childhood dilemma in reverse. As kids, the boys desperately wanted to be friends with the girls and share in their activities. However, because of their male anatomy, the girls usually excluded them from their inner circle. Now that these same boys are teenagers, they are welcomed by the girls, who suddenly want their company *because* they are male. They are now considered prospective beaus, which is very different from the girl-to-girl friendships that transsexual boys typically want to have with girls. As a result, since they do not wish to play the role of male suitor, many transsexual males choose to exclude *themselves* from the girls' company and refuse to date.

Timothy was one of these boys. "The teen years were easily the most unhappy time of my life," he said. "I didn't date. I felt out of place because I didn't feel male or female. I didn't belong anywhere. By the age of fourteen or fifteen, I became aware that there was a female inside my male body. Then later I read a story about a French transsexual and saw it as a replay of my life."

Some transgendered teenagers of both genders do go ahead and date to try to prove to their parents, family members, and friends (and in some cases themselves) that nothing is wrong with them.

George's parents constantly pressured him to date, and he was fairly certain that it was related to their concerns about his femininity. "They were always bugging me to go out with girls," he said. "I guess they expected me to follow in the path of my two older brothers, but I just wanted to be alone. I never dated much. Every time I did ask someone out, I would get turned down. It was almost as if the girls knew that something was different about me. But I often didn't even mention these rejections to my parents because I knew these 'failures' would disappoint them and serve to confirm their suspicions about me. It was easier to act disinterested."

Margaret was interested in dating girls but afraid to admit it. As an athletically inclined teenager, she spent most of her free time playing ball with the "other guys." Whenever girls were in the vicinity and the boys would sneak sidelong glances or laugh and joke about who they'd like to take out, she'd grit her teeth and try to ignore their conversations. She felt no more a part of their world than she was a part of the girls' world. And what would her buddies think if they knew that she, too, was looking at the same girls with considerable interest?

Some gender dysphoric teenagers date as a way to be close to teens of the other gender—with whom they self-identify. But in such cases, they are usually consumed with feelings of envy. Male patients who do this also describe feeling guilty and frustrated about their deception.

As Carl said, "I felt like a total sneak, a fraud. Here was a girl I really cared for and I was more or less leading her on because what she wanted was very different from what I wanted. I wanted companionship, the opportunity to spend time with her, talk to her, go shopping for clothes. Basically I wanted to do 'girl stuff' with her. But I was aware that what she wanted was something entirely different."

## "I Must Be Gay"

Transsexual teens can't help but notice that most of their peers are interested in dating, and in some cases becoming romantically or sexually involved with members of the opposite sex. They feel that everyone must perceive them as odd or abnormal because they don't share those interests.

If they have any romantic interest at all, it is often toward individuals of their own anatomical sex, and these teens feel that if they act on their true feelings, they will likely be perceived by others as gay (since their cross-gender identity is invisible). Since few teens realize that being gay and being transsexual are two separate things, they themselves often begin to wonder whether all the kids who taunted them during their early years about being homosexual might have been right after all.

It's not hard to see how they could reach this erroneous conclusion. How would they know that homosexual males don't feel like a woman inside or that lesbians don't feel like a man inside? They wouldn't. Usually they've never *knowingly* spoken to a gay person and don't know much about the gay experience. As a result, these teens sometimes wrongly conclude that their childhood gender confusion is typical of the experience of growing up gay.

Some gender dysphoric teens may therefore experiment with a gay lifestyle. However, if a transgendered teenage boy develops a friendship or relationship with a gay male, he generally becomes very unhappy when he realizes that his gay friend views him as another male, is attracted to him as a male, and treats him like a male instead of the female the transsexual knows he really is.

The same is true for females, except that generally they are able to integrate more easily and more comfortably into the lesbian community, at least temporarily. Whereas some female transgendered teens find that they can play a somewhat satisfying version of the male gender role and sex role, eventually it is not enough because they are still playing it in the wrong body. Ultimately, they find that homosexuality is as emotionally unsatisfying to them as heterosexuality.

As Jane put it, "I had occasional lesbian encounters in high school and college, but I never felt lesbian. I felt male, and when I would go to mix with lesbian groups, their issues seemed vastly different from mine. It was *one more place* I didn't belong."

Jack expressed similar sentiments. "I came to the common but false belief that feeling as if I should be a woman meant that I was gay. So I set out in earnest in my first semester of college to see if this was the case. Though I would place myself in situations where I could have easily had sex with a man I found attractive, I never found myself ultimately able to be comfortable with the idea of being in the situation of a gay male and always backed out."

To dispel the notion that they are homosexual, some of these teenagers go out of their way to date a lot in order to get parents and friends off their back. If they do so, however, they typically run into problems if and when their partner wants the relationship to progress to a sexual one. Some try to avoid the situation altogether by keeping their social interactions to a minimum.

Marlene, another patient, was a teenager whom everyone assumed was gay all through high school because she didn't have a boyfriend and didn't talk about boys, kept her hair short, never wore dresses or makeup, and was an avid athlete. She remembers being attracted to females during her early teens but didn't give it a second thought at the time. Despite the talk, she knew that she wasn't lesbian because she had a male identity herself.

Just as a certain percentage of the general population is gay, a certain percentage of the transsexual population is also gay. Because homophobia (irrational fear of, aversion to, or discrimination against homosexuality or homosexuals) and transphobia (irrational fear of, aversion to, or discrimination against transsexuality and transsexuals) still prevails in our society, some patients describe being transsexual *and* gay as a "double whammy."

## "I Must Be Crazy"

Transsexual teens have a long-standing inner perception of themselves that doesn't match the image they see in the mirror. Nor does their perception match that of anyone else they meet and interact with. Day in and day out, they face the harsh reality of a world in which parents, family, teachers, friends, and even strangers view them in a way that is the diametric opposite of how they view themselves.

Eventually, this serious distortion can cause them to doubt the validity of their own perceptions. It is not surprising that at a certain point, many transsexuals begin to question their own sanity. Sometimes their parents or peers have even told them so in so many words: "Are you crazy? Boys don't talk like that," or "How could you possibly not be a girl? Of course you're a girl!"

When enough people have told them, even in jest, "You must be nuts," it eventually seems to transsexuals to have the ring of truth. They assume that something must be wrong with them mentally, since gender classification in our society is considered an either-or proposition. To some people, questioning gender is akin to contradicting indisputable facts, as in insisting that black is white or that $2 + 2 = 5$. With all the negative feedback and all of the questioning (both self-questioning and questions posed by others), it's no wonder that transsexual children, teens, and adults often find themselves thinking on occasion, "I must be crazy."

Judy was such a girl. "I never felt right as a girl, and I spent fifteen years trying to fit in but never made it. I doubted myself every other day. Yet since this was the way I was born, I couldn't help but ask myself, 'Would God or nature make such a mistake?'" She wondered if she was crazy. This was clearly what her parents thought. They had told her so in anger on more than one occasion.

The suspicion of mental illness is terrifying to transsexuals, but many of them are at a loss for any other explanation. If they have heard of transsexualism at all, it is ordinarily in such negative terms that they would be far too ashamed to pursue the subject, seek more information, or discuss it with other people.

Typically, transsexuals feel as though they are leading two completely different lives—an internal one and an external one. This causes some to worry that they might be psychotic. Gina was one of those individuals. "I continually worried," she said, "that I had a multiple or split personality. The dichotomy between the public Gina and the private 'Gene' was enormous. I flip-flopped back and forth between the two so much that I couldn't help but question my sanity."

One patient, Bob, said, "After a point in time, I ceased to know what was real. I kept wondering how I could have these thoughts that I was trapped in the wrong body if I wasn't downright crazy. After a while, my perception of reality became so completely affected by that that I figured I must be losing my mind. I feared that I would reach a day where I would not be able to take care of myself and would be locked up in a mental institution."

Some patients describe becoming extremely outgoing during their teen years. It is almost as if by doing so, they hope to "fool the world" or somehow "learn to become normal." Just because they suspect they might be crazy doesn't mean that they are willing to let other people reach the same conclusion. Often their acting skills, honed through long years of practice, lead them to believe that they can continue playing out a role and fool the world about their "mental illness" as well. Some teens withdraw deeper and deeper into a shell or a formidable fortress that they have constructed over the years to protect themselves from the expectations, the reprisals, the fear, the loneliness, and the pain of growing up transgendered. Others may turn to substance abuse in an attempt to numb their pain.

## Escape Through Alcohol and Drugs

Amid the natural turbulence of the teen years, many teenagers seek psychological crutches or temporary escape routes in order to cope with what they consider insurmountable problems. Many turn to alcohol and drugs. Gender dysphoric teenagers are no exception. They typically have all of the problems characteristic of the average teenager, compounded by the additional burden of gender conflict.

Marianne starting drinking when she was twelve years old. Her gender problems completely overwhelmed her, and the only time she felt any release was when she could forget her dilemma for a period of time. Consequently, every time she got the chance, she would sneak a bottle from her parents' liquor cabinet into her room and drink herself into oblivion. "At some level, even at that age," she said, "I knew that I couldn't solve anything by going on a drunken binge, but it sure seemed like I could at least have short spurts of reprieve from the dungeonlike darkness in which I felt confined."

However, she found that the more she drank, the more depressed she got about her female body. Then she would fall even further into despair when she realized that she could not find lasting refuge at the bottom of a bottle.

Dwayne jumped right in not only with alcohol but with drugs as well. "I drank every day for six years," he revealed. "I found my body so disgusting and my options so nonexistent that I gave up all hope of ever living a normal life. All I cared about was getting high on anything at all. Drinking was easier because booze was cheap, but I also took any kinds of drugs I could get my hands on. Since I was so miserable and never expected to live beyond my teens, I had no hesitation about what I was doing to my body. After all, my body had nothing to do with who I was."

Another patient, Sandra, began drinking at age fifteen as a way to escape from her all-consuming gender conflicts. She thought that perhaps with the help of alcohol and drugs, she might better assimilate the feminine behaviors that everyone expected of her. She explains:

I wanted to fit into the group, but I wanted to be a male, not a female. And I remember how bad I felt whenever someone put down effeminate or gay men. It really hit home because my secret dream was to leave home and move away to someplace where I could live as the man I knew I was. But I knew that even cross-dressed, I'd still be a fairly feminine-looking man, and it hurt me to think that there was no way on earth

I would ever be accepted for who I really was. This realization made me drink even more, and I became far too hostile to interact with anyone in that state.

For these teenagers, their early tendencies toward substance abuse may set the stage for destructive behavior patterns that will extend well into their adult years.

## Self-Mutilation and Suicide

For some transsexual teens, their gender conflict may escalate to the point where it leads to debilitating depression and despair. Nothing they have tried to do has provided any lasting relief from their dilemma, so eventually it seems as though they have reached the end of the road; they see no solution in sight. They feel as though there is no one to turn to, nowhere else to go, and nothing to look forward to in life. This overwhelming sense of hopelessness about their condition may lead them to take such dramatic steps as self-mutilation. Considering the nature of gender dysphoria, it is not too surprising that the parts of the body that transsexuals usually seek to mutilate are their genitals or their breasts. Some females pound or hit themselves in the chest area until they are covered with black-and-blue marks or in some cases cut their breasts. Males use razors or other sharp instruments in crude attempts to sever their penis or castrate themselves. Several self-destructive male patients have admitted to fantasies (or actual attempts) whereby they injured their penis in some "accident" hoping that they could then get a physician to finish what they started.

This was Rick's intention. When talking about his gender conflict with his parents didn't work, Rick decided to take a far more self-destructive tack in "waking them up" to his pain. "I took the scissors to my genitals," he said, "fully intending to cut them. But at the last minute, I couldn't go through with it. I guess I hoped my action would make my parents see the severity of my anguish. They knew about my transsexualism but were in complete denial about it." He was also worried, like many transsexual teens, that his parents might "put him away" if they knew the seriousness of his dysphoria.

Some teens seek to end their lives. As indicated in Chapter One, the suicide rate (and attempted suicide rate) among trans-sexuals is considerably higher than that in the general population. Among those who do not actually take action, thoughts of suicide are still frequently present. At least 70 percent of my patients admit that they have considered suicide at some time in their lives.

I have little doubt that in a large number of unexplained teen-age suicides—cases in which the family and people close to the teenager can cite no plausible explanation—the victim is either secretly gay or transsexual. Since these teenagers frequently feel as though they have no options, that people will not accept them, and that they are never going to have a satisfying life, suicide may appear to be the only way out.

A patient named Darryl describes his suicidal teenage years in terms of entrapment. "I saw no reason to live. I saw no solution to my problem because there was no path out of where I was. I felt like a rat stuck in the middle of an endless maze. I was running around and around but getting nowhere at all."

Another patient, Gail, said, "I remember that when I was four-teen years old, I had this incredible desire to jump off a cliff. I felt such unutterable despair. The only thing that saved me was my mom. She reached out to me and helped me through this difficult time." But Gail's depression did not go away. At age seventeen, she intentionally drove head-on into a tree but managed to survive the accident, which the insurance adjusters claimed should have killed the driver.

Andy remembers contemplating suicide on a regular basis. "I had so much anger all through my growing-up years because of a situation that was not of my choosing," he said. "It seemed so unfair. My exis-tence, my maleness, was a nightmare and a purgatorial madness that was particularly acute during my teen years. My mind didn't want to deal with my body because it was so inferior. It seemed pointless to go on. I wanted to be rid of the female side of me because I couldn't live with it any longer." He felt that the fact that he would die if he destroyed his female side was unfortunate but unavoidable.

Gender dysphoric teens who attempt suicide or self-mutilation are often unaware of the options available to them. More important, many teens may not even know that gender dysphoria is the underlying cause of their conflict, confusion, misery, or alienation until much later in life. As teenagers, they may never have heard that transsexualism exists or that hormonal and surgical procedures are available for people like themselves.

This is particularly true of those who were teens prior to the late 1960s. It was not until 1965 at the University of Minnesota Medical Center that the first sex reassignment surgery was performed in the United States.

Though hormone treatments and surgical procedures are commonly available today, young people rarely have the funds or the freedom to pursue such options. And it is highly unlikely that their parents would agree to these procedures, much less pay for them.

Although the cost of treatment, especially sex reassignment surgery, is often prohibitively high, the mere knowledge that such options do exist prevents some transsexual teenagers from taking self-destructive actions.

Despite all of their gender-related problems and the resulting unhappiness that pervades nearly every aspect of their lives, most teenage transsexuals begin their adult years resigned to living their lives as best they can in the bodies they have—at least for the time being.

# 4

---

# The Adult Years

The gender discomfort experienced by transsexuals during their childhood and teen years does not dissipate as they grow older—instead, it intensifies. By the time they mature into adults, however, most have become adept at keeping their dysphoria under wraps. They learn from their early experiences that if they value their family, friendships, and career, they have little choice but to bury their cross-gender feelings and identity. To do otherwise might jeopardize the life they have struggled to create.

---

## Functioning in Daily Life

Driven by their need to cover up their true nature, transsexuals typically develop a series of coping techniques, defense mechanisms, and diversions that allow them to function reasonably well in the gender role that matches their anatomy.

### Coping Techniques

Some of the coping techniques my patients have used over the years are stress reduction processes such as visualization, guided imagery, and meditation. A common visualization is one in which they mentally create an impenetrable shell or container, not unlike a steel vault, into which they deposit and lock away all of their cross-gender feelings, yearnings, dreams, behaviors, and manner-isms. They insulate that container with layer after layer of rein-forcement until it is strong enough to enable them to cope, at least temporarily, with their internal trauma and conflict.

## Defense Mechanisms

Whereas coping techniques tend to be inner-directed, defense mech-anisms are primarily outer-directed, external methods that transsex-uals use to avoid detection, rejection, and scorn. These methods include role-playing, conforming, and distancing themselves from others and are necessary tools in their arsenal for successful func-tioning. By playing the gender role that is consistent with their anatomy, transsexuals attempt to fit into the mainstream of society. They dress the part, develop their body, join groups, immerse them-selves in careers, date the opposite sex, get married, have children—in short, they do everything they possibly can to live a "normal" life. As one patient said, "If I don't fake it, I won't make it."

Many male-to-female transsexuals seek the most rugged, stereo-typically male profession or job they can find. They may go into law enforcement, become auto or airplane mechanics, drive big rigs, or work in steel mills, auto manufacturing plants, or heavy construc-tion. Some are considered by their coworkers among the more manly members of the group. As a patient named Earl said, "I did a better cover-up than any politician could. I was so successful that people used to tell me all the time how macho I was. I exaggerated the male role to such an extent day in and day out that it almost killed me."

Military service is a route that many male-to-female transsexu-als follow in their quest for confirmation of their masculinity. Over half of my male patients served in one of the branches of the mil-itary. Many transsexuals not only become career military officers but also frequently request the most rigorous or dangerous missions they can find in their desire to exaggerate their gender role. Their bravado serves a double purpose. First, it provides an excellent cover-up. Nobody would ever suspect that these rugged military men are not what they appear to be. Second, if the mission were to end in death, the transsexual would be permanently freed from a lifetime of gender pain.

In a further attempt to conform, some transsexuals purposely seek out the most obvious trappings of the gender associated with their anatomy. Male-to-female transsexuals may work out, grow a beard or mustache, or favor haircuts, demeanor, and clothes that make them look more masculine. Female-to-male transsexuals may overcompensate and wear lots of makeup and jewelry, choose traditional female hairstyles, or dress in ultrafrilly clothes to make themselves look more feminine.

As a female-to-male patient said, "I had to consciously develop female traits and a female image so that I could exist in a woman's world. Because, sadly, in this life, you are judged by what your body looks like and not by what you feel. But it is extremely distressing to have to go around pretending to be a female when I am so comfortable in the male world."

Another defense mechanism often used by transsexuals is to divert their attention away from the source of their anguish. They may do this by immersing themselves in work or studies, improving their mind and body, pursuing hobbies, or participating in politics, sports, or religious activities.

## Diversions

Computers are a primary diversion for many transsexuals. Not only do they provide easy access to information about transgender issues, but they also significantly broaden the boundaries of the transsexual's world. Through the vast resources of computer online services as well as electronic mailboxes and bulletin boards, transsexuals can communicate with individuals around the world who have similar concerns and issues. This helps combat feelings of alienation and enables them to form lasting friendships with other transgendered individuals they meet online.

Some transsexuals may find that a demanding career or a time-consuming outside interest may take the edge off their dysphoria for a while, but such diversions cannot completely eliminate their discomfort.

Carl found himself able to succeed only up to a point by making his job the prime focus of his life. He explains:

> I was a super computer-kind-of-fast-tracking character who went in five years from making twenty-two grand to one hundred grand. I found that I could do that by behaving in this stereotypical macho kind of way that they seemed to expect from me. I threw myself totally into my work. I would fly around the world and speak to people about our products and develop relationships but not really be there. It was just this character I was doing. But it really affected me. I was so tired of being deceitful internally, I felt like I was dying little by little living that half-life. After a while, I couldn't deal with it anymore and left the corporate world.

## Paying a Price

All of the techniques described here enable transsexuals to hide their true feelings—for a time. But repressing so much that is integral to one's being and living a life that is a lie in such a fundamental way demands tremendous energy and concentration. Transsexuals spend a great deal of time worrying that some small detail or gesture will arouse suspicion or give them away. Thus they must forever be on guard. This exacts not only a terrible psychological toll but often a physical one as well.

Many of my patients report suffering from medical conditions such as ulcers, colitis, migraines, high blood pressure, and respiratory and cardiovascular diseases. Others have eating disorders, suffer from anxiety attacks, or have difficulty sleeping. Whatever the physical ailment, it is most likely to occur during times when gender-related stress is at its highest level. Many transsexuals have found that their physical and emotional health begins to improve when at least one of the following occurs:

- They go into therapy and are able to release some of the intense emotions they had repressed for so long
- They "come out" (reveal their condition) to family and friends and are able to lead a more honest life
- They embark on cross-gender living or undergo hormone treatments or sex reassignment surgery

Most adult transsexuals, however, suffer in silence and isolation for a long time before letting *anyone*, even a therapist, know about their gender conflict. Instead, they try to create the most satisfying life possible within the limitations of the body in which they were born.

## Adult Cross-Dressing

The need to wear clothing of the opposite gender continues to be an important part of most transsexuals' lives. But finding a place to cross-dress and locating stores where the clothing can be obtained are continuing problems. For a transsexual who is a college student, a young adult living at home with parents, or a married person with spouse and kids, opportunities to cross-dress are rare. These individuals have to wait for the chance to be alone in the house, rent a hotel room, or find some other private place in which to cross-dress. For a single transsexual living alone, cross-dressing is easier because the prime component—opportunity—is seldom an issue.

A patient named William described how his adult cross-dressing differed from his childhood experiences: "I always cross-dressed from the time I was nine or ten years old. At that time, I wanted to do it but didn't understand why. By my teen years, I had some inkling because the gender stuff was driving me to the brink of despair. At some level, I knew it was important to my identity to wear clothing from time to time that was closer to who I really was.

Now, as an adult, cross-dressing is like breathing to me. It feels utterly natural."

Some adult transsexuals begin to venture out in public cross-dressed, usually in places where they don't know anyone or where they feel comfortable. They may go to another city or seek out support groups where they find a safe haven for interacting with others like themselves. These outings often act as a release from the pressures of living the lie. Many patients describe how good it feels to have opportunities outside of their home life where they can cross-dress and begin to relate in the world as their true selves.

## Acquiring a Wardrobe

Acquiring a wardrobe is not always easy, particularly for male-to-female transsexuals who are tall or large in body structure. They must find clothing stores and shoe stores that cater to larger women or else purchase clothing through mail-order catalogues.

Finding clothes that fit properly is another major hurdle. Because in most stores transsexuals are unable to use gender-appropriate fitting rooms to try on clothing, they must make their purchases based strictly on size labels alone. This is problematic because sizes often vary with the manufacturer, style, and cut of the garment. Transsexuals frequently make countless trips back and forth from stores buying and returning garments until they find something that fits them. And imagine buying a pair of shoes without the benefit of first trying them on. A male-to-female transsexual cannot try on women's shoes without attracting attention unless he is cross-dressed at the time. And even then, people may stare or cast disapproving glances.

Male-to-female transsexuals often feel embarrassed about purchasing feminine garments and feel compelled to explain that they are shopping for gifts for their mother, sister, girlfriend, wife, or daughter. But then they have to remember what they said if they consistently shop at the same stores. As one patient explained, "Once you find a store that carries your size, you always have to keep your stories straight. After all, 'Mother' can have only one birthday a year!"

Female-to-male transsexuals have a far easier time shopping for male clothing because it is not unusual for women to purchase and wear clothes that men typically wear or to purchase clothing for their husbands, boyfriends, or sons. But there are still problems. FTMs don't have access to men's fitting rooms to try on garments. In addition, women who are extremely small in stature cannot shop in the men's department at all. Often they must make their purchases in the boys' or teen department because men's garments are too large. This is discouraging because children's clothing styles are not what grown men usually wear—and what adult male wants to shop in the kids' department?

## Guilt and Shame

Adult transsexuals, just like their child and teenage counterparts, experience some degree of guilt, shame, and fear about their cross-dressing because they know how negatively their spouse, parents, friends, and colleagues would react if they found out. These transsexuals feel guilty and embarrassed about their inability to control, reduce, or eliminate their cross-dressing behavior. And they worry about the risk—they fear getting caught cross-dressing and being ridiculed and scorned. For these reasons, male-to-female transsexuals especially have a tendency from time to time to "purge"—to get rid of all female clothing, wigs, makeup, jewelry, and accessories. Many MTF transsexuals purge their wardrobes at least two or three times during their lifetime. They literally throw away everything or give it to charitable organizations. But since cross-dressing is an important expression of the transsexual identity, it is merely a matter of time before most replace everything they have discarded.

Jeremy, like most transsexuals, fluctuated between indulging himself in cross-dressing and chastising himself. He explains:

I often felt very guilty that I felt a need to cross-dress. I thought that this might be a sign that I was sick or deranged.

I went through periods of time where I gave in to doing it and then hated myself for it. Many times I considered getting rid of my entire female wardrobe, and once I actually did so. I reasoned that if I got rid of the clothing, I wouldn't be tempted to cross-dress. I guess you could say I was literally attempting to purge myself not only of the clothing but also of all my thoughts of looking like, living as, and being a woman.

Though cross-dressing is usually a satisfying part of transsexuals' lives, it also, at times, causes them distress. Even adults who have their own home or apartment sometimes find it difficult to cross-dress on a regular basis because they run the risk of being discovered by people who drop in unexpectedly. Whenever male-to-female transsexuals invite guests or family members to their home, they take special care to be sure that there are no female clothes, cosmetics, or other telltale signs in view. Gender-related books, magazines, and support group newsletters must also be tucked away.

Transsexuals may get to a point where they feel so good wearing clothing of the opposite gender that they begin to cross-dress almost daily. However, many become discouraged because there doesn't seem to be a logical next step that won't cause a major upheaval in their lives. They can't help but wonder where they can go from there.

Many consider talking to a therapist but may be too afraid to proceed. Several of my patients, for instance, were referred to me by a doctor or a friend but carried my phone number in their wallet for a couple of years before summoning the courage to call for an appointment. Transsexuals worry about confessing their secret, often dread facing up to it themselves, and harbor fears about the possible implications of acknowledging their condition. As one patient said, "God, if I admit to cross-dressing, they may think I'm loony and lock me away."

Some adult transsexuals don't cross-dress at all or may opt for an androgynous look. While this gives them some freedom of expression, it tends to keep friends and coworkers guessing because the transsexual generally looks not quite female and not quite male.

## Relating to Others

A troubling aspect of gender dysphoria, according to the majority of my patients, is the effect it has on their relationships with friends and loved ones. On the one hand, good relationships with family and friends are based on mutual openness and honesty. On the other hand, there is so much that transsexuals must keep secret if they are to live up to the expectations of their friends and families that it is not possible for them to share their feelings openly. Inevitably, this dichotomy gets in the way of their relationships and friendships and causes them to put up barriers to keep people from getting close enough to discover their secret.

As one patient said, "It seems like most of my adult life has been spent in a locked room or a closet, and even though the closet didn't feel secure, at least I felt like I owned it. I knew how the lock and the key worked and how to keep people out and at a distance."

Transsexuals often feel sad about the superficiality of their relationships. Nobody really knows them. Since they are afraid to tell the truth, people see only the false front that is projected. As Carol put it, "When you immerse yourself in maleness, you learn the language and the idioms. You understand the female role well but are never really living it because it's just a role. You simply follow a script, just like an actor does on the stage, and so you're not free. You're never allowed to shed the character role you play."

Transsexuals inevitably feel guilty about their dishonesty and as a result may retreat even further into their closet or protective shell. Yet the dysphoria is always there, insidiously doing its damage. They may become sullen, sarcastic, argumentative, and confrontational with the people they care about most.

## Family Relations

Some patients can't help but feel that the people closest to them should be able to see through the deception. They look at their loved ones and think, "If you really loved me, you would know that something's wrong."

Ironically, although transsexual adults need the love and support of their families as much as other adults (or maybe even more), they are often less likely to get it because of the distancing and alienation that results from all of the things that remain unsaid.

A patient named Mark explains:

I loved my parents and wanted to have a normal, warm family relationship, but whenever we got together, I could still sense their disapproval and their reluctance to accept me the way I was instead of the way they wanted me to be. It was all just swept under the rug. They didn't confront me in the same way they had when I lived at home, but there was this gap, this space that existed because of all the things we could never say to each other because I am transsexual but don't have the nerve to tell them that. I think they would like more closeness too, but as it is now, it's like we're playing on two different playing fields.

Ellen, a middle-aged patient, described her family relations as strained for more than three decades because of her overwhelming feelings of guilt. "Sometimes it feels like my whole life is one big hurt," she said. "I can block it out for a while, but it keeps coming back. I've been crying almost every day for months, but I don't talk about it with my family. I'm tired of bringing pain into the lives of others like my parents and my husband. I've brought too much pain already."

Another patient, Theresa, said, "I found myself often unable to let myself really befriend people because of my secret. Never being able to tell the truth but only half-truths got in the way of communicating. It was painful to talk to old friends and not be honest."

This kind of interacting limits friendships and causes ongoing problems for both male and female transsexuals. "I had to monitor everything," a patient named Carolyn said. "I had to censor and edit what I said and forever try to match some female profile created eons ago by who knows who. It becomes lifeless to interact that way. There is no joy in it. Eventually, even with my husband and kids, the constant gender issues robbed me of my sense of pride and pleasure."

## Dating, Sex, and Intimacy

By nature, human beings need and want affection, companionship, and intimacy in their lives. Most people want someone to love, someone who will love them back, and someone with whom they can share their lives. Gender-conflicted individuals, just like everyone else, grow up with family and societal pressures to pursue traditional goals. And in many cases, in their quest for conformity, they enter into relationships and marriages even though it doesn't feel entirely appropriate to them, given their gender conflict.

Dating, intimacy, and sexual relationships are even more difficult for adult transsexuals than they were during the teen years. All of the confusion and complexities of teen dating and courtship remain unresolved and follow these transsexuals into adulthood—only the consequences of not dating are more serious in adulthood. Because dating is the usual prelude to developing a lasting relationship, people who don't date are more likely to end up living a lonely life.

No matter how much transsexuals desire the warmth, intimacy, sexual expression, and tenderness of a loving relationship, many of them are unable or unwilling to date and be sexual in a body (and gender role) that does not match their identity. And although as adults they may have greater physical and emotional needs than they had in their teens, they refuse to act on them in the wrong body.

If they do date, transsexuals find that dating and sexual relationships often prove disappointing and unfulfilling because— assuming they are heterosexual—they generally do not feel desire for partners of the opposite anatomical sex.

As one patient said, "I had to eventually stop dating altogether because it felt so unnatural. There was no joy for me in dating or making love to a woman. There was no meaning in it. I wanted to be made love to, not to be the male aggressor. I didn't want to date women, I wanted to *be* like them."

As another patient said, "I noticed in my peers that what they were looking for was primarily to get laid, and that didn't make sense to me at all. I was always looking for deep relationships to form. I was much more interested in affection and companionship than in making a conquest or developing a physical relationship."

## Sexual Behavior

Generally, married transsexuals, or those in man-woman relationships, engage in sexual behavior less frequently than nontranssexuals do. Usually, their relationships with partners have more of a best friend or sister-brother aspect.

When transsexuals engage in partnered sexual activities, male-to-female transsexuals generally are more comfortable in a passive role and, if they have intercourse, prefer to be on the bottom. Conversely, female-to-male transsexuals prefer to play the active or aggressive role. They would rather stimulate their partners than be stimulated. Typically, they are uncomfortable having their own breasts and genitals touched.

Transsexuals who do establish sexual relationships usually rely on sexual fantasies to help them become sexually aroused and achieve orgasm. Those fantasies generally revolve around putting themselves in their partner's place. Male-to-female transsexuals typically report that they fantasize during partnered sex that they are female, have a vagina, and are being penetrated by a male. Female-to-male transsexuals report that they fantasize during sex with a partner about being male, having a penis, and penetrating a female. A patient named Edward described the somewhat confusing elements of this common fantasy scenario very nicely and also touched on some of the most common concerns that my patients report about their sexual relationships:

> In any sexual act, I always put myself in my partner's position in my mind. There were even occasions where I mentally "took over" my partner's body and eliminated her from the

picture. The female body was mine, not hers, and there was no male body present. This is why I would so much enjoy caressing a lover but preferred no action at all on her part, and definitely no involvement with my body at all. This allowed me to maintain the image in my mind with no sensory input contradictory to my "perception" of the situation, nothing to "break the image."

The absolute worst action to break this image would unquestionably be to perform the actual act of intercourse. This has always been extremely distasteful to me and has only ever been performed for two reasons. The first was curiosity. Having heard so much about it my whole life and about "how wonderful it is," I, not surprisingly, felt a need to know what something like that would actually feel like. Even after not really enjoying it the first few times, I continued several more times in the hope that I just needed to "get used to it" or "let it grow on me" and then I would enjoy it. Needless to say, neither of these things occurred.

The second reason was for the sake of my partner—to let her think I wanted to. I know how it must hurt a woman to be wanted in bed but not to go "all the way." Nevertheless, I could not bring myself to face the act very often. The most common complaint that I got from my ex-fiancee was that I didn't "complete" our lovemaking anywhere near often enough. Despite dating for five years and living together for eighteen months, the number of times we completed intercourse could probably be counted on three hands.

The thing I remember most about intercourse is that I seemed to have no instincts for it at all. Oh, I did for all the preliminaries or foreplay, but when it came to the actual act, if it were not for reading I had done, conversations I had heard, or just reasoning, I would have had no idea what to do. At almost any given time, my instinct was simply to stop and go back to petting. It was only my conscious mind that knew that we weren't "done" yet.

My inability to perform as a male sexually is probably the largest single factor that led to the cancellation of my wedding. My fiancee was very happy with my "performance" but disturbed by its rareness. She often said that she felt somewhat undesired by me. In the purest sense of the word, I suppose she was. This, of course, did not mean that I didn't love her, simply that I did not desire her as a sexual partner.

Female-to-male transsexuals report a strikingly similar dependence on fantasy and role-playing in order to maintain romantic and sexual relationships. As Meredith described it, "My relationships with men were based around effecting feminine stereotypes that I learned in my neighborhood as a teenager, from my parents, or from living vicariously through men. I found that if I got intoxicated enough, I could create a lifestyle sexually with men whereby I could avoid myself. My sexual relationships depended on sexual fantasy. I would fantasize myself as a male with a female so that I could become aroused and get my body to do whatever I needed it to do."

Some transsexuals find that it is possible for them to maintain a relationship if they find a partner who is willing to play a more flexible, less stereotypical role. "If I found strong, aggressive women," one male patient said, "they would take the initiative. And that worked a lot better than me trying to do anything because I wasn't clear about what to do or where to go with things of a sexual nature. Left to my own devices, I probably wouldn't have lost my virginity until my late twenties."

Some transsexuals who have a heterosexual orientation date individuals (usually gay or bisexual) who have the same anatomy. That is, males date males and females date females in what may appear to an observer to be a gay or lesbian relationship. However, the transsexuals themselves consider this heterosexual dating. Assuming the masculine role for female-to-male transsexuals and the feminine role for male-to-female transsexuals may ease their gender dysphoria for a time because they can play their preferred sex and gender role. Ultimately, however, most heterosexual transsexuals cannot continue indefinitely in same-physical-sex relationships. Such a pairing may take away their loneliness for a while and allow intimacy, but it is never quite right because the relating is done in the wrong body. The female-to-male transsexual needs her body to be male in order to match her gender identity, and the male-to-female transsexual's body must be female if he is to feel whole as a person.

Anna's story exemplifies this plight. "I am not bisexual or gay. I've explored those possibilities, but they don't work for me. I need a heterosexual relationship with a woman. I need to be recognized as the man I am, the man that I've been hiding inside me. I want to be able to give a woman what a man could, but I don't know how."

What this means is that, although these transsexuals are attracted to members of the same anatomical sex, they consider themselves heterosexual (given their gender identity). Furthermore, because gender identity and sexual orientation are two entirely separate things, it is also possible that a male-to-female can self-identify as both female and lesbian and that a female-to-male can self-identify as both male and homosexual.

This is often one of the most confusing aspects of transsexualism and is a direct result of the unfortunate human need to label everyone. Though society's social groups are often based on these labels—male, female, homosexual, heterosexual—it is apparent from the foregoing discussion that labels are futile and lose their standardized meaning when discussing transsexualism.

Despite their gender dysphoria, most transsexuals are able to love deeply. Most want to find a mate and have loving and meaningful relationships.

## "But He's (She's) Married with Children"

People are sometimes surprised to discover that many transsexuals are married or have been married and have children. Transsexuals marry for many of the same reasons everyone else does—to have love, companionship, intimacy, bonding, and security, and to have a lifemate, sexual partner, and family. But the need for conformity is frequently a strong motivating factor. The role of "husband" or "wife" is often one more in a long series of roles that transsexuals assume in life.

Some, however, simply fall in love with someone of the opposite sex despite their own gender conflict. They think that their love is strong enough to obliterate their yearnings to be the opposite sex. It sometimes works, but only for a limited time. Some transsexuals marry knowing full well that their dysphoria isn't going to change, but they marry anyway so that their family and friends will be happier by seeing them function in a socially approved role. "I tried very hard to fit into that 'woman' mold," one FTM said. "That's why I married Tom and got pregnant right away. It was important to me that I was doing what a woman was supposed to do. I didn't want to be considered sick, a freak, or crazy."

Many transsexuals report how bittersweet their wedding day was because of their cross-gender longings. An MTF patient remembers how he couldn't help but feel jealous of his bride.

> I'll never forget the terrible contradiction in my heart and head that day. I knew it was the wrong role for me. I had a lovely woman for a bride, I was young and had so much to look forward to, yet I felt frustrated. The pressure I had felt all my life was there. I felt guilty, confused, and upset, and that ruined what should have been a totally beautiful event. When I saw my wife walking down the aisle, I almost burst into tears. People thought it was just a sentimental moment, but it was really because *I* wanted to be the one walking down the aisle in a wedding dress.
>
> How do you tell your bride, "I love you but I am a woman too?" And when our son was born, I felt the same pride as if he had come out of me. I always felt like his mother.

Many male-to-female transsexuals express similar sentiments about their role as husband and father. They regret that they were the groom instead of the bride, and they express sorrow about their inability to become pregnant and bear children. They envy their pregnant wives' growing bellies. They dearly wish that they could become pregnant, give birth to a child, nurse it, and perform the primary nurturing role.

Based on my clinical experience, although many male-to-female transsexuals marry, the percentage of female-to-males who do so is much smaller. Instead, many FTMs maintain "lesbian" relationships, sometimes for many years. If at some point the female transsexual transitions to male via hormone treatments or surgical procedures, and if the partner is bisexual or can adjust to the new dynamic, the relationship may remain intact. In those cases, they move from a lesbian (female-female) relationship to a heterosexual (male-female) relationship or marriage.

Some transsexuals function successfully in a marriage for a number of years. Eventually, however, even married transsexuals find that nothing takes away the pain, frustration, hopelessness, and despair of gender dysphoria—not the love of a good spouse or an exciting job or a successful career. Their gender conflict remains, always there just beneath the surface.

As Katherine said, "Even though my love for my husband was deep and sincere, my deluding myself was the cruelest mistake because it intimately involved another person, an innocent one who knew nothing of my feelings. I submerged my feelings in that marriage for several years and started to think that my 'problem' was gone. Unfortunately, as I grew older, I became less and less satisfied with the solution and with myself. I gradually became an angry and disagreeable mate due to feelings of unhappiness, guilt, and extreme discomfort with myself."

## Gender Dysphoria Takes Its Toll

Eventually, the plight of being transsexual—the gender conflict—must be resolved if the person is to live an honest, satisfying life. The frustration, hopelessness, and despair build to a point where transsexuals feel they cannot fake it any longer without dire consequences.

"Eventually I saw no reason to live," a patient named Marion reported. "I tried every kind of escape I could think of—marriage, parenthood, career military, skydiving, and even alcohol and drugs—but nothing seemed to work. I was a wreck until I finally realized that I just had to face my dysphoria. It was my only hope for survival."

When the gender dysphoria reaches the point that it becomes so severe that it interferes with daily functioning, most transsexuals turn to therapy. They might seek out a therapist who specializes in working with individuals who have a gender identity disorder, or they might go to a more general therapist who recognizes what is happening and either works with them or refers them to such a specialist. In the next chapter we discuss the issues that transsexuals bring to therapy and the type of therapy they can expect.

# 5

## Therapy

Sooner or later, most transsexuals reach the point where their gender dysphoria dominates their lives to such an overwhelming extent that daily functioning becomes difficult, if not impossible. Although they may have been able to contain their cross-gender feelings, longings, and behaviors in an internal "vault" for many years, eventually that coping technique no longer works. The combination of internal and external stress causes "cracks" to appear. In addition, defense mechanisms that may have served them in the past are no longer effective. The dysphoria begins to slip out. And once it's out, it is nearly impossible to force it back inside.

Debilitating depression often sets in. Things that used to be important in their lives are no longer meaningful. The pleasures previously experienced from relationships or personal interactions fade. Even simple joys like listening to music, communing with nature, or engaging in creative endeavors may diminish to the point of extinction. Nothing seems to matter. Transsexuals eventually find that they cannot ignore or deny their gender dysphoria any longer; something has to change.

"I felt like I was in an endless maze," one patient said. "I'd gotten to the point in my life where I felt like the path I was going down was spinning wildly around in ever-decreasing circles, finally to disappear. I had to do something or die."

It is at this critical juncture that most transsexuals turn to a gender therapist for help. This is often a frightening step because up to this point, many transsexuals have never told another soul about their condition. They may be nervous about articulating their feelings, even to a therapist, as they are not sure what kind of response they'll get. Yet they realize they must confront their dilemma if there is to be any chance of resolving it.

## The Turning Point

Although severe gender dysphoria is what motivates most transsexuals to seek gender counseling, the majority can also pinpoint a specific life circumstance—a turning point—that prompted them to seek professional help.

During a recent MTF group therapy session, eighteen new patients were asked why they were beginning therapy at that particular time. Their responses were representative of most of the patients I have seen over the years.

Three members of the group had recently experienced changes in their family or marital status. One had just gotten divorced and felt "free to move on" with her own life. (Because these patients all self-identify as female, the female pronoun will be used.) Another had just gone through the breakup of her fourth marriage and had finally decided to stop and look at who she was "before running for refuge into another marriage." The third had waited until her kids were finally grown. "I always knew," she said, "that I wanted to live life as a woman, and now I can do so with the least amount of damage to my family."

Debilitating depression marked the turning point for four of the new patients. "Up until now, I stayed in my box so nobody could hurt me," the first person in this foursome said. "I couldn't handle the stigma. But over time, the pain of remaining closeted was even worse. I was desperate. There seemed to be no place to turn, nowhere to go."

"I'm here tonight," the second person said, "because I felt like I was going to blow up inside. I'm forty-three years old, and I can't wait any longer." The third admitted that she had been ready to "jump off the bridge." She had felt as though she was the only person "like this" until making phone calls and finding out about my group. The last patient suffering from severe depression said that she, too, had been ready to kill herself but as a "last-ditch effort" had called a local church and had been given the phone number for my group and for a local gender support group.

Changes in health status also cause transsexuals to begin therapy. One patient who had recently become physically disabled (she is confined to a wheelchair) felt depressed and not in control of her life. She said that "transitioning" from male to female was something positive and empowering that she could do for herself.

Another patient described herself as "not ready emotionally and financially to go forward until now." Yet another had just turned twenty and said that her decision to seek therapy was a matter of becoming old enough to take charge of her own life.

One patient had been in two serious car accidents in a three-month period and had interpreted that as a subconscious message that she didn't want to go on. She had decided that she'd better get help.

Another patient had just moved to California from a small town in the Midwest where she had been unable to find a gender specialist. For her, exploring her gender identity issues had been put on hold until she was able to move to a place where it was easier to find the help she sought. Another member of the group said that she had gained courage to move forward from her interactions with an online computer group.

One patient said, "I ran out of ways to keep my mind occupied on something other than my gender problems and decided it was time for therapy." Another said that she had reconciled her religious beliefs with who she is and saw that she could go forward. "It's taken me forty years to realize that I am not perverted and that there is nothing wrong with being who I am and to see that I won't go to hell because of it."

Two patients stated that the death of someone close to them had prompted them to seek therapy. While the death of a loved one usually causes great sorrow, it can also bring renewed appreciation for one's own life and a greater awareness of the passage of time. Transsexuals may be more inclined to feel that "life is too short" and take steps to improve the quality of their own lives after losing someone close to them. Moreover, one patient said that she had refrained from moving forward with therapy until after the death of a family member who would have been distressed by her transsexualism.

Another patient had a greater sense of urgency about her gender because she had recently been diagnosed with heart disease. "Even if I only get to live as a female for one month, one week, or just one day for that matter—I'll still be happy. After that I can croak."

## Finding a Gender Therapist

Once individuals decide to explore their gender conflict, they go about finding a gender therapist in any of several ways. Some seek a referral from their physician, clergyman, non–gender therapist, or family counselor. Others ask transgendered friends or seek gender-related information from computer online services or gender newsletters and publications. Still others contact local hospitals, gender clinics, sex or gender information hotlines, and national referral sources such as the American Educational Gender Information Service (AEGIS) or the Harry Benjamin International Gender Dysphoria Association (HBIGDA). (Addresses and phone numbers for these and other organizations are listed in the Resource Guide at the back of this book.)

## Types of Patients

Transsexuals seeking therapy arrive via different life paths, for a variety of reasons, and from different stages in their journey of self-exploration. Insofar as their gender problems are concerned, they fall into one of two categories, "knowing" or "confused."

## Knowing Patients

Knowing patients are those who know with certainty that they are transsexual, although they may not know what they want to do about it. Their initial aim in therapy is informational; they want to know what their options are and what is involved in exercising those options. Furthermore, knowing patients, like their confused counterparts, usually have serious personal and interpersonal issues to work through in therapy as a result of their condition. They need the help and guidance of a skilled and knowledgeable therapist who works with transgendered patients.

Certain knowing patients view therapy as a means to an end. They know what they want—hormones and sex reassignment surgery—and they may be somewhat reluctant patients. They undergo counseling for the sole purpose of obtaining referral letters they must have from a primary therapist to proceed toward their goal through the standard medically approved path. They are often impatient with the process and want to speed it up. As a result, instead of learning how to cope with the intricacies of their condition, some may limit themselves to superficial work and not derive full benefit from the therapeutic process.

## Confused Patients

The confused group is composed of individuals who are unsure or conflicted about their condition, their options, or both. As one patient said, "I was determined not to be bound by everyone else's labels, but I had no real way to define myself. I knew who I *wasn't*, but had no idea who I *was*. I called myself a transsexual with no real understanding of what it meant to be transsexual, without ever having met people who thought of themselves as transsexual to see if we were talking about the same thing."

The confused patients are usually nervous about starting therapy and are worried about what may come out. They are fearful that their disclosure will throw their lives into chaos. As one patient said, "I had perfected the art of avoidance and was frightened about what would be uncovered, even in a therapist's office."

Many of these patients feel trapped, depressed, and anxious. But they may not readily recognize that a lot of their problems are gender-based. As one patient described it, "I was living in the darkest depths of hell. But I didn't realize that my anguish centered around my gender issues."

In spite of lifelong gender confusion, many manage to deny their dysphoria or block it out over the years and live relatively well-functioning lives for a while.

"I had incidents all the way from childhood on," one MTF patient said, "but they didn't mean much to me at the time. I just assumed that I was all screwed up. I did all the 'guy' things, played sports, got married—twice, in fact—had kids, and just assumed all guys dreamed about breasts. It wasn't until much later that I realized that guys' fantasies about breasts did not include wanting *to have them themselves*. Years later, in therapy, I finally put all the pieces of the puzzle together and life began to make sense."

Nearly all patients, knowing or confused, have two things in common: they experience considerable emotional pain, and their lives "do not work" because they are not in the right body. They need therapy to deal with their anxiety, depression, and emotional pain. The psychotherapeutic process provides the environment and the exploration techniques necessary to resolve the patients' gender dysphoria and the guidance they need to allow them to make decisions concerning their future needs and goals.

Gender therapists who work with these patients follow well-defined guidelines called Standards of Care (sometimes referred to as SOC) that protect patients, both knowing and confused, from acting hastily in their decision-making process.

## Standards of Care

Most gender therapists, physicians, and surgeons follow the Standards of Care developed in 1979 (and regularly updated) by the Harry

Benjamin International Gender Dysphoria Association (HBIGDA). The SOC were designed to provide clinicians and other health professionals who treat transsexuals with a set of minimum guidelines and prerequisites that should be met before patients can begin hormone treatment or proceed with sex reassignment surgery. Considering the invasive and permanent nature of many of the medical interventions for the treatment of transsexualism, these protective SOC guidelines are critically important. They have built-in time constraints and safeguards so that, contrary to the misconception and fear that many parents and families of transsexuals share, a person can't impulsively or easily rush into hormone treatments or sex reassignment surgery.

Neither hormone treatments nor surgery can occur overnight. In fact, the SOC call for a minimum three-month period between the time a health professional begins work with a transsexual and the time the patient begins hormone treatments. Generally, most HBIGDA therapists wait six months for FTMs. These precautions are taken because some of the physical changes resulting from taking male hormones are permanent and irreversible. (The effects of female hormones on MTF transsexuals, by contrast, are usually reversible.)

## Real-Life Test

Prior to sex reassignment surgery, the SOC call for a minimum twelve-month period during which the patient lives full-time in the social role of the "genetically other sex." This one-year period is referred to as the "real-life test" (RLT). It provides transsexuals with an opportunity for a "trial run" whereby they cross-dress and "cross-live"—live in the gender role that matches their identity—full-time, seven days a week, twenty-four hours a day for at least a year (sometimes referred to as "seven-twenty-four-ing"). This gives patients time to determine how effectively they will be able to function in the opposite gender role. (The RLT is discussed in more detail in Chapter Six.)

It is important to keep in mind that the time periods outlined in the SOC are the *minimum* amounts of time required. Because every patient has different life circumstances, it frequently takes a year or more, instead of three months, to reach the point where both patient and therapist are comfortable about beginning hormone treatments. Similarly, a responsible decision regarding sex reassignment surgery (SRS) can sometimes take several years to make. This also applies to the RLT. Some patients who desire SRS cross-live for many years before going ahead with surgery.

All of these protective measures, as well as the others outlined in the SOC guidelines, help ensure that patients have the benefit of ongoing counseling about their specific gender issues and adequate time to consider all of the ramifications of hormone treatment and surgery before taking major steps that will change their bodies. Sex reassignment surgery is a drastic step. It is very costly— both emotionally and financially. Gender therapists, almost without exception, urge patients to consider surgery as a last resort rather than a first option.

## Gatekeeper Issues

Not all transsexuals are happy with the SOC guidelines. Some view them primarily as a control device and resent what they characterize as having to "jump through hoops" to obtain the letters they need for hormone treatment and surgery. Essentially, they want "treatment on demand" and see the gender therapist as strictly a "gatekeeper"—in this case, someone who denies or grants access to hormones or surgery.

These transsexuals maintain that since people don't need permission to have a face-lift, a nose job, or other kinds of cosmetic surgery and medical procedures, they should also be able to have hormones and SRS on demand. They argue that, as adults, they can make their own decisions, medical or otherwise.

One transsexual at a recent professional conference phrased it this way: "I'm fifty-two years old, I've been married for thirty years, have raised three children, and run my own successful business. I find it incredibly frustrating to have to explain to a therapist why I need to do this. It's hard for me to sit back and have somebody else control my life and tell me whether or not it's OK for me to do something to my own body. Plus there is always the fear—what if they don't sign the damn letter?"

Yet the system works. Few professionals who work in the gender field want to forestall or limit a patient's right to pursue hormone treatment or SRS as long as it is a well-considered decision and one that the patient is absolutely sure will significantly improve his or her chances for a full and satisfying life. However, the exploration and decision-making process requires time. Considering whether or not to change sex is certainly one of the most radical and far-reaching decisions patients will make in their lifetimes.

Transsexuals and their therapists and physicians generally understand that the standards were developed to assist and protect them. Although there are some physicians and therapists who are unaware of the SOC or for some reason choose not to adhere to them, most take their responsibilities in this regard very seriously, as do most patients themselves. Some patients, however, are so overanxious to move forward that they circumvent the established guidelines and obtain hormones illegally on the black market, or find surgeons who do not adhere to the SOC, or in some cases "buy" their SRS letters from unethical therapists without undergoing therapy. Fortunately, such cases are the exception, not the rule.

Though nearly all preoperative transsexuals express the feeling that "the world is speeding by without me" or "I don't want to spend one more day than I have to in the wrong body," most understand the wisdom and reasons behind the caution and care associated with adhering to the SOC. In fact, most postoperative patients report that the time they spent dealing with their gender issues and exploring their options was necessary and well worthwhile when weighed against the possibility of making a very serious mistake.

## Determining a Diagnosis

One of the reasons that gender dysphoric individuals consult a gender therapist is to have their condition diagnosed. For knowing patients, the diagnosis validates what they have known or suspected all along. In addition, the diagnosis of gender identity disorder or transsexualism serves to depathologize the condition and make it seem less "abnormal" to patients and their families. The diagnosis reinforces the fact that transsexualism is a medical condition, not a mental illness or perversion. People are often more comfortable with a medical or psychological condition when they have a name for it because they can then begin to learn about it and understand it. A diagnosis also provides reassurance to patients that they are not alone and that other people also suffer from the same disorder.

Yet some individuals think of a diagnosis in negative terms. They attach a stigma to it or see it as a label that automatically pushes the patient toward one course of action—hormones and SRS. This is not so. Diagnosis as a transsexual does not mean there is any predetermined path that must be followed. A number of options are open to transsexuals, and SRS is just one of them.

## Initial Assessment

An accurate diagnosis requires careful evaluation by a qualified therapist over an extended period of time. It is an evolving process. A determination of such importance and with such far-reaching consequences clearly cannot be made after only a few therapy sessions. Many areas of the patient's life have to be explored—family dynamics, psychological stressors, sexual orientation issues, substance abuse problems, and any history of physical or sexual abuse. As these and other areas are thoroughly investigated, the therapist watches for any inconsistencies or "red flags" that might come up.

I ask my patients to write an autobiography detailing their background and life experiences. It is important that I get a clear picture of how they perceive themselves. Detailed social and sexual histories are also taken that go well beyond the scope of their self-histories and serve as an important part of the diagnostic process. The patients' motivation for presenting themselves for therapy is another consideration. Why now and not ten years ago or twenty years ago? And what are the patient's goals and expectations?

Another important part of the diagnostic process is the therapist's ability to differentiate between transsexualism and other possible conditions or problems. Some patients who go to a therapist stating that they are transsexual and want to change their sex may not be transsexual at all; for example, they may actually be any of the following:

- Gay men or lesbians in denial or confusion (who may either be reluctant to face their sexual orientation issues or confused about the differences between sexual orientation and gender identity)

- Transvestites for whom the initial eroticism of cross-dressing has been replaced by feelings of comfort (which causes them to wonder if this *shift* might be an indicator that they are transsexuals rather than transvestites)

- Effeminate men or masculine women who are uncomfortable in their gender role but not with their own gender identity (they may deem it easier to change sex than to struggle in their roles or deal with their issues)

- Men with severe erection problems (who, prior to the availability of penile implants and injections, thought that being female might be better than having to live the rest of their lives with their impotence)

- Individuals who were sexually abused or assaulted at some point in their lives (who may, as a result of their early trauma, find their bodies so distasteful that they'll go to any length to change them)

- Individuals who have inappropriate sexual impulses toward exhibitionism, rape, molestation, or other antisocial or criminal behaviors (whose fear of engaging in such acts leads them to seek genital amputation or castration via hormones or surgery)

- Criminals who wish to change or disguise their identity (who may, in rare cases, seek a sex change in an attempt to avoid detection and prosecution)

- Individuals with Munchausen syndrome (a rare disorder in

which individuals claim to have various medical problems—which may be totally fabricated, self-inflicted, or an exaggeration of preexisting physical conditions—as a way to get medical attention, care, and concern)

- Individuals with psychiatric disorders (who may, if they have certain thought disorders such as schizophrenia, have delusions that they are members of the opposite sex)

- Individuals who have multiple personality disorder (one of the personalities may be gender dysphoric even if the others are not; improper diagnosis could lead to disastrous results for the other personalities)

In my years as a gender therapist, all of these types of patients have sought gender counseling because they wanted to "change their sex." *Yet none of them was transsexual.* Had they been improperly diagnosed as transsexual, the resulting treatment could have led to disastrous consequences. Careful diagnosis, therefore, is of paramount importance.

## The Need for Caution

Even when working with patients whose histories clearly meet the American Psychiatric Association's DSM-IV criteria for a diagnosis of gender identity disorder (as set forth in Chapter One of this book), caution must be exercised and adequate time taken. Sometimes transsexuals seeking surgery are so worried about whether they will be considered appropriate candidates for SRS that they may not represent themselves honestly. They study the literature, talk to other transsexuals, and formulate a story to present to a therapist. Obviously, reciting a "classic" transsexual history that is not based on their own experience is counterproductive to the patient and to the therapeutic process. However, experienced gender therapists usually know when this is happening or are at least able to detect it over time.

Because the differential diagnosis (which distinguishes between transsexualism and other disorders) can sometimes be so difficult to make, non–gender therapists often refer their patients to a HBIGDA therapist or work in consultation with one to determine a diagnosis. Furthermore, whenever there is any question of psychopathology, it is important to work in conjunction with a psychiatrist who can do a comprehensive evaluation and provide treatment and medication, if necessary.

Transsexualism and psychopathology can and do coexist. Transsexualism left unresolved can create enough emotional stress over time to produce severe clinical depression and other psychiatric disorders. Psychopathology can also arise from a cause unrelated to the patient's gender dysphoria. Regardless of the cause, current thinking among gender therapists is that psychiatric disorders, even severe ones like schizophrenia, are not considered contraindications to hormonal or surgical sex reassignment as long as the gender disorder does not fluctuate with the illness and the patient is reasonably stable emotionally.

It is necessary, however, to control psychiatric disorders before dealing with the transsexualism so that they do not interfere with the clear thought process necessary for a patient's honest self-examination in therapy.

## The Therapist's Role

Therapists tend to wear many hats. Depending on the needs of their patients, they serve as professional observers, diagnosticians, supportive nurturers, guides, and facilitators as they assist their patients in exploring and dealing with their issues and concerns. They act as the "human connection" for patients who are isolated and without a support system.

Given the unique nature of the transsexual phenomenon, additional roles come into play when working with this particular population. For example, gender therapists are companions on the transsexual's exhaustive and groundbreaking journey of self-exploration and self-redefinition. Together, patient and therapist examine and slowly break through the facade the patient has created, uncovering the patient's true self—the often tortured soul that has been buried and is crying out for release and expression.

## Forming an Alliance

The long and arduous journey to knowledge and self-acceptance begins with the development of an honest and trusting relationship between patient and therapist. Patients need to feel secure that at least one person—the therapist—is on their side and will be there to guide them. The trust between therapist and patient leads, in turn, to the patients' trust in the psychotherapeutic process and ultimately to trust in themselves and their feelings.

A gender therapist acts as an "anchor point" for the confusion and turmoil that transsexuals experience in what could be described as a turbulent sea on their journey of self-discovery. Transsexual patients need a "captain" with a "map and compass" to keep them on course and moving in the right direction. Much of their cross-gender feelings and longings are so extraordinary—if viewed within the strict confines of an ordered universe—that they are in dire need of a context in which to approach them. Gender specialists need to be knowledgeable about the various stages of the transsexual journey and the various options available at each stage. The therapist's role is to guide and help pace the transsexuals' progress along their chosen path. This is done without bias on the part of the therapist toward the outcome. Whether patients choose to make the transition or live as male, female, or someplace in between makes no difference to the therapist as long as the patients are comfortable with the choice they make and with themselves.

Gender therapists may also function as social workers, educators, or advocates. They sometimes act as consultants to employers and coworkers of transsexuals, providing information and education on transsexualism. They also often meet with family members who need assistance in coping or adjusting. For instance, in my practice,

I've worked not only with parents, siblings, spouses, and kids but also with groups that include relatives, neighbors, and friends of a particular patient.

In addition to writing referral letters for hormones and SRS, therapists are also called on to write letters in child custody and visitation cases and to help patients obtain health insurance coverage. They also work in conjunction with physicians and other health professionals who treat people dealing with gender identity issues.

In addition, gender therapists provide information on a wide range of transsexual issues and concerns. They serve as a referral source to their patients for medical and legal needs, support groups, and transgender services (such as electrolysis) and hard-to-find products (such as large-size women's shoes).

## Special Skills

When working with transsexual patients, the therapist's theoretical orientation and individual approach are not as important as a knowledge and understanding of transsexual issues and his or her comfort level with transsexualism. Whatever techniques therapists have historically used to help nontranssexual patients uncover buried material and pull them through severe emotional turmoil will work with transsexual patients as well, provided that the therapist is flexible, open-minded, and nonjudgmental.

This is especially important during the early sessions when a patient's visual gender presentation may be quite different from his or her gender identity. For example, a therapist may see a six-foot four-inch balding, muscular, hairy male patient walk into the office and learn that this patient has self-identified as female all of his life. Thus gender specialists learn over time to fine-tune their senses so that they can see through the misleading exteriors and hear the true voice of the patient's hidden gender.

During their first session, regardless of whether patients are dressed as male or female, I ask them the name by which they wish to be addressed, both for that session and in the future. Most prefer to be called by a gender-appropriate name that they may have had for many years but had seldom been able to use. Being called by their "true" name is a positive and even exhilarating experience for them. They have waited a long time for this to occur.

Family members sometimes frown on therapy because they believe that talking about gender concerns and addressing transsexuals by their "preferred" name authenticates the patients' condition or encourages them to "become" transsexual. Some worry that this will influence their loved ones to proceed down a predetermined path to SRS and that the therapist is "going along with" or "catering to" the patients' wishes. They worry that therapy will reinforce their loved ones' "delusion" or "pathology." But this is not how gender specialists view the process. They see it rather as a matter of respect and common courtesy. Calling patients by the name of their choice is not going to steer them toward transsexualism. Despite fears to the contrary, no therapist, or anyone else for that matter, can "create" a transsexual from an individual who is merely confused.

Indeed, therapists are quick to point out to patients the negative ramifications of undergoing such a major change. The transsexual journey is treacherous by anyone's standards. Patients report, without exception, that coming out and going through transition are the hardest things they've ever done. Gender therapists caution their patients about rushing too quickly into any step that may jeopardize their psychological health. They tend to paint a bleak picture of transition to be sure that patients won't have unrealistic expectations about what life will be like as the opposite gender. Much care and attention is given to ensure that they *don't* believe that changing their bodies in a physical way is magically going to improve their entire lives, solve all their problems, and bring them that elusive thing called happiness. Transsexuals, like the rest of us, have many problems to face during the course of their lives, and sex reassignment surgery does not automatically eliminate those problems.

## Issues in Therapy

In the journey that comprises the therapeutic process, transsexuals have to confront and deal with emotions and issues that have become an integral part of their gender dysphoria. When they first begin therapy, many transsexuals are overcome with feelings of hopelessness and depression about their condition and about what the future holds. Most are afraid to stay where they are but even more afraid to go forward. Various negative emotions, such as shame, fear, anger, guilt, and low self-esteem, are often their constant companion and must be confronted and defused before progress can be made. Patients need to be stabilized psychologically and emotionally before they can make rational decisions about their lives and the future.

Although some patients are more conflict-ridden than others, because of the nature of gender dysphoria, *all* transsexuals struggle with at least some of the following negative emotions and issues.

## Fear

Fear is the emotion that transsexuals struggle with above all else. Whereas most of us have occasional fears—of flying, having surgery, going to the dentist, meeting financial obligations, or giving a speech—*most transsexuals experience debilitating fears nearly every day of their lives.* These fears can affect every area of their existence and can be so all-consuming that considerable time must be spent in therapy to resolve them before progress can be made. The following are some of the more common fears:

- Fear of challenging the status quo and losing family, friends, and everything they value
- Fear of losing their livelihood and becoming indigent
- Fear of the unknown and what will become of them: Will they function well or "crack up" under the stress?
- Fear that they will never "pass," that people will always be able to tell that they are transgendered
- Fear of societal intolerance, persecution, and discrimination
- Fear of being ridiculed, rejected, beaten up, or even killed

- Fear of never having anyone love them again or never being in an intimate relationship, of being alone for the rest of their lives

## Anger

Transsexuals are often indignant about the injustice of their condition and angry about the intolerance in our culture of anyone who doesn't fall neatly within the traditional definitions of masculinity and femininity.

Theodore Rubin states in *The Angry Book* that anger alienates us from others and from our own feelings. Anger turned inward against oneself also results in self-hatred. Angry people are often accident-prone and may behave in ways that are potentially harmful to themselves and others as they try to express or work off their anger.

Patients may feel anger directed against various targets:

- Anger at God

  For giving them a body that doesn't match their mind; for making them different from everyone else

  For causing them to suffer so intensely with such a burden; they often ask, "Why me? What did I do to deserve this?"

- Anger at loved ones

  For not realizing or understanding what they have been through

  For expectations placed on them

  For not accepting them as the person they truly are

- Anger at themselves

  For living a lie and not having the courage to be true to their nature

  For being ashamed of who they are

  For allowing others to dictate how they live their lives

- Anger at society

For being so narrow in vision and lacking tolerance, understanding, and acceptance for anyone who is different

For not believing them or acknowledging transsexualism
as a valid condition

- Anger at the medical and health care profession

For the power to make them wait for referral letters, access
to hormones, or surgery

For the high cost of medical care; for charging top dollar for
medical services

For not taking them seriously or not having adequate information about their condition or issues

For trying to "cure" or "reform" them

## Guilt

Transsexuals experience considerable guilt because they are deceit-
ful with the special people in their lives. By not sharing what they
are going through, they are withholding a vital part of themselves.
"Due to the fact that I couldn't share this with my partner," one
patient said, "there was this dark side. I was deceiving her and also
lying to friends and coworkers and everyone I came in contact with.
I felt like a con artist, a charlatan, a fraud. But I didn't know what
else to do."

Transsexuals also feel guilty about the presumably terrible consequences of telling the truth. They don't want to hurt the ones
they love. This double-edged guilt results in a lose-lose situation for
many; it's a "damned if you do and damned if you don't" scenario.
In the first instance, by living a lie, they hurt themselves, and in the
second, by sharing their truth, they hurt others (and themselves by
extension).

Although they did not choose to be transsexual, most have a
strong "inner critic" that blames them for their condition. They
harbor considerable guilt for all their perceived "sins," for being a

member of an "undesirable" group, and for the negative way others feel about their condition.

Thus the guilt transsexuals experience takes several forms:

- Guilt about deceiving everyone
- Guilt about not living up to family expectations
- Guilt about "ruining" the lives of their parents, spouses, loved ones, and children

## Shame

Shame is a painful feeling that arises when something we have done is perceived as inappropriate, dishonorable, or ridiculous. Although most people experience embarrassment or mild shame at various times in their lives, profound shame is a destructive negative emotion that many transsexuals experience. Sometimes the shame is self-induced by the patient's own sense of self-blame and self-hatred. Other times, transsexuals are made to feel shameful by family members or other people. One patient explained, "My mother keeps telling me that I'm 'a sick boy with a very rich fantasy life.' Consequently, whenever I'm near her, I'm filled with shame."

In his book *Understanding Shame*, Carl Goldberg writes that self-condemnation and the self-loathing that shame precipitates are part and parcel of a pervasive, persistent, and destructive set of emotions and a crippling sense of terror and pessimism.

The following are some of the kinds of shame that transsexual patients experience:

- Shame about their bodies, especially their genitals
- Shame that they are flawed and will never measure up to non-transgendered individuals (this is especially strong among postoperative female-to-male transsexuals)
- Shame because some segments of society consider transsexuals sick, perverted, scary, or inferior

## Poor Self-Esteem

For most of their lives, transsexuals have had to hide their true selves from the world. This deception, carried out over an extended period of time, results in feelings of unworthiness. Furthermore, their self-esteem is generally very low because they are keenly aware that in the eyes of the world, they are one of "those people"—a member of a marginal or even freakish group. Low self-esteem runs rampant among transsexuals and causes many of them to become loners and underachievers, to take dead-end jobs, and to develop problems with health, grooming, and body image.

An important goal in therapy is to help transsexuals build confidence and a sense of self-worth and to empower them so they finally feel as though they have more control over their own destiny.

The self-esteem issues that transsexual patients struggle with include the following:

- Poor self-esteem because they are different from other people and have a hard time fitting in or being accepted
- Poor self-esteem because it's hard for them to like or love themselves when so much of their existence is based on deception
- Poor self-esteem because they have the wrong body and genitals

## Group Therapy

A helpful adjunct to dealing with the various negative emotions just discussed and other transsexual issues is group therapy. Group therapy is beneficial to patients in several ways. The group provides a unique environment in which transsexuals can safely share their innermost thoughts and feelings and get feedback from an empathic and sympathetic audience. After years of thinking that they were the only one "like this," they discover a roomful of people who are in a similar situation. This provides some comfort; they see that they are not alone.

Group dynamics create a climate of camaraderie and solidarity. Patients who have always been loners and have never experienced a true sense of kinship with others at last make contacts and develop friendships with other transsexuals. The group situation provides a forum, perhaps for the first time in their lives, where there is no need for lies or false fronts. An honest bonding process can begin. When they need to talk or want the company of someone who understands what they are going through, they now have people to reach out to.

Certain group sessions are also designed to provide patients with resources and information specific to their needs. Professionals such as endocrinologists, surgeons, voice therapists, electrologists, and fashion consultants are invited to speak at these meetings. This not only provides patients with information they need but also saves them the expense of private consultations in these areas. Dealing with these practical issues during group sessions frees up valuable time during individual therapy sessions for working on patients' emotional issues.

Group therapy also provides patients with a useful "reality check," an opportunity to compare themselves with others in similar (or different) places in the gender spectrum. A few patients drop out after attending several group sessions because they become discouraged by the comparison. They conclude that their prospects for the future are poor and that they will never "make it" in society as a member of the opposite sex. But for most patients, group therapy provides an opportunity to learn and benefit from other patients' experiences and to develop the self-confidence and self-acceptance necessary to come out of their self-imposed closet.

## Coming Out to Self

The expression "coming out" in our culture can refer to a person's formal introduction to society—as in the case of debutantes—or to a person's proclamation or revelation of his or her true (and formerly hidden) self to others—as in the case of gay or transsexual individuals.

The coming-out process for most transsexuals involves two steps. The first step is what I call "coming out to self." This is a process whereby transsexuals acknowledge *to themselves* their true self—the self that has been concealed and denied for so long—and then learn to accept this newly emerged self with pride. This is an essential part of gender therapy.

The second step is coming out to others, revealing one's transsexualism publicly to family, friends, coworkers, and society. Coming out to oneself is a necessary precursor to coming out to others. Patients who cannot accept themselves will project this and thus be less likely to gain acceptance by others.

In therapy, patients begin the "coming out to self" process by communicating their long-repressed cross-gender longings; their inner turmoil, fears, and shame; and whatever else they need to work through in the safety of a judgment-free environment. For the first time, they can throw off the old chameleon self and discover their real self. It is akin to a molting process. Before their true identity can emerge, they must shed their many layers of defenses bit by bit and lose the tremendous "emotional baggage" they have carried for so many years.

Coming out to oneself can be a slow and difficult process, but most patients report that it is a positive and personally satisfying experience—one that provides a tremendous sense of freedom and renewed strength.

For some, the process will stop there. They will have examined their options and decided not to go beyond coming out to themselves. Responsibilities toward their family, financial considerations, health issues, or fear of losing everyone and everything they value may outweigh their wish to go further. With so much at risk, they may choose never to tell anybody else about their condition and thus may never proceed to step two. They will maintain the status quo, no matter how unsatisfactory it may be—that is, they will continue to live in the wrong body, guard a formidable secret, and suffer chronic emotional pain so that their family life and professional life can remain unchanged. Though they will continue to hide their condition, they will do it with a new sense of freedom knowing that they are now doing so as a conscious choice after having weighed the available options.

For these patients, coming out to themselves is a powerful therapeutic end in itself that results in newfound self-acceptance and self-esteem. The therapeutic process provided them with a safe haven where feelings were aired, lives were examined, choices were made, and coming out—if only to themselves (and their therapist)—was accomplished.

For the majority of transsexuals, however, coming out to themselves is not enough. After living what most of them describe as a "diminished, unsatisfactory life" for so long, they are determined not to hide any longer. They find that they have no choice but to come out to others.

## Preparing to Come Out to Others

While patients feel a sense of relief at the thought of no longer having to live a lie, they are also aware of the obstacles that lie ahead—interpersonally and financially—as they seek to come out to other people.

### It's Different from Coming Out as Gay

It is often mistakenly assumed that the coming-out process for transsexuals is the same as for gays. Although the basic concept of revealing a long-held and deeply personal secret (to which people may react strongly and negatively) is the same, coming out as gay does not challenge people's basic notions about human nature—at least not in the same way that the transsexual's revelation that he or she is really of the opposite gender (and is seeking to change his or her gender role and body).

Another major difference relates to the *changes* that occur following the coming-out process. Coming out as gay typically involves a revelation to others about one's inner feelings and desires. Though reaction to the revelation can be severe, the gay person's outward appearance, gender, and social roles remain the same (except, perhaps, in the case of drag queens). Coming out as a transsexual, by contrast, involves not only the revelation of one's inner life but also of the dramatic process of outer changes and social role changes that will follow.

Moreover, gay men and lesbians can be openly gay without their family and friends ever having to know about it or having to meet or become involved with their partner (if they have one). Neighbors, casual friends, and coworkers never have to know unless the gay person wants to tell them because the gay individual's outward presentation and gender role will remain the same. For example, if parents had a daughter before, they still have one after she comes out as gay. She continues to live and work as a female and attends family functions as a female. However, if parents have a daughter who is openly transsexual and cross-living as a male, then she works as a male and attends family functions as a male. The change from female to male can't be hidden. It will be obvious to those who knew the transsexual previously. As one patient described it, "We're right there in everyone's face."

Parents will now have to start seeing their transsexual daughter as their son. Friends and family will have to learn to relate to the transsexual in an entirely new way—new name, new appearance, new voice, new role—whereas for a gay man or a lesbian, nothing dramatically changes. Adjustments by family and friends are far fewer and relate more to the concept of homosexuality than to physical appearance or outer presentation.

## The Momentous Decision

The momentous decision to proceed toward coming out to others requires a great deal of preparation in therapy, as the anxiety of disclosure can be severe. And each new disclosure carries its own set of anxieties, depending on the people involved and their relationship with the transsexual.

These anxieties are examined and worked through by having patients do "practice run" assignments. These assignments include role-playing, letter writing, and going out in public in their new gender role.

Role-playing in therapy gives patients a chance to put their feelings into words, to rehearse their words, and to develop effective strategies for coming out. Patients first make a list of the important people in their lives. We discuss the relationship they have with each of these people as well as the personalities involved. We then formulate the best approach for communicating with each of them. We role-play by having the patient assume the role of the family member, friend, or coworker while I play the role of the patient, and vice versa. Role-playing allows transsexuals to prepare themselves for some of the reactions they might get. Letter writing is another therapeutic exercise patients are asked to do even if they plan to come out in person.

Both role-playing and letter writing are effective ways to help prepare patients for coming out to family, friends, and coworkers. Preparation and presentation are important in these sensitive situations and can help lessen the chances of damaging important relationships. These techniques will be discussed in more detail in Chapter Eight.

## Coming Out to Others

Before coming out to family members, some patients find it helpful to do their first trial runs with casual acquaintances or strangers and then with a trusted friend or relative who is likely to be understanding and supportive. This allows patients to "test the waters" before moving on to the formidable task of telling their secret to the most important people in their lives.

Coming out to others doesn't necessarily have to happen verbally. Rather than talking about it, patients sometimes start by just doing it—going about their daily lives as the opposite gender and keeping appointments with individuals with whom they have had a long-term, albeit casual, relationship, such as their doctor, barber, accountant, or mechanic. Patients don't necessarily want to break off contact with such people just because they are "transitioning" (switching from living as one gender to living as the other).

As one patient explained:

> There was no way I was going to sever the tie with the trusted mechanic who has worked on my Porsche for seven years. I just jumped right in the last time I was there to pick up my car and saw his puzzled look. I said, "Yes, I am the same person who has always owned this car, but I am a transsexual in transition." He handed me the bill without skipping a beat, and that was that. Although it was somewhat awkward and uncomfortable for me, I figured it was much easier to do than trying to find a new mechanic!

Transsexuals have little to lose by coming out in this way. Although mockery or rejection from people they know only casually can certainly be hurtful, it is nothing compared to the pain of rejection from loved ones. With them, so much is at stake. The impact of coming out to family members is discussed in detail in Chapter Eight.

## Preparing to Pass

One therapeutic assignment I use is designed to help patients build confidence in their ability to "pass"—to be seen and accepted as a member of the other gender. They are first asked to spend a couple of months (or as long as they need) practicing how to walk, talk, move, and gesture in ways appropriate to the other gender.

Next they are asked to go to public places such as shopping malls, laundromats, or grocery stores dressed in the attire of the other gender to find out what the experience is like. Do passersby do double-takes or stare? Are the patients able to interact with people with some degree of success, or are they reduced to abject terror? Many venture out slowly at first and find it very frightening. Some patients report going to a shopping center and sitting in the car shaking for two hours, unable to go inside. And if they do manage to go in, they usually don't want to risk speaking for fear that their voice will give them away. Many pick very public places because they are afraid of running into trouble or of putting themselves in situations where they might be confronted, attacked, or beaten up.

Practice runs such as these are valuable because they help decrease the emotional risks involved in coming out and act as a form of desensitization for the patient. They help transsexuals develop the thick skin they must have in order to deal with the inevitable slings and arrows of society. Patients who go into a deep depression every time they think they cannot pass are obviously going to have a hard time functioning and shouldn't consider transitioning—at least until they work through more of their fears and anxieties.

Issues about passing are carefully explored in therapy well in advance of transitioning. It's important for therapists to examine not only their patients' fears of passing but also their expectations. Patients can set themselves up for failure if they have perceptions or expectations that are unrealistic. For example, some transsexuals think that they are totally passable when they are not—they are certain that *everyone* will accept them as the other gender; others are such perfectionists that even though they are totally passable, they unreasonably expect that *nobody* will accept them.

## Boulders and Barriers

My patients' most significant problems usually relate to their negative expectations and fears about family, finances, and career. Examples include "My grandmother will have a stroke if I tell her" or "I'll probably end up destitute and friendless if I transition." And some of the most frequent and critical concerns my patients express are related to passing: "I'll never pass because my shoulders are too broad."

In therapy, I refer to these self-imposed obstacles as *boulders*. These boulders, whether large or small, are created out of fear and function as roadblocks or barriers that impede the patients' progress. They also give the patients something to hide behind. By examining these underlying fears in therapy, we chip away at them. We don't necessarily have to break them down completely, but at least enough so that patients can squeeze through and continue moving toward their goals.

Because of these boulders, practice runs are essential stepping-stones on the road to transition. Transsexuals have to be willing to take risks because if they let the boulders stand in their way, they will never succeed in their quest for a satisfying life in the new gender role. On the eve of transition, one patient eloquently summed it up this way:

> My fear has been like a prison. It has kept me from living the life I wanted to live. It kept me from going to the movies, from going to concerts, from going hiking, from going grocery shopping, from going to my company picnic—in general, it kept me from fulfilling the life that I now have. I hated being stared at by people. It hurt. It's like I was mortally struck each time I saw someone gazing with amusement at me. Fear breeds negativity, and negativity breeds discontent.
>
> But I think I've finally learned through therapy that fear and negativity are human artifacts born of simple habit. If you make it a habit to be afraid, you will be. And then if it is your habit to be negative, you will be. I also believe that the opposite must be true. It has to be. And I intend to find out. Now, every chance I get, I affirm to myself that I am strong and that I am impervious to hate and ill-will. I tell myself that people cannot hurt me; that I empower only myself; that if I am negative and unhappy, it is by my own choice; that I am worthy of living on this planet; and that I am a survivor. I will take everything I've learned and summon all the strength I have as I joyously move into transition.

# 6

## Beginning the Transition

Transitioning—going from living as one gender to living as the other—is incredibly exciting for transsexuals. At long last, their hopes, dreams, and yearnings to be the opposite sex are finally within reach. For the first time in their lives, they no longer have to live a lie. They are free to live in the appropriate gender role and to move toward becoming whole.

As their true selves emerge from hiding, dysphoria is frequently replaced with euphoria, health problems improve, and depression lifts. As one MTF patient said, "At last I can be true to myself. I have integrated my feminine gender identity and feminine gender presentation. I no longer have to deal with the conflict and pain of being someone other than who I felt myself to be internally. It was time for my light to shine. Now it radiates outward for all the world to see."

At the same time, however, the enormity of what lies ahead can be intimidating. There are so many changes to make, so many things to deal with. Transition is a time of increased expenses but diminished job security or even joblessness. It's a time when many transsexuals must restructure or end their existing marriages, relationships, and friendships. Transsexuals have to be prepared to encounter disapproval and intolerance from the people around them and prejudice and discrimination in the workplace. Not all transsexuals can handle the psychological challenge and strain.

As one MTF patient said, "Transition is tough. I have to make a stand for myself, but as a new person. I can't (nor do I want to) go back to being male, yet I'm not always being accepted as female. It's kind of a double bind. It's also kind of frightening. I've never done anything like this before."

Transition (also known as gender reorientation) is a time of insecurity, uncertainty, and unknowns. As transsexuals begin the real-life test (RLT), they cannot help but worry about whether they can "make it" in the real world as the other gender and whether friends, family members, and coworkers will accept them. The possibility of rejection, loss, and a lifetime of loneliness is an overriding fear for many patients.

"Sometimes I wonder if my losses will be too many and too great to recover from them," said one FTM, "especially when constantly facing an uneducated, unsympathetic world and ceaselessly wondering whether time and hormones will ever allow me to escape their scrutiny and judgments."

One MTF patient expressed similar sentiments about her fear of the unknown. "What really strikes home for me," she said, "is that all transsexuals lose something once they come out. The question I ask myself is, How much will I lose? I've laid everything I've achieved in life—job, relationship, family, health, future—on the table, and it seems that fate will decide what I will be allowed to keep, if anything. It's kind of like starting life all over again."

Transsexuals need stamina, courage, emotional stability, and determination to survive the challenges of gender transition. Many describe this stage as "living life without a safety net." There is much to learn and a long road to travel through uncharted territory.

The gender reorientation period is a time when transsexuals' lives will be dramatically affected by the myriad changes that will occur as they alter how they look and behave. This reorganization and restructuring of their entire being is, in fact, the *essence* of the transsexual's transformation. The true rebirth occurs for them when they can at long last live in the world as the opposite gender, *not* when they have the actual sex reassignment surgery. Such surgery, if it does occur, is what many patients describe as "the icing on the cake."

Their comfort level during the RLT will depend on how well they are able to adapt to and function in their new gender role. Before the RLT, transsexuals could go out cross-dressed on "trial runs" (or cross-live on a part-time basis) but could always fall back on their "former selves"—on the gestures, responses, and behaviors that worked in the past whenever they encountered difficult situations. Once they begin the RLT, however, the former self—at least the overt, external one that carried them through life until that time—must be discarded, and without the benefit of a well-developed "new self" to put in its place. As one patient said, "I was frightened because the comfort and safety of my male persona was no longer there, but I was also excited because I was finally finding my place in the world and seeing how I fit in."

## Restructuring Identity

As transsexuals slough off the outer shell of the male or female persona they have presented to the world, they must create a new identity. Having repressed their instincts about their true gender for such a long time, even though they are finally in a position to demonstrate it outwardly, they are unskilled and awkward at the outward expression of their new role.

Most adults have the benefit of years of societal cues, parental guidance, and the cumulative effects of social learning skills on which to base their gender role. Transsexuals, by contrast, are more or less back at square one. What comes naturally to everyone else as a result of their socialization as either male or female does not apply to transsexuals. They cannot simply emerge "full blown" as the other gender. They must rebuild themselves psychologically, socially, and interpersonally by integrating elements of their old self into the new one. One MTF patient described this as follows:

There are aspects of John that are useful and powerful. I don't want to lose those and have absolutely kept and incorporated them. I've noticed that people try to carve off their past and set it adrift, but it has a nasty effect of following you wherever you go. So I'm not trying to make John disappear. It's more like I'm looking to embrace that aspect of myself. There's a lot of useful things in John. He gets the job done, and he got me this far, but that's not who I am now. So I can have the best parts of John but not *be* John.

The task of integrating, reorienting, and restructuring identity, however, is not easy. It takes time, patience, and perseverance. Nobody but transsexuals find themselves in the position of having to acquire the identity and social skills of a whole other gender. Moreover, they must do so without the benefit of years of socialization.

They need encouragement and guidance while undergoing such dramatic changes. For most, therapy continues to be a valuable source of support and feedback. To some extent, the gender therapist serves as a mirror, reflecting what the transsexual is implicitly or explicitly expressing and objectively assessing how well the person is functioning in the new gender role. This feedback is essential to help patients develop a sense of identity in their new gender. This process is similar to the parental feedback and social learning that occurs during a child's formative years.

The more practical "presentation" adjustments—learning to walk, talk, gesture, and express themselves as their true gender—are generally accomplished through observation, practice, and the help and feedback of family, friends, and therapists. But it is a time-consuming process and seldom comes easily. The early months of transition are an awkward, uncertain, "hit and miss" time when transsexuals use trial and error to establish themselves in their new gender role. As one patient said, "I am a female without experience, without a past. I don't know how to do this. There are so many unknowns. Part of me feels like a scared child waiting to see how the changes will manifest themselves. It seems to go layer by layer."

One patient named Melody eloquently described what transition was like for her "through a woman's eyes":

For me, transition began the moment I allowed myself to look fully at the world through a woman's eyes. The world shifted, and I was no longer in a familiar place. My perspective had changed, and so had the expectations of others. The more I walked through this new world, the sharper my current vision of reality became. I had always viewed the world from a female perspective, but as a protected spectator and not as a participant. A participant must know much more than a spectator. It was frightening and tremendously exciting at the same moment.

For a long time, I thought that my female side must be the fantasy because, after all, I am a genetic male. I mean, how could I dare to think that I had a female soul? I am woefully lacking in experience as a female, so I can't really be female, can I? But I am! Once I really looked through my own true eyes and not the eyes I had worn for society, it was so clear that my male side was a convenient armor and a passport to certain freedoms. I felt as if I had shed my armor and removed the filter that protected me from society. I realized that my interactions with people had always been from a female perspective. I also realized that I was in trouble.

I could either try to fake it as a male or try to live as a forty-five-year-old woman with no experience. The interesting thing is that I am actually having great difficulty faking the role of the male. So I don't seem to have a choice; I am going to have to face up to the fact that I have a lot of catching up to do. I have to learn to live without the male privilege on which I have relied for so long.

For me, this means the end of a magnificent marriage and possibly the estrangement of my wonderful child. I really don't want this to happen, but it is moving in that direction and I am powerless to stop it. The good news is that I finally feel real. God help me, but I do feel that this is my only alternative. If I stayed in my marriage, I would show my child that it is OK to bury one's personality to pacify society.

Now that I am committed, I am amazed at the magnitude of my ignorance; there is so much to learn! The excitement swells within me. I am really like a child again. How many people have wished to go back to childhood—but I am there again. At this moment, I am aware of the pain in my breasts from undergoing puberty a second time, but it is not unpleasant. It is a reminder of things to come.

This time around, I also realize that I have a gift that has not been bestowed on many others. I know what it's like to be either sex. This is the advantage that will keep me alive. Because of this secret knowledge, I am really better prepared than many of my female predecessors. But best of all, I know that I am finally being true to myself and I will not spend the rest of my life as an actress but instead as a willing participant.

## Making Legal Changes

As they begin the real-life test of living full time in the opposite gender role, transsexuals are eager to erase all traces of their former identity. To accomplish this, their driver's license, social security card, bank accounts, credit cards, and school and employment records must all be changed to reflect their new name and gender.

During transition, most transsexuals rename themselves with a gender-appropriate first name (unless they have already been using their preferred name). Many also adopt new surnames. Some accomplish these changes through court order; others do so through what is known as common usage. In either case, they must go through the tedious process of updating all pertinent documents to reflect their new name and gender.

The driver's license is usually the first document changed, as it is the most widely recognized form of legal identification. As such, once it has been corrected, it can be used to transfer other documents to the new name. In California, getting a new driver's license is accomplished by having a physician fill out a form (DL 328) provided by the Department of Motor Vehicles (DMV) specifically for this purpose, taking this form to the DMV, paying a fee, and having a new photograph taken. A new driver's license is then issued with the new name and new gender designation. This is a highly significant event for transsexuals. They proudly show their new license in therapy and exclaim, "Look, I'm finally legal!"

The next step is to obtain a new social security card. After that, correcting additional documents is relatively easy. Their driver's license and social security card serve as proof of their new identity, which in turn facilitates changing other records and documents such as bank accounts, charge accounts, and school, military, or work records.

Changing birth certificates is sometimes more difficult, and the laws regarding doing so vary by state. In California, a person who can document having undergone sex reassignment surgery and has changed his or her name through court order can obtain a new birth certificate that indicates the new name and new sex. Some transsexuals engage the services of an attorney to assist them in changing official records such as passports, deeds and titles to property, stock records, patents, professional licenses, credentials, wills, and stocks and bonds. Transsexuals also need to establish credit in the new name. Needless to say, accomplishing all this is time-consuming and often frustrating.

Care must be taken, however, that they do not destroy all past records during this process in the event that their prior identity needs to be proved, as in the case of inheritance. Surprisingly, it can sometimes be more difficult for transsexuals to prove who they *used to be* than to substantiate their current identity, especially once records have been destroyed or updated.

Transitioning transsexuals often experience anxiety about problems that can occur in establishing their new identity. For example, they worry about being stopped by the police for a traffic violation, having an accident and being hospitalized, or being confronted or questioned about their gender in public places such as rest rooms, fitting rooms, and locker rooms. Because unforeseen circumstances can arise that can be inconvenient, uncomfortable, or even dangerous, as a protective measure, some transsexuals elect to carry a "letter of passage" from their therapist or physician identifying the patient as a "transsexual in transition."

More than verbal challenges or abuse can befall transsexuals when their outer presentation is questionable. On occasion, some patients have been beaten up because others apparently disapproved of their appearance or mannerisms. In our rigid two-gender society, there is little understanding of or tolerance for individuals of ambiguous gender. For these reasons, transsexuals go to great lengths to create an outer presentation that is as gender-appropriate as possible.

## Changing Outer Presentation

Months or even years before transition (and for a long time during and after transition), transsexuals make physical changes for their own sense of well-being, as well as to increase their ability to "pass," so that others will be more likely to perceive them as belonging to the gender they self-identify as.

Transsexuals pursue hormone treatments and various types of surgeries to masculinize themselves (if they are FTMs) or to feminize themselves (if they are MTFs). In addition, they must learn to behave, walk, talk, move, gesture, dress, and present themselves as the opposite gender. This process is similar to the intensive type of practice and training actors engage in as they prepare to play a role entirely different from their everyday life.

Even though transsexuals have long identified with the opposite gender, they usually do not have the opportunity to actually assume that role until transition.

To achieve a more masculine outer presentation, FTMs usually get a traditional male haircut, put together a male wardrobe (including men's shoes, underwear, and shoulder pads), and practice the body movements and postures that are typical of men.

As one patient admitted, "I've been allowing myself to observe men to learn how their pants really hang on them, how they walk and move. I'm not embarrassed to do this anymore. I also allow myself, although still somewhat secretly, to look at women in an admiring way. I'm still somewhere in the middle, so I'm not fooling myself into thinking that I'm coming off as totally masculine yet, but that's my goal. I want to be a man, not a butch woman."

In addition, FTMs typically begin to work out or exercise. This not only helps them build a more muscular and more masculine body but also enables them to become more confident about themselves and the way they look. As one patient said, "My diligence and hard work at the gym paid off. I was able to reduce almost all physical female characteristics to virtual nonexistence."

MTFs learn to apply makeup and style their hair from willing friends and relatives, from books, and by trial and error (just as teenage girls do). They begin to assemble a gender-appropriate wardrobe. Even if they have cross-dressed in the past, they usually need to acquire clothing that will be suitable for their work environment and lifestyle, as well as fit their new, ever-improving image of themselves.

MTFs practice walking in women's shoes, sitting down and crossing their legs when wearing dresses and skirts, and perfecting the gestures and body movements that will add to, rather than detract from, their overall femininity.

For MTFs, electrolysis and voice training are two important contributors to a credible cross-gender presentation.

## Electrolysis

Although the amount of body hair on MTF transsexuals is reduced as a result of hormone treatments, facial hair is not affected and continues to grow unless it is permanently removed by electrolysis.

Electrolysis is performed by inserting a fine needle adjacent to the hair and applying an electrical current that destroys the hair's germination cells in the follicle. The follicle containing the hair is then removed. The process is painful and leaves the skin swollen and tender for about four hours after each treatment. One patient described electrolysis like this: "First you take a bunch of bees and get them really angry. Then you stick them in your face!"

Since males have approximately thirty thousand coarse, deep facial hairs, the process must be repeated at least thirty thousand times. This typically amounts to three hundred to five hundred hours of treatment, which, at a cost of $30 to $65 per hour, can end up costing as much as, if not more than, sex reassignment surgery (SRS).

Some patients, over the course of several years, have electrolysis done not only on the face but also on the chest, back, and hands to eliminate the need for regular shaving, waxing, or depilations.

Improperly done, electrolysis can leave unsightly scarring and pockmarks and can cause premature wrinkling. It is important, therefore, that transsexuals find a skilled professional who has medical-grade equipment and is used to working with transsexuals.

Arduous as it is, electrolysis is an important part of transition because MTFs will not be very convincing with an obvious beard. Once the process is complete, patients gain considerably more self-confidence about their appearance and about their ability to blend into society.

## Voice Training

Most of us, with the exception of actors and singers, take our speaking voices for granted. Transsexuals, however, must give a great deal of thought to their voice because how they sound is a significant factor in their ability to be accepted in their new gender role.

This is particularly so for MTFs. Even the most natural-looking "passable" MTF will draw raised eyebrows and have her overall presentation questioned if she sounds like a man when she speaks. This is especially so in job interviews or professional situations.

Whereas testosterone injections cause FTMs' vocal cords to thicken (which deepens their voices), estrogen treatment has no feminizing effects on the vocal cords of MTFs. Therefore, for most MTF transsexuals, considerable time and effort is necessary to train their voices—even the way they cough and clear their throat—to become as gender-appropriate as possible in register, pitch, inflection, and intonation.

## Passing

The ability of transsexuals to "pass"—that is, to be unquestioningly perceived by others as the gender with which they self-identify—is of primary concern for them, particularly prior to and during the initial stages of transition. However, these are the times when they are least likely to pass, as most transsexuals will have just begun taking hormones and other preliminary steps toward changing their bodies and still exhibit many of the contours and features of their original gender.

Passing allows transsexuals to blend unambiguously into mainstream society, thus reducing the possibility of social stigma. If transsexuals can pass, they have a far better chance of developing relationships and finding jobs. In fact, many patients assert that their success (or lack of success) in the RLT depends on how well they pass and that unless they are able to do so, they won't be comfortable in their new gender role.

### "Being Read"

The opposite of passing for transsexuals is "being read"—having people privately or publicly question their gender or recognize that they are transsexual. Most of us never worry about or even consider being questioned or challenged about our gender, but for many transsexuals, it is a daily concern. Some feel as though wherever they go, they are under the constant scrutiny of everyone and that everyone knows their secret.

As one MTF said, "I am so worried about how I look and act that anytime somebody glances my way in the mall or on the street,

I automatically assume the worst. I panic and immediately try to figure out what the person saw—what was wrong, what gave me away."

A certain amount of apprehension and paranoia about being
read is to be expected. The public bathroom, for example, is a formidable challenge for transsexuals; it is the place where they are
most likely to be questioned or confronted if there is any obvious
gender ambiguity.

Passing is very important to transsexuals. They want others to
look at them, talk to them, and relate to them as their true self,
their true gender. But it's not enough for transsexuals to pass only in
society's eyes. They also want to pass in their own eyes and meet
their own expectations and standards of masculinity or femininity.
"I may not look beautiful to the world," one patient said, "but when
I can gaze in the mirror and see an image that matches the mind,
that's what it's all about, that's when I will be free."

The intense desire of patients to pass pushes many of them to
undergo cosmetic surgeries of various types (discussed in Chapter
Nine). They go to great lengths to look and act either superfemi-
nine or supermasculine in their attempts to achieve acceptance by
conforming to societal stereotypes. Sadly, what some transsexuals
are doing is trying to force themselves into yet another box into
which they don't fit, another stereotype that allows for no ambiguity. This is a replay of their childhood struggles when, because
of their gender dysphoria, they could never quite measure up to
their peers.

Some patients pass easily. Others, even after long-term hormone treatments and various cosmetic procedures, still find it difficult to appear as masculine or feminine as they would like. Gender
therapists strive to de-emphasize their patients' fears and fantasies
about passing. Upsetting as it may be, not passing as well as the
individuals (or society) would like does not mean that transsexuals
should abandon their transition. They must be true to themselves.

Rigid cultural standards for masculinity and femininity have
been pervasive for years, and in the past, even gender professionals
sometimes discouraged transsexuals from continuing their program

if they did not meet those standards. In recent years, however, there has been a shift in thinking toward recognizing the enormous diversity in the ways that gender and gender roles can be expressed. It is not simply an either-or, black-or-white situation. There are many shades of gray.

## Accepting Uniqueness

As society moves toward acceptance of diversity, so transsexuals must move toward accepting their uniqueness and not care too much about matching an artificial standard. They must recognize that despite their best efforts, they will never overcome certain physical attributes. A large MTF can't reduce the size of her hands, shoulders, or feet, just as a petite FTM can't enlarge his hands or feet. In these cases, they simply assume that certain people will read them no matter what they do. One such female-to-male named Troy lamented: "I ask myself which is the lesser evil, being seen as female or as transsexual? No matter how depressing this is, I'd still rather be regarded as a transsexual than as a female."

Patients like Troy who have difficulty passing may choose to seek acceptance not as a male or a female but rather as a "transsexual male" or "transsexual female." For them, it's less about looks and passing and more about being free to live life as their true selves— the gender that matches their core identity. They may never be entirely happy with the way they look, and they realize that they will undoubtedly be taunted by some people. But what are their alternatives? Living life as the wrong gender is even worse. They know because they've been doing that for years.

Even transsexuals who pass successfully may choose to identify publicly as transsexual. Some live in such fear of being discovered that they feel it is easier to simply come right out and tell people that they are transsexual. Making sure everybody knows frees some transsexuals from their prison of fear. It spares them the potential pain of rejection from those who seemed to accept them prior to their disclosure, only to abandon them later.

There is a tendency to conclude that passing and acceptance are the same, but they are quite different. They may go together, or they may not. Passing is largely superficial and particularly important in dealing with mainstream society, where image predominates. But acceptance—being appreciated as an individual—is more important and is the cornerstone of any relationship.

## Internal Factors

Though transsexuals often tend to focus on the more obvious observable features of body, face, and demeanor, they also recognize the importance of making the necessary psychological progress on their journey toward self-acceptance. Passing is much more than outer presentation alone.

As one FTM patient phrased it, "For me, the secret of successfully passing was based as much on internal factors as on the way I presented myself in terms of my clothing and demeanor. I found through experience that as soon as I began truly to accept myself, others began to accept me more readily as well, regardless of whether they were relating to me as a transsexual or as a man. My own attitude has changed."

If transsexuals can hold their anxieties about passing in check during the early months of transition, the combination of the effects of hormones and the practice of living the role day in and day out eventually makes it easier for them to blend in, or at least gives them enough confidence not to take it to heart if they can't.

One male-to-female patient explained:

I honestly feel much less nervous about being out in public, and I think the feeling stems from the fact that I no longer have to justify to anyone why I'm projecting a woman's image. People have noticed. Finally, after so many years of frustration and torment, I'm increasingly, day by day, getting the chance to be *me*. And oh, does it ever feel good! I've never felt so alive, so vibrant, so full of feeling in my entire life. So feeling as I do in my heart and soul, I need justify nothing except to myself. Many people in this world might still like to interject their opinions—to prevent me from my right of self—but I simply can't worry about them. I have the right to appear as and to be the woman I am inside. Because of a strong sense of dignity and pride, though, I also want to do nothing to dishonor either women or transsexuals, and this is the reason, more than anything, I want to be the best-looking woman I can be.

## Sex and Intimacy

Love, sex, and intimacy are an important part of most people's lives. Transsexuals, however, because of their gender conflict, face some intimacy problems that most others don't have to deal with.

In Chapters Three and Four friendship, dating, intimacy, and sex are discussed from the perspective of transsexuals who were "closeted." Here we examine these areas for transsexuals who are living full-time in the opposite gender role—without or before SRS. Post-SRS intimacy issues are also described here but SRS itself is addressed in Chapter Nine.

### Friendships

After they transition, transsexuals generally maintain most of their former friendships, although old friends may be somewhat taken aback at first. After all, seeing an old army buddy for the first time as a female can be mind-blowing and takes some getting used to. But time and the years of shared experiences, respect, and mutual caring usually help keep the friendship alive.

Sometimes friendships may actually improve during and after transition, as the walls closeted transsexuals had erected to hide their gender conflict come down. Transitioning transsexuals are usually more open, less angry, and less withdrawn than before, and friends may see them laugh or dance for the first time. Old friendships are often uplifted to a more honest and more intimate level.

Developing new friends can be difficult for transsexuals. They generally feel insecure and lack the self-acceptance and self-confidence needed to feel comfortable in new friendships. Furthermore, same-sex friendships are generally different for women than for men. Women are more likely to maintain emotionally intimate and intense friendships with other women, whereas male friendships with other men are generally more casual and less intimate. As a result, an FTM transsexual who has been accustomed to having several very intimate friendships may suddenly feel quite lonely in the male world of friendship. Conversely, for MTF transsexuals, it may be very difficult to dissociate intimacy from sexuality.

## Dating, Sex, and Intimacy (Preoperative)

Most transsexuals don't date during transition. Dating with the wrong body feels inappropriate and uncomfortable, and it perpetuates a lie. There are also limits as to how far they can go sexually. Most patients state that they would rather be lonely and frustrated than date or be sexual during transition. But realizing that the transition period may last several years, transsexuals frequently find other ways to bring intimacy into their lives.

For example, they may spend time on computer chat lines. There they have anonymity, can assume their desired gender role without any visual contradictions, and can test their powers of masculinity or femininity using the written word. At times, the communications can become sexual. One patient described it like this: "I find that engaging in 'cybersex' is really a form of harmless fun and safe sex, especially right now. Part of the attraction to this form of communication is that the interactions are all invisible and people do not have a preconceived notion about my sexuality."

For some transitioning transsexuals, "vicarious sex" is not enough, and they miss the tactile sensations of physical contact. Hence some will pair up with other transsexuals or transgendered individuals. Whether these relationships are brief or continue even after SRS, they allow for emotional intimacy, holding, and touching at a time when transsexuals may feel uncomfortable sharing their bodies with less understanding partners.

Some transsexuals who want to date but are fearful of the possible consequences if their secret is discovered place personal ads in the newspaper. These ads typically begin "Preop MTF seeks . . ." This eliminates surprises; potential dates know the situation in advance.

Certain transsexuals who pass well might brave the straight dating scene. They may flirt and go out for dinner or dancing, but they usually avoid intimate time alone with their date. Still others find some comfort and sanctuary in the gay and lesbian social and dating scene. Other transsexuals seek partners during transition who are bisexual and are attracted to both genders. Many FTMs have been in relationships with women for years before they seek gender therapy.

Some FTMs date heterosexual females who relate so strongly to the transsexual's true male self that they are able to "bypass" the transsexual's genitalia and relate intimately with the man within. This seemingly lesbian relationship is viewed as heterosexual by both the transsexual and his partner.

As the female partner of an FTM expressed:

I've always been heterosexual. I'd dated and been attracted only to men—I was married for eight years—I'd never, ever thought of another female in a sexual way. Then I met Danielle at work, and we hit it off instantly and became best friends. One night, we were sitting on the sofa drinking wine, and I don't know how it happened, but suddenly we were kissing and it felt great! I was so confused. How could I be responding romantically to a female? Then she told me that she was FTM and that my attraction was to Danny (the male inside her). To make a long story short, she began therapy, got hormones, and had SRS. We've been married for ten years now and have two beautiful adopted kids. I've never been happier.

Relationships or marriages that existed pretransition may remain intact but will take on a different form. For example, a heterosexual couple might live as two males (as with FTMs); or as two females (as with MTFs), either without sex or with an altered form of sex.

## Dating and Sex (Postoperative)

After surgery, transsexuals have to "relearn" how to attract, relate to, and respond to a potential mate in their new gender role. They also have to learn how their new bodies function. Most people acquire this knowledge during adolescence, but the information transsexuals acquired then seldom applies in their new gender role. Transsexuals have to go through adolescence a second time and learn anew from the perspective of their new gender and gender role. As one person said at an FTM conference, "We weren't socialized as men; we never had the advantage of growing up as a boy. We want to have sex with women in a heterosexual way, but some of us don't even know what a penis looks like in real life. We have to learn from scratch."

Some postoperative transsexuals discover that although they may have been inhibited in their old body, with the right body, they feel freer to date, are more comfortable and more willing to become intimate, and are frequently more responsive.

Some transsexuals find their sexual orientation altering after SRS. One MTF expressed her surprise: "I tried to be sexually active with a genetic woman and discovered that as a woman, I felt no polarity sexually with women. This came to me as a great surprise, given my previous two marriages and sexual history. I do feel an emerging natural polarity sexually with men and have begun to see men socially with a different eye."

Some transsexuals, however, change their gender and gender role but not their partner preference (that is, the sex of the partner to whom they are attracted). In other words, a married MTF transitions to living as female but remains attracted to her "wife."

## To Tell or Not to Tell

*Whom* postoperatives choose to tell about their condition and *when* they choose to do so depend on the individual and the circumstances.

With regard to the general public, most transsexuals prefer not to make an issue out of their status and their past. "Once you make this change in your life," one FTM said, "unless you become romantically involved with someone, I don't think you have to tell everyone you meet. You're the person they know, they are comfortable with you. You are not hiding anything from them; you are who you are now."

Another states, "Like your sex life—how many people go around talking about it? That's our private business. If you had cosmetic surgery to have a terrible scar removed from your face, would you have to tell everyone, 'Years ago, I had this terrible scar'?"

For casual relationships, the decision not to tell can cause some embarrassing moments because transsexuals don't have the appropriate past history for their new gender. They may slip up and make an inappropriate reference. For example, an FTM might mention menstrual cramps or say something about "when I was in the Girl Scouts." An MTF might mention a past locker room event with the boys or make reference to being an altar boy. These individuals must then rush to correct themselves— "Oh, I just meant I always dreamed of things like that." Some postoperative transsexuals have developed an entire false history that they rely on to carry them through awkward moments, but most transsexuals refuse to do anything in their new lives that involves perpetuating a lie.

Postoperative transsexuals may not feel inclined to tell everyone they date that they underwent SRS, but once the relationship has progressed to a point where they are about to become sexually intimate, most disclose their past to their date or potential lover. This disclosure can be painful because the news is not always well received. In some cases, the repercussions can be devastating to the transsexual. "It's awful to lose someone because of who you once were" is how one patient put it. Some patients' dates have become angry or verbally abusive, and some ended the relationship immediately upon learning the truth. Some have even resorted to violence.

## Discrimination and Violence

Unfortunately, transition (and thereafter) is a time when many transsexuals experience discrimination because of their transgendered condition. They may find it difficult to find a place to live, a community in which to make their home, or a work environment that offers them the same opportunities afforded other men and women. Some even find themselves thrown out of their living quarters, driven out of or summarily dismissed from their jobs, or denied basic human rights. As a result, some transsexuals wind up jobless, homeless, and in the streets. This is yet another reason why passing is of paramount importance to most transsexuals. They believe that they must pass successfully if they are to avoid discrimination.

But it goes beyond passing. Discrimination can be a life-or-death situation. Transsexuals have been attacked and beaten up in the streets and in their homes. Medical professionals have refused necessary medical treatment to transsexuals upon becoming aware of their situation. And one transsexual who was involved in a car accident was denied lifesaving treatment by fire department rescue workers when they discovered her male genitalia. She died at the accident scene, and onlookers reported that in the last minutes of her life, she was laughed at and humiliated by the rescue workers.

Though some progress is being made—some cities are beginning to pass ordinances to protect the rights of transsexuals and other transgendered individuals—there is still a long way to go. Political action groups are being formed to fight discrimination against transsexuals and to help pave the way toward extending to them the same basic inalienable rights of freedom, dignity, and respect that the rest of us enjoy.

For some transsexuals and their friends and family members, being involved with these kinds of groups provides a special type of therapy. By helping transsexuals and their loved ones to take control of their lives, they can effect social change for themselves and others like them. Such involvement can help mend broken dreams, create hope, and give individuals an opportunity to make a difference as they help break the chains of discrimination for transsexuals now and in generations yet to come.

# 7

**Transition and the Workplace**

An important and challenging requirement of the Standards of Care for transsexuals who are contemplating sex reassignment surgery is the real-life test (RLT), as discussed in Chapter Five. The RLT requires that transsexuals live as the genetically other sex for at least one year before they can be considered candidates for surgery. Simply cross-dressing and staying at home during that year is not enough. As part of the RLT, transsexuals must demonstrate their ability to function *socially* and *economically* in their new gender role. Consequently, months before they begin their RLT, they examine in therapy how transition will affect their jobs, their income, their career path, and their ability to make a living.

Although transsexuals welcome the opportunity finally to live and work as their true selves, the prospect of "changing on the job" at their current workplace or else finding new employment provokes a great deal of fear and anxiety. The possibility of losing their jobs or facing a prolonged period of unemployment is of great concern, especially since transition is a time when their cost of living increases dramatically. They now need to pay for therapy, hormones, a new wardrobe, and electrolysis (if they are MTF) and to save money for various gender-related surgeries.

Donald, a police sergeant who transitioned on the job, worried for months about the effect his transition would have both on his fellow officers and in the community he served. "I was very, very fearful," he said. "I knew they didn't have the right to take my job from me—I'm an honorable, upright, taxpaying person. Yet each step carried its own fear. I wondered if it would ruin my career as a police officer."

Even transsexuals who are self-employed professionals or owners of small businesses worry about whether or not they will be able to retain the continued trust and loyalty of their employees, clients, patients, or customers. They wonder whether their business or private practice will be forced to fold as a result of their transition.

Susan, a tax attorney, expressed her concerns this way: "I had spent over twelve years establishing my practice and had a good clientele, but I was not at all sure how my longtime clients would react to my transition and gender change. I had to face the serious possibility that it might all go down the drain and I'd have to do something else to make a living. If starting all over again was what it took, I was willing to do it, but I desperately hoped that it would not be necessary."

## Whether to Stay or Leave

Transsexuals who are employed must decide whether to transition at their present place of employment, find a new job, or enroll in school to prepare for a new career.

### Staying at the Present Job

There are two primary advantages to remaining at a current job. By doing so, transitioning transsexuals have the best chance for financial security. They are able to keep their salary at its current level and retain their seniority, health insurance, profit sharing, bonus plan, and retirement benefits.

Furthermore, it is stabilizing and comforting for transsexuals to remain in familiar surroundings and with coworkers with whom they already have established relationships. At a time when so many major life changes are occurring, staying with their present employer can be far less stressful than trying to prove themselves to new people in new job situations.

There are, of course, negative aspects to transitioning on the job. Coworkers may not be able to abandon their image of the transsexual's former identity. Name slips and use of improper pronouns frequently occur, even among supportive coworkers (especially if they have known the transsexual for a long time). It is disheartening for an MTF transsexual who is elegantly groomed and smartly dressed in appropriate female business attire to be referred to as "he."

Transsexuals may find that no matter how well they are able to pass, it may be difficult, if not impossible, to be considered an ordinary male or female employee. He or she may always be regarded as the "company transsexual."

Certain coworkers may be so uncomfortable with the transition that they avoid transsexual employees, exclude them from meetings or events, and ridicule or harass them. Employers may subject them to discriminatory practices such as demotion or removing them from positions in which they interact with the public.

One patient named Joan had worked as an auto mechanic for nine years. She had little doubt about how the other mechanics in the shop would take her transition. And she was right. "You have no idea what it's like to tell a group of six rugged guys that you're a girl! It's like stepping off the edge of a cliff."

Indeed, after she transitioned, her hours were significantly cut, and some fellow mechanics were cruelly vocal. "I had hoped things would go OK," Joan said, "but I was the token 'TS' on the job, the 'weirdo.' The stress of daily taunts and catcalls was too intense. I finally had to quit. I lost my house, I lost my car; I fixed bicycles and cleaned houses to make ends meet. There just wasn't much call for a female mechanic."

For reasons like this, many transsexuals start fresh in a new work environment where nobody knows them or return to school to learn new skills and develop alternative careers.

Yet despite the difficulties, for financial reasons, many transsexuals choose to change on the job—either in their current position or by transferring within the company to another department or facility. Some remain as loyal employees for many years, especially if the transition proceeds smoothly. Others may decide after a year or two to move on to a new job. By that time, they are not only more comfortable and confident in their new gender role but, more important, they also have work experience and references in their new name and gender.

## Leaving to Find a New Job

For a transsexual who decides not to change on the job, finding new employment where nobody knows about his or her past has obvious advantages. By starting anew, there is a greater likelihood of being accepted as a man or a woman instead of being categorized as a transsexual.

But finding a new job may take a long time and has its own set of difficulties. In general, transsexuals face three problems in the search for a job.

1.   *Work history.* Most transsexuals do not have a work history or job references in their new name or gender. It is therefore difficult, if not impossible, for a forty-year-old MTF, for example, who has worked only as a male, with a male name, to produce documentation for a prospective employer to account for a twenty-year work history. Usually the only way this can be done is for the MTF to come out to the former employer and request a change in documentation to indicate that it was Jane Doe rather than John Doe who worked for that company. Transsexuals are understandably reluctant to do this, however, as the whole purpose of going to a new workplace environment is to leave their past behind them. But they often have no choice. In addition to work records, other documents such as school records, diplomas, credentials, union cards, and licenses all have to be changed to the new name prior to applying for a new job.

2.   *Interviewing.* Going out on interviews and conducting a job search is stressful for anyone seeking employment. For transsexuals

in transition, however, the interviewing process is especially anxi-ety-provoking. They must not only impress potential employers with their background, qualifications, and ability to fulfill the job requirements but also must do so in a gender role that they have just recently taken on. They want to project an air of confidence, but this can be difficult and intimidating if they are at an awkward stage in their transition.

3. *Ethics*. Transsexuals often face an ethical or moral dilemma when job-hunting. Some applications include a question regarding whether the applicant has ever worked under another name. Most transsexuals answer truthfully and consequently don't get the job. They also face the possibility that the interviewer will read them and ask if they are transsexual. Again, most tell the truth and don't get the job. When they do find new jobs, they may have to take positions with far less status and salary. Some of my patients have had their income go down by a third or even half. Some can barely survive and may have to file for bankruptcy. Some end up living in a car or even on the street.

## Ways of Coming Out at Work

For transsexuals who decide to change on the job, careful prepara-tion is necessary. Transsexuals rarely walk into their boss's office and simply blurt out the fact that they are transsexual. Timing and pre-sentation are important, as is making their transition as minimally disruptive as possible to the workplace routine.

Some transsexuals decide to "ease into" the disclosure by subtly (or not so subtly) changing their appearance on the job. Some MTFs may begin to let their hair and fingernails grow, pierce their ears, and dress more androgynously than usual. Some FTMs cut their hair, abandon makeup and jewelry, and dress in more mas-culine attire. Then they wait until coworkers become inquisitive enough about their changes and ask point-blank questions about what's going on. At that time, they go ahead and make the disclo-sure. Some feel that this softens the shock and allows coworkers to adjust to each new change.

Most transsexuals, however, take a more direct approach and come out at their jobs by means of a letter or a combination of face-to-face disclosures and a letter (or e-mail message).

## The Letter

To help my patients be as prepared as possible for their disclosure, they are asked to write a "Dear fellow employee" letter that includes everything about their situation that they want their boss and coworkers to know. We then discuss and refine this letter during therapy sessions. Here is an example of an open letter from a patient named Jane regarding her transition.

> *Dear friends and coworkers:*
>
> I have known many of you for some time now, and I count you all as my friends. What I must tell you is very difficult for me and is taking all the courage I can muster. I am writing this both to inform you of a significant change in my life and to ask for your patience, understanding, and support, which I would treasure.
>
> I have a gender identity problem that I have struggled with my entire life. I have been in therapy for it for nearly four years now and have been diagnosed as a transsexual. I have felt imprisoned in a body that doesn't match my mind, and this has caused me great despair and loneliness.
>
> I cannot begin to describe the shame and the suffering that I have lived with. Toward that end, I intend to have sex reassignment surgery. The first step I must take is to live and work full-time as a woman. On the first of next month I will become Jane Johnson.
>
> I realize that some of you may have trouble understanding this. In truth, I've had to live with it every day of my life, and even I don't understand it. I have tried hard all my life to please everyone around me, to do the right thing and not rock the boat. As distressing as this is sure to be to my friends and

family, I need to do this for myself and for my own peace of mind and to end the agony in my soul. Through it all, I have learned that life is an adventure, and I would like to think that the best is yet to come. I hope we can all enjoy it together.

*Jane Johnson*

## Presenting the Letter

Patients must decide how, and to whom, they will first present the letter. Usually, although not always, their immediate supervisor is the first person they inform. Some patients, especially if they work in a large corporation, approach the human resources department first. Others may seek assistance through their union representative. Typically, an appointment is scheduled with their boss, and when the time comes, the patient hands over the letter and sits there, often in a cold sweat, waiting for the reaction.

The response, at least initially, is usually a positive one. Then together, the transitioning transsexual and his or her supervisor or human resources representative usually decide who should be informed next and how the information can best be disseminated to the company at large.

Gender therapists sometimes work with company executives to educate them about transsexualism in general and to suggest ways to help them handle their own transsexual employees' transition. These executives then inform their various managers and department heads, who in turn inform the people working for them.

Some companies elect to inform coworkers by sending out a company or interoffice memo stating the company's support and position, as illustrated by the following letter:

> *To all members of the International Sales
> and Marketing Department:*
>
> We are writing this to notify you of a change that concerns one of our employees here. Although this change is of a

personal nature, it is also one that may be surprising to many of you and may even be uncomfortable for some of you. Consequently, we feel that it is important to let you know about the change and to take this opportunity to reinforce our company's position and desire to support the right of our employees to make personal decisions.

One of our long-term sales managers, John Smith, will be continuing a personal transition that began during the past several months. Beginning next Thursday, December 5, John will be taking a major step in a gender transition whereby he will fully assume his life's role as a woman.

Some people in John's department are already aware of this change. Others will be surprised. While there are many who have expressed general support for John's choice, we anticipate that a variety of personal reactions will surface as this change occurs. We want to take this opportunity to reinforce the fact that our company remains committed to certain principles as an employer, including our support for the right of employees to make personal choices. As always, our responsibility is to ensure a safe and healthy environment where employees of diverse backgrounds and beliefs can work free of harassment, intimidation, or discrimination. In addition, our management group expects employees to perform well in their jobs and to contribute to the overall success of the company. In John's case, he has demonstrated his commitment in this regard and has reinforced this commitment as he assumes the identity of Jane. (Jane will be the name on her cubicle sign and e-mail addresses after December 5.) We have designated certain women's rest rooms that will be available to Jane. However, to respect the wishes of any women who might be uncomfortable with sharing a rest room with her, we have reserved certain rest rooms in each building to be unavailable to her.

Our management is working to support Jane during this transition period and in the performance of her job and ask that you do the same. If you (or any of your employees) are interested in learning more about this subject, please contact the Human Resources Department.

Sometimes, before this type of memo is distributed, a gender therapist is asked to meet with all of the employees who work with the transsexual or, in the case of small companies, the company as a whole. The therapist provides an overview of transsexualism, answers questions, and deals with employees' fears, prejudices, and misconceptions. If employees are informed at a company meeting, the "Dear friends and coworkers" letter is distributed either prior to the meeting or at the meeting, or else the information is conveyed via e-mail at some point.

Usually the transsexual is not present at these meetings so that coworkers are free to ask questions and express their concerns. Many coworkers are surprised and even shocked by the revelation. Frequently, although they may have worked side by side with the transsexual for many years, they had no suspicion of their colleague's transsexualism. However, because some employers are unsure about how to explain the transsexual's situation, sometimes the transitioning employee does participate in the meeting.

Here's how the progression of events occurred for a patient named Mike:

I set up an appointment and met with my boss. I explained that I had been diagnosed as gender dysphoric and briefly outlined the Standards of Care my doctor was following in my transition from female to male. I answered his questions about when I would begin dressing and living as male and how my family was reacting. He told me that I had no worries about my job, stating that I was doing fine work. He also said that gender dysphoria was a recognized medical condition in his country, India, and that individuals transitioned and were absorbed back into society. I was then asked when I would like to explain my situation to the others in our small company.

Within ten days, we held a company meeting, and I

explained my situation to my coworkers and what changes they could expect and provided each with a copy of my letter. Before opening the meeting to me, the company president prefaced my discussion by stating that I had discussed the situation with him and that the company was in total support of me. The meeting went well, and my coworkers, though thoroughly surprised, were very supportive.

## Logistics of Transitioning

Generally, transsexual employees take a planned vacation or medical leave of absence for a week or more. This gives them a chance to prepare physically, psychologically, and emotionally for returning to work and assuming their new gender role. It also gives coworkers time to adjust to the radical changes that will occur. Companies that implement educational programs regarding transsexualism usually do so at this time so that everyone is informed before the transsexual employee returns. Usually, any necessary changes to company records, directories or telephone lists, name or identification badges, and security clearances are also made during this period. As one patient described the process: "When I returned to work, everything had been updated, and there were very few glitches. For all practical purposes, I was treated as if I were a new employee."

The first day back at work, understandably, is frightening for most transsexuals. They have no idea what their coworkers' reactions will be and whether they will be supportive. What has worked well in many workplace situations to help ease the transitioning employee's stress is for one or more supportive coworkers to have breakfast with the transsexual before work the first morning back as a way to break the ice. The transsexual can then be escorted into the building and "introduced" to everyone.

On the day of the transsexual's return, some companies have had flowers waiting or have scheduled a party. There may be some commotion for a couple of days, and the transsexual may receive lots of attention the first week. This is to be expected and stems from coworkers' desire to offer support, from simple curiosity, or from both. After all, John may have left for vacation two weeks ago as a balding male who paid little or no attention to fashion; now Jane is back in his place with a beautiful wig, makeup, and stylish clothes.

## Coworkers' Reactions

Ordinarily, most coworkers accept the change quickly, react positively, and are encouraging and supportive of the transsexual. Olivia, a computer programmer who works in a company with four hundred employees whom she advised of her transition via an e-mail message, received direct replies from nearly half of the people in her company:

> They were very positive, very moving messages and in some cases came from individuals who were near strangers. The one from the company president was one of the first to arrive. "I wish you the best in your transition," he wrote, "and look forward to having you remain as a member of our team for many more years. I didn't realize you were experiencing these difficulties with your gender, but I don't see how your future plans to resolve them affects your job in any way. Your gender has nothing to do with it. It is not a factor in the quality of your work."

Another patient's supervisor said, "Please don't be apprehensive. I think most people couldn't care less whether you have a skirt or pants on. It's you, the person, they know and like."

A number of other reactions from coworkers are presented at the end of this chapter to show the range of responses, the concerns that come up for some people, and the level of understanding and support that is typical in most cases.

Most employers recognize that all the same personal attributes and professional abilities, skills, talents, education, and experience that the transsexual employee originally brought to the workplace will remain intact. A gender change does not alter any of those things. Whether the job is carried out by a man or woman makes no difference. *Indeed, employees are not hired on the basis of gender.*

Although there will be adjustments to be made—on the part of the employer, the transitioning employee, and coworkers—most are related primarily to interpersonal relationships. Coworkers will have to get used to seeing the transitioning individual dressed appropriately for the new gender role and to get used to using the new name. Once everyone gets over the initial surprise, work goes on much as before. The employee will continue to perform his or her job functions as before, except now as the other gender. The only significant, long-lasting effect of transitioning is that transsexuals are often more productive than ever in the workplace because they no longer have to struggle under the constant burden of gender dysphoria.

## Hostility

Not all transsexuals, however, meet with acceptance, understanding, and support. Some coworkers are uncomfortable, resistant, or even openly hostile. They may be reluctant to change their perception of the transitioning employee. Sometimes their behavior stems from not knowing how to behave or interact with the transitioning employee in the new gender. Men generally seem to have more trouble than women in this regard.

Transsexuals may, at least initially, be the object of animosity and disdain. Many of the previously mentioned negative aspects and fears associated with transitioning on the job—name slip-ups, use of improper pronouns, distancing by some colleagues, exclusion from meetings, even harassment—may materialize.

Ironically, in some cases, coworkers have a hard time adjusting because they really liked the individual as they were. As one MTF patient described it, "People were angry because the male belonged. He put on a terrific act. They liked and respected him, whereas she seemed immature and less confident."

Although transsexuals' expectations about the realities of transition are examined in therapy, and despite their realization that
"you can't win them all," it's nevertheless painful for them to be
rejected during transition by coworkers who were once warm and
friendly. When transsexuals are excluded from meetings and are no
longer invited to join their fellow employees for lunch or for social
gatherings, it obviously takes an emotional toll.

At business meetings, some transitioning transsexuals have
found that coworkers no longer listen to their presentations or
value their opinion. It's almost as though the transsexual's intelli-
gence, knowledge, and abilities are now invalid. Some coworkers
have gone so far as to sabotage the transsexual's projects.

There have been instances where certain managers, who previously gave the transsexuals excellent job reviews, have put them on
probation for poor performance after transition. For this reason, it
is important that transsexuals keep copies of all their job reviews,
commendations, performance reports, and records of pay raises for
the time period before transition as protection in the event that
they are now unjustly demoted or fired.

Some employers have used more subtle methods in an effort to
force transsexuals to quit, such as bypassing them for promotion,
extending their work hours in an attempt to exhaust them, cutting
back their hours, or giving them only inconsequential projects.

Another tactic has been to place transsexuals in unpleasant or
even dangerous situations. In one case, an MTF police officer named
Carol, despite having been on the force for five years as a male
officer and having no problems, found that after she transitioned,
problems began. For instance, when she would call for backup in
dangerous situations, the other officers would not send anyone to
assist her. Thus her life was endangered. Another patient who
worked for the telephone company was given work assignments
that she had never done before, such as climbing sixty-foot poles
without the benefit of proper training or safety equipment.

Others have found, much to their dismay, that their positions
have been eliminated altogether. Twelve years ago, a male corpo-

rate executive and chief design engineer for a major auto manufacturer, who now goes by the name of Rachel, helped design one of the most popular cars on the road today. She was well respected in her field and earned a six-figure salary. After she came out as a transsexual, a representative of the company came to her house one evening, demanded that she hand over her corporate credit cards, and eliminated her job on the spot.

Rachel went for more than two hundred interviews for jobs directly related to the automotive industry, in which she had more than twenty years' experience. Once they checked her references or social security number, however, and found out that she used to work as a male, nobody would hire her. Some gave excuses such as, "You're overqualified" or "too senior." As a result, she worked many menial jobs to make ends meet. Eventually she lost her car and her home and had to move into a friend's garage.

Ironically, at one point after trying for two years to find work as a female, she cut her hair, put on a shirt and tie, and sought work as a male and was immediately hired. But she felt terrible and could contain her gender dysphoria for only so long before she had to revert to female. She became unemployed and severely distraught once again.

Unfortunately, this is not an unusual story. Transsexuals from every field, with years of experience, have been refused jobs and have remained unemployed for months or even years. They have gone from working as corporate executives to being employed as potato peelers, dishwashers, and housecleaners. Those who are not yet established professionally often have even more difficulty. One patient who recently transitioned while in medical school applied to 150 hospitals for residency before finding one that would take her. And even the people at the facility that finally did take her do not treat her with respect. She fights every day for her dignity. Transsexuals must be prepared to deal with these kinds of difficult situations, even though some protection is available through the legal system in most states.

Most employers today, fortunately, are far more attuned to the broad range of diversity in the workplace and not only accept it but also value it. Bias on the basis of gender is no longer accepted or tolerated, and many companies have antidiscrimination policies. Many transitioning transsexuals have reported that their employers and coworkers have given them lots of encouragement and treat them with the same respect or, in some cases, with even more than before.

One area, however, that elicits some concern and discussion, (even in companies where the transition occurs smoothly), is the use of gender-specific areas of the building, such as bathrooms or locker rooms.

## Bathroom Issues

Both practicality and logic dictate that someone dressed as a woman does not belong in the men's room—just as someone dressed as a man does not belong in the ladies' room. And yet, which bathroom the transsexual employee should use often becomes an area of concern in many companies.

Some employees are uncomfortable using the bathroom when a transsexual employee is there. This discomfort may arise from their perception that their privacy is being violated—rest rooms and locker rooms are often considered restricted, almost sacred same-sex areas. This discomfort may stem from an irrational fear that their transsexual coworker may have voyeuristic inclinations. Though it seems ludicrous to believe that a transsexual would go through the financial and emotional costs of transitioning just for the opportunity to be voyeuristic, some people have stated this concern.

These are some of the solutions companies have devised to address the bathroom problem:

- A separate facility is designated for the transsexual that may not be in regular use or is located on another floor or in another part of the building.

- Certain rest rooms are made "off limits" for the transsexual, to accommodate the needs of employees who are uncomfortable sharing a bathroom with the transsexual.

- An existing unisex facility is used, or one is designated to be used by both sexes and a lock is installed.

- A specially devised procedure is initiated whereby a "flag" or sign is posted on the door whenever the transsexual is using the facility. This system, which is humiliating to most transsexuals, is designed to allow any of their coworkers who are uncomfortable to wait, if they wish, until the flag or sign is down before entering the bathroom.

- A supportive coworker accompanies the transsexual to the rest room and "stands guard" while he or she is inside.

From a legal standpoint, transsexuals in transition are not prohibited from using public facilities designated for the opposite anatomical sex. However, companies have the right to control their private property and a few have instituted less-than-ideal policies, such as some just discussed. Transsexuals who go on to have SRS, however, have a legal right to use the rest room that corresponds to their new gender without corporate interference.

## The Transsexual's Reactions to Transition

After transitioning, nearly all patients report being happier, healthier, more productive, and better able to communicate and interact in a positive and professional manner with fellow employees. They are especially pleased when they are included in the inner circle of their new gender. As one MTF patient said, "The women are mostly supportive. The bathroom has never been an issue for me, and I am included in women's functions. Sometimes one or another of the women interface with me in ways I can only assume will happen between two women. In one case, a female coworker told me things about her life that I don't think she would ever have discussed with a man. I've longed for this kind of 'girl talk' since I was a teenager."

Not every patient, however, is so lucky. As one said, "I feel a bit exiled at times. Except for one woman who has been an especially good friend to me, the only time I'm invited to social get-togethers is when large groups of people are expected. I know of several occasions when I should have been invited but wasn't. It's clear that people prefer not to be seen socializing with a transsexual."

What is important to transsexuals is that their work responsibilities continue as before and that they are not relegated to the back room. "I must say that my company has been wonderful in doing its part to make sure that my transition has never interfered with my professional duties," one patient said. "I have often been introduced to important business clients, made presentations to them, visited their facilities, and interviewed prospective employees. I've even been made a project manager on a very important project."

## Letters

The following letter will give you a further idea of how some transsexuals who transition on the job approach telling their coworkers about their condition.

> To:        All employees
> From:      Marlene
> Subject:   Gender transition: An open letter to my coworkers

I know that some of you are probably wondering what it is about me that makes me so different, why I have gradually changed my physical appearance and behavior. This letter will, I hope, explain much of me to you and will also announce a major change in my personal life that will have a significant impact on my interaction with the everyday work environment.

I have been medically diagnosed as having a condition called gender dysphoria. This condition is characterized by extreme discomfort with one's anatomical sex and a continuous, extremely strong desire to live as the opposite sex—in my case, as a female. Currently, I spend virtually all of my time away from work living in the female role as Marlene, which is my preferred name. I have decided, after careful evaluation and soul searching, to live full-time as Marlene.

This decision didn't come easily; I have resisted it for many, many years. I have cross-dressed all of my life, starting at age seven, and have struggled for many years to stop doing it. I have seen more than twenty therapists and psychiatrists over a period of twenty-five years, all without success. What I didn't know is that this is almost impossible to stop; the "cure" for me is living full-time as a woman.

In my former gender role, I was very successful, as success is defined by our culture. I had everything one could want: I was happily married, with a beautiful child, a house in a great neighborhood, a sailboat, a BMW, and a hefty bank account. Yet I was miserable because there was something inside that I was denying, a very major part of myself. Something was missing; I knew what it was, but I repressed it.

As time went on, however, it became clear that I would have to deal responsibly with my own personal gender issues, which is what I intend to now do.

I know that this will be a shock to some people, a serious consideration to some, a relief to other people who already know about me, and, I hope, a nonissue for most.

It is my sincere desire to make this major change in my life as minimally disruptive as possible; I want to retain my good working relations with all of you and will do whatever I can to make that happen.

## Coworkers' Responses

Here are examples of e-mail messages that transitioning transsexuals have received in response to their "Dear coworker" letters. Most patients report that while they may receive a few negative responses, the overwhelming majority, like those reprinted here, are messages of encouragement and support.

Friendship has no gender. I wish you the best of luck in your
new life/persona/identity.

GOOD FOR YOU, MARLENE. Congratulations! (After all,
this is a rebirth of sorts.) I don't envy you the soul searching
and intense work that you had to go through to get to this
point of self-acceptance, but I admire the fact that you had
the courage to ask hard questions of yourself and have committed yourself to find out the truth. I support your efforts to
become who you really are, just as I would support anyone in
transition in ANY facet of their lives.

You have my strongest credit and respect. I have to say that
I admire your strength and openness in dealing with this.
Indeed, the way you announced the change is, in my mind,
the best way it could possibly be done.
    People are afraid of what's different, but you have one
life to live as you need to and TO BE HAPPY. Good luck.
Head high!

Wow, I must say, I am nearly speechless. I want you to know,
though, that I really respect your courage, and I am thankful
that you included me in your message. I cannot even begin to
imagine what you must have had to go through to reach this
point. I can only salute your strength and wish you the best of
luck. As far as I am concerned, this has no effect on your role
with the project or on your value to us. Your contributions
and talents are needed and appreciated.

Some coworkers, though supportive, express their surprise about
the revelation or acknowledge that it will take some time to get
used to the change:

I had no idea that you were unhappy with yourself as a guy.
You seemed more nurturing and stuff than most guys, but it

never occurred to me that you were considering changing. I'm a bit taken aback with what you're doing, but I am glad that you are following a path that will take you away from the pain, conflict, and confusion that no one deserves.

If I said I wasn't a little shocked at first, I would be lying. One reads about cases like this without ever thinking it would relate to someone you know, especially a friend. It will probably take a while to get used to thinking of you as a her, instead of a him, as well as getting used to the new name. So, feel free to point out any lapses on my part.
   Take care, stay well, and don't be a stranger.

Some coworkers use a touch of humor to express their feelings and as a way to communicate their comfort level with the change:

What fabulous news! I wish you all the best in your new life as a woman. You have the advantage of having lived as a man. I look forward to conversations with you about the treatment of women in technical fields. We need more great woman engineers, and whatever you do, don't take any salary cuts over this!

Congratulations! This must have been a major decision. You know there will be pain ahead because people are often unfeeling. Also, pantyhose are damn uncomfortable! I don't know what support I can be, and I can't say I completely understand your feelings, but I can support you in your decision. If I can be of any help, let me know.

Sandra, Sandra, Sandra . . . I fear this is going to be hard to remember. Maybe the change in appearance will remind me. And thanks for letting me know. I'm so dense in these matters, I could have been confused for months. I wish you happiness. For what it's worth, as long as she's as smart and nice as you are, I don't care whether I'm working with Tom or Sandra! And I've often thought that hair as fabulous as yours was rather wasted on a guy.

Whether responses from coworkers express total support, are more lighthearted in tone, or focus on the changing nature of the relationship, transsexuals are touched and overjoyed at how heartfelt most of the messages are. Often they lay the groundwork for maintaining, or even improving, the relationship in the future.

# 8

## Bringing the News Home

Coming out to family members is usually much more difficult for transsexuals than coming out at work. Though the possibility of job loss and decline in living standards may be upsetting, the thought of rejection by family members, especially parents, can be devastating. There are few losses greater than that of the family bond. A warm, loving relationship with our family can be one of the most satisfying aspects of our lives.

Yet despite all that's at stake, transsexuals realize that they must come out of their closets and be true to themselves if they are to live satisfying and meaningful lives. At the same time, however, they fervently hope and pray that their families will continue to love and value them despite the changes in their outward appearance. To that end, transsexuals spend many hours in therapy and many sleepless nights agonizing over the best way to tell their families.

One female-to-male patient expressed sentiments typical of many patients:

I'm terrified. I know I shouldn't be. I come from a close-knit, loving family who support each other emotionally, but what if my revelation is more than they can handle? I've played out the scene many times in my head with so many twists and endings. I keep asking myself, If I knew with absolute certainty that my family would reject me, could I remain female for the rest of my life so that our relationship could stay as it is? The answer is no! I've already tried—that's what I've been doing for the past twenty-five years. At a certain point, I realized that not transitioning could leave me as either a young corpse or a very unhappy old woman. Neither one was acceptable to me. I owe my family the opportunity to know the real me, instead of the automaton that I've been. I owe it to myself too.

In the following pages, we describe the most common concerns and fears about coming out to family from the transsexual's perspective, as well as typical reactions from family members. We place special emphasis on parental reactions because every transsexual is somebody's child, whereas only some transsexuals are spouses, parents, or siblings.

This information can help family members see how others like themselves have reacted to the transsexual's disclosure. It can also help medical professionals, therapists, and counselors working with transsexuals or their families to understand the enormous impact that transsexualism can have on family members.

## Parents

Relationships with parents are among the most significant and complex we have. Although these relationships may sometimes be tense, the emotional attachment between parent and child is such that from infancy on, we look to our parents for love, support, nurturing, and acceptance.

My patients, almost without exception, have said that their greatest wish is to keep the love of their parents after transitioning. They fear that their revelation will lead to distancing between their parents and themselves or, worse yet, cause their parents to reject them. We can always find a new job or make new friends, but we can't replace our parents. For these reasons, patients often postpone their transition as long as possible. Some wait until they are in their forties or fifties to come out. They want to please their parents and are almost as afraid of hurting them as of losing them.

"Whenever others asked me why I waited over twelve years to transition," said one patient, "the answer was always the same. I said I was afraid of losing my Air Force career, I thought I was far too masculine to be a woman, and I was way too poor to transition. Yet the *real* reason was always my family—I was afraid of losing my parents and family."

Another patient, whose parents were intolerant, feared that they would deal with her transsexualism with the same prejudice that they exhibited to others. "We once had a neighbor who turned out to be transsexual," she explained, "and you should have heard the laughter when my family talked about her. I used to feel my heart sink each time they discussed her. Of course, I didn't want my family ever to laugh at me like that, so I pushed my secret even further into my inner recesses and agonized about how on earth I could break the news."

For some patients, the thought of coming out to parents is so frightening that they develop eating or sleeping disorders, migraine headaches, or other physical ailments. "I waited to tell my parents until I felt that I could physically look good enough as a female so that they wouldn't throw me out when they saw me," one such patient said. "And yet, now that I'm finally ready to tell them, I've been so riddled with anxiety that I've lost twelve pounds in the past month and broken out in hives. If I could keep on going as their son, I would do it for them, but it's just not possible anymore. I cannot leave this path now that I've found it. I'm not going to my grave as a male."

## "The Telling"

Although most transsexuals come out to their parents in person, I have my patients prepare, as a therapeutic assignment, a "Dear Mom and Dad" letter explaining their situation.

Writing is an effective and useful process. People tend to get flustered or upset when talking about emotionally charged topics, and in the heat of the moment, crucial points may be overlooked. Writing, by contrast, allows patients the time to organize their thoughts and to find the right words to express themselves. There is ample opportunity to refine the letter to the point where they can actually send it if they decide to come out in that manner. The same letter can also be modified for other family members.

The letters patients write are varied. Some individuals express themselves with angry and emotional words, others prepare intellectually detached discourses about the transsexual condition, and still others compose beautifully phrased, heartfelt letters about their lifelong emotional pain.

After completing the letter, the patients read it aloud in therapy so that they can hear their own voices saying the words. We then discuss how their words feel to them and what they forgot to include or might wish to omit. After giving them my feedback, we anticipate how their loved ones might respond, and we role-play "the telling," based on what they have written in their letters.

When the letters have been rewritten and refined, patients then decide how they actually want to tell their parents. Most do it verbally and in person. Others come out by phone or by handing their parents the letter and letting them read it in their presence. Patients who are geographically separated from their families or are fearful of making an in-person disclosure generally send the letter by mail.

When coming out by mail, patients usually include a separate sealed envelope containing pictures of themselves dressed appropriately for their new gender role. Patients make a special point of mentioning these photographs in their letter, telling parents (or family members) that they can either look at the photographs right away or set them aside to view later when they feel more emotionally prepared.

Coming out by mail has the advantage of allowing parents the time to digest and adjust to the information and the visuals. They can have their initial reactions—screaming, crying, laughing, or having violent outbursts—without the transsexual being there to witness it.

Here is an example of a "Dear Mom and Dad" letter written by a female-to-male transsexual:

*Dear Mom and Dad,*

I have something very important to tell you about myself. You might not approve of it, but please try to keep an open mind as I try to explain this. Also, please understand that what I'm about to tell you is not your fault. So whatever you do, please don't blame yourselves.

I know you've wondered why I never had a boyfriend. You might have noticed that all of my guy friends are more like my "buddies." Well, I'm not a lesbian, but I am very much attracted to the ladies. You see, my body doesn't match the way I think and feel. Mom and Dad, I feel that I'm a man. My body might tell you the opposite, but I know I am male. It's what comes naturally to me. I have felt this way for as long as I can remember. I know you thought I was just a tomboy, but it went much deeper than that.

At the age of four, I remember thinking that I was a boy. Then I learned that boys have a penis. So I waited for mine to grow. Obviously, it never did. So every night I asked God to please change my body into a male body. It hasn't happened yet.

Up until age twelve, things were just OK. I had some really good times with my buddies, but I was still very sad and lonely. Then in junior high and high school, things got a lot worse. There were so many things I wanted to do but couldn't. There were girls that I really liked and cared about, but I had to keep my feelings locked up deep inside. I always had to pretend to be someone I wasn't. I couldn't just be myself. You have no idea how hard it was for me to try to act like a girl. It was extremely humiliating for me! To this day, it really tears me up inside! At one time, I came close to committing suicide, but I just couldn't do it. I didn't want to die. I just wanted out of this body!

Every day is a struggle for me because I know I have to play a role I'm not comfortable in. It stresses me out so much! I'm sick and tired of the whole charade! At work, I present a cheerful image. So they expect me to be all feminine and happy. They're used to seeing me with a smile on my face all the time. If they only knew the pain and torture I'm going through!

Well, Mom and Dad, what I'm trying to say is that I am going to have a sex change. Now you don't have to understand me, but please try to accept me. I know you had so many hopes and dreams for me. But I can't be who you want me to be. I've got to do what I know is right for me—not what anyone else might think is right.

Mom and Dad, you've been so good to me. I just want to thank you for all you've done for me. I feel truly blessed to have parents like you. I love you. Please don't ever forget that, no matter what.

*With love,*

*Alice*
*(soon to be known as Adam)*

P.S. Inside the envelope marked "Don't open me yet" are a few current pictures of me. You can look at them if you want to.

Other transsexuals do their coming out in a more lighthearted manner, as illustrated by the following excerpt:

. . . Please understand that I am completely clear about this in my own mind. I am certified by the experts to be sane and rational, and I am not being pulled into this by anyone else. This is not a religious cult, nor have I been abducted by aliens. Nope, Mom and Dad, I've got all my marbles together on this one. I am what I am, and now I'm simply making a decision to deal with it after more than twenty years of thought.

Just when you thought it was safe to glide through those golden years in Florida, I drop my bombshell. Oh, well. If nothing else, life is going to be interesting over the next couple of years!

## Parental Response

The revelation that their child is transsexual leaves most parents shaken—even parents who may have seen signs or had suspicions that something was wrong. It's the last thing in the world that any parent expects to hear. Even the most loving and supportive parents require a period of adjustment. Their expectations, hopes, and dreams are shattered. There are so many unknowns, and so much is at stake.

Initial reactions by family members are difficult to predict. Parents may be positive, supportive, and accepting, or they may be negative, angry, and rejecting. The type of relationship that each parent has with a transsexual son or daughter plays an important part in determining how the parent will deal with the child's disclosure.

Some parents react to the news as if the child had died. They go through a period of grief that can last for months, or even years. Although their child is very much alive and is in fact the same person they've known and loved, many mourn the loss of the external image and the significance attached to that image ("my son, the doctor," "number one son," "my darling little girl," "my only daughter"). They may be unable to let go of their long-standing perceptions or expectations for the person and have difficulty learning to adapt to their child's new gender role.

Some parents express resentment at even having to try to deal with the impact of transsexualism in their lives and say, "I wish you'd never told me. Before you told me, I could pretend that this wasn't so. Now that I have heard your 'shameful secret,' I have to deal with this whether I want to or not. Now I have to go through this pain, this trouble." One father in his anger shouted: "I wish you'd kill yourself and save us all from having to go through this. You'd be better off dead than transsexual."

Parents often experience many of the same negative emotions that their transsexual child has been dealing with—confusion, denial, fear, anger, depression, guilt, shame, and low self-esteem. Any or all of the following emotions and reactions can apply to other family members of the transsexuals as well, especially their spouses and children.

•   *Confusion.* Many people simply don't understand what their son or daughter's announcement means: "How can this be? I never saw any signs. He was always such a macho guy." "She was the prettiest, most feminine of all our daughters." "Does this mean he's gay?" "Does it mean he's psychotic?"

•   *Denial.* Frequently, family members just aren't ready or willing to acknowledge the transsexualism. Denial for them serves to dismiss, cover up, or block out distressing suspicions or knowledge: "It's just a phase he's going through." "This is only a response to stress, a reaction to her divorce." "If we don't acknowledge it, it'll go away. It's just a whim."

•   *Fear.* Parents may have fears both for their child and for themselves and their family unit. Fear for the child: "What on earth will happen to my daughter now?" "I'm afraid she'll be miserable." Fear for themselves: "What will our friends and relatives say when they find out? Will they think we caused it? Will they reject us?" "What's going to happen to us? Are we going to be strong enough to survive this shock? What do we do with this, where do we go from here?"

•   *Anger.* Many parents take the revelation as a personal affront: "How dare our child disrupt and discredit our family this way! We'll never be able to hold our heads up in this town again." "How can he be so selfish? Why is he always trying to hurt us?" "Will her rebellious streak never end? What did we do to deserve this?" Sometimes the anger is so extreme that parents throw their children out of the house, ban them from family celebrations unless they come as their former self, cut off their money for school, or disown or disinherit them. Some parents are so unrelenting in their anger that they would give up their relationship with their child rather than try to come to terms with the transsexualism.

•   *Depression.* The grieving and negative emotions get so intense for many parents that they begin to sleep poorly, eat poorly, and function poorly in their jobs and in life: "I can't go on." "I'll never recover from this blow." "I've lost my child; I want to die."

- *Guilt.* Some parents feel as if they are to blame for their child's transsexualism: "If only we had somehow been more attentive, more loving parents or better role models, or if we had been less permissive and set more boundaries, our child might not have turned out to be transsexual." Some parents also feel guilty because they cannot readily offer their child unconditional love and support. Some feel they may have genetically passed this on to their child. Mothers may fear they "caused" this condition by taking certain medications during their pregnancy.

- *Shame.* Society as a whole looks down on transsexualism and sees it as strange or sick. Many parents look at their children as an extension or reflection of themselves. Thus if their child is "not okay," the parents or family unit are "not okay." The parents may take on the stigma that society attaches to the condition. "How can we face people?" they ask. They often retreat into semi-isolation and guard a secret that they are too embarrassed or too fearful to share.

- *Low self-esteem.* The guilt and shame just discussed often threaten the parents' sense of self-worth. Their egos are shattered. "What a mess we have made." "We certainly have failed as parents." "I raised Joan on my own; I must have turned her off femininity."

Over time, many parents of transsexuals (though unfortunately not all) are able to rise above their initial negative feelings and express their continuing love for their transsexual son or daughter. They recognize that this transsexual is still their child and that everything that they always loved about that child is still there. This shift is illustrated by the following letter and subsequent interview with the mother of an MTF:

Dear Bob,

I'm having a real problem with this "Betty thing," and it's easier to make my point in a letter to you rather than talking face to face. It's one thing for you to put on a wig and behave as a woman and quite another when you start believing you *are* one. It is insulting to me, as a woman, that you assume that the outer trappings of femaleness somehow entitle you to all the other baggage that women carry—baggage that can only be acquired by growing up female in a male world. For you to think that donning female attire entitles you to appropriate and fully understand all that being a woman encompasses is unfair to me and to women in general. It denigrates my experience. The way you appear to grasp all this is so *male*. Whatever your fantasy is about being a woman, the reality is that you're a man. You can share my makeup and wear my wigs, but you do not and never will share the lifelong experience of growing up female in America. And for you to insinuate your man-dressed-as-a-woman self into the whole *process* and *actuality* of being a woman is arrogant and insulting. In so doing, you discredit and discount not only my own experience of being female but the entire community of women.

The mother who wrote this negative letter, when interviewed two years later, had the following to say:

When I first heard about all this, I must admit, it really threw me for a loop. Certainly, Betty has always definitely taken her own path and "done her own thing," but never something like this. Much of the upset I experienced initially had to do with my irritation about her attempts to simulate being female without the benefit of having been born that way. I guess I really resented her for a while.

But I spent the last year in therapy, and I came to understand that Betty or Bob, there's really no difference. That's my child. That person is flesh of mine and I can't deny that child. I want to be there for her and help ease her pain.

## Relief and Support

All parents require time to adjust to the fact that their child is transsexual, but some are able to give immediate support and unconditional love. They are almost without exception sympathetic to what their transsexual child had to go through. They realize how difficult it must have been to experience lifelong gender dysphoria. They regret that their child had to travel such a painful road all alone. Here are some typical responses:

"Why didn't you tell us sooner? We never would have abandoned you."

"Why would we want to withdraw from someone we love? Did you really think this was going to change the way we feel about you?"

"We always knew something was wrong but wanted to respect your privacy. We hoped that you would tell us and let us carry some of the load with you."

"Is that all? I'm so relieved. We thought maybe you were in trouble with the law or something or that you had a terrible illness and we might lose you."

"How could you think this would change our feelings? It doesn't make a difference. You'll always be our child, and we'll always love you."

"We're proud of the courage and strength you've shown in dealing with your gender dysphoria. We're lucky to have a child like you. We're sorry that you've suffered so long."

Many times, with this type of family, the relationship gets even better because with love and acceptance, the transsexual becomes a happier, more genuine, and more functional person. Moreover, transsexuals' love and appreciation for their parents often intensifies when they receive this level of acceptance and support.

"My parents and I talked from eight in the evening till four in the morning," a female-to-male patient said. "Mother hugged me on the way out and said, 'Goodnight, son.' My parents phoned the next day to say that they loved me. We talked about whether to tell the rest of the family, and they said they'd rather not hide it. A balance shifted in our relationship because now I can be real. We've never been this close before, and I've never been prouder of them or loved them more."

What follows is an excerpt from an interview with a mother of an MTF whose relationship with her child underwent significant positive change:

There was a distance between us. Gloria held resentment inside of her. I always thought that it was something I said or did. Once she told me about her transsexualism, I immediately said to her, "Now maybe I'll have the daughter I always wanted." We were never close before, but now we are. The news was a shock, but I accepted it right away. I suppose if I had been younger, I would have had trouble. But you come to a certain age and you learn to accept things you can't fight.

I was eighty-five when I found out. I'm happy that Gloria is happy. I can't imagine parents rejecting their child! There are too many ties to break them off. There are a lot of things worse than transsexualism. I'd rather see Gloria like this than a drug addict or a criminal. Now we spend a lot of time together. We go for lunch or shopping and laugh and have fun. I never knew what was wrong with him. Now it's a world of difference. He saw so many therapists and was still confused and unhappy. Sometimes I miss Glen, although I like Gloria much better than him. The neighbors saw Gloria coming and going, sometimes in jeans and sometimes in a dress, and asked me, "What have you got, a son or a daughter?" I told them that I had a son who had a sex change and is now my daughter. I'm grateful to live to see my child happy. Fifty years ago, they handed me a baby in a blue blanket, but they were wrong. It was a girl. My only regret is that she had to go through this for so long without my help.

Parents frequently show their support by accompanying their transsexual son or daughter to surgery and helping to nurse them back to health when they get out of the hospital. Though some may still need to grieve for their "lost" son or daughter, they are ultimately able to look at it in terms of gaining a son or a daughter.

One patient's mother went through her son's entire transition with him as an active participant. She accompanied him to the appointment with the physician who would be performing the surgery. "It's really nice for me from a parent's perspective to meet the doctor and see who this person is. I feel really lucky to be here and involved in the process. I see that some people don't have family support, and that breaks my heart."

She described what it was like when Mark/Marilyn first told the family:

It was really interesting. Marilyn (we knew her as Mark then so I'll use that name when referring to the past) came over late one evening after my husband had already gone up to bed. I could tell that something was going on, but I didn't know what. All of a sudden, he dashed out to the car and came back in with these papers in his hands that he had all rolled up. I knew something big was going on. For months I had been aware of something brewing. I felt Mark pulling away from us. I was really concerned about that but couldn't figure out what was happening or what to do about it. But we found out that very night. Mark was sitting in the living room in my husband's chair, with me and his two sisters, and handed out these letters he had written to all of us. All I did was read the first paragraph, and I started crying. "Is this all that's going on?" was my first reaction.

I had a thousand questions at that point, but I also felt a sense of overwhelming relief. We are a stepfamily with six children in all—three of my husband's and three of mine. Our first son joined the army and left home, and the other two left abruptly to go to their moms' even though we had custody, and that separation was painful. Even though I didn't expect that to happen because our family was so much closer, you just never know. Mark had been out of the home and on his own for a couple of years, so I wasn't sure what to think. There was just the fear that maybe he didn't want to see us anymore, maybe he was moving away, whatever. I had no idea. I knew that Mark had broken up with his girlfriend a while back, but I didn't think it had to do with that.

My husband was very upset initially. He just didn't understand. He's a very macho kind of man and has said many times how much he loves being a man. So for him, having a child who says, "I'm not a man even though my body says I am" was really hard. For a couple of months, he would hide upstairs whenever Marilyn came over. But eventually they worked through that. Time was the most important factor.

The unconditional love and support expressed by this mother and by the one in the letter that follows is every transsexual's dream:

> *Dear Doris,*
>
> I must admit we've all been kind of numb since our talk—can't quite take it all in yet—it was *so* unexpected.
>
> I'll say this for you, hon, you never did things on a small scale. And this one was a 10 on the Richter Scale. In time, I guess this will seem like nothing. But for now, it will grow on us. I love Dorian, though, so don't bury him too deep. He is highly intelligent and has a great sense of humor and a very soft heart (that's Doris).
>
> It's a funny feeling at age 58 to be giving birth to a daughter, but you're the one going through all the terrible labor pains. I know how hard this is for you—you have to give up so much to gain your sanity. Since you are one of the most intelligent human beings I know, I'm sure you have given this all the searching time needed to come up with your decision. If you say this is the only way you can live, I believe you.
>
> Your road now is long and hard, but I know that you are going one step at a time and you can handle it. I only wish we

lived closer so that we could be more help to you and be able to be there when you need a hug or help, but this can't be—so hug your pillow and pretend it's me. I'll do the same. I miss you very much.

Remember, we'll always love you and you'll always be our child. And as always, as a family, we will work things out. Tomorrow is another day.

*Love you much,*
*Mother*

## Spouses

Approximately 50 percent of the MTFs and 10 percent of the FTMs in my practice were married or had been married when they first sought therapy. Because we have more information on wives of MTFs than on husbands of FTMs, we will focus on the wives' reactions, although some of the information could apply to husbands as well.

Most transsexuals dearly love their spouses and don't want to hurt them or damage the marriage or upset their family life in any way. They hope and pray that their spouses' love is unconditional and will remain so once the former outer image is gone.

If transsexuals have not told their spouses prior to marriage about their cross-gender feelings, they generally experience guilt at having withheld such important information. "I know my wife will feel confused and betrayed," one MTF said. "That was never my intention. I've loved her deeply through all these years and will always love her. I honestly thought that my love for her and our kids would keep my gender dysphoria at bay forever and that I would never have to disclose my condition to her. But now I see that I have no choice. I can't go forward without confronting the issue with her."

Single transsexuals, if they wish, can proceed through transition without ever telling parents or other relatives. But married transsexuals must discuss and plan transition with their spouses because the decision to cross-live will obviously have major repercussions for the spouse as well.

Certain spouses know before they get married that their partner has a gender identity problem, but their love often overpowers their concerns about how this problem will affect the marriage. They marry and become their partner's friend and supporter, even when the transsexual's cross-gender desires are outwardly expressed. Most spouses, however, are not aware of their partner's transsexualism when they first marry. Instead, they discover it or are told at some later point in the marriage. For them, the revelation is generally shattering. They usually say they had absolutely no idea that they were married to a severely gender-conflicted person. A closeted MTF husband, for example, may have been distant, irritable, or depressed, and marital sex may have been infrequent, but from these clues his wife could hardly be expected to make the quantum leap to "Aha! He must be transsexual."

## Initial Reaction

The initial reaction for many wives is often anger at the injustice they feel was done to them and at what they perceive as deception and betrayal throughout the marriage. They are often furious that such a big secret was kept from them. "Why did you want to get married in the first place?" and "What other secrets have you kept from me?" are typical cries.

As one wife said, "How dare you, after all these years, tell me this? Now what am I supposed to do? This is the worst possible thing you could say to me. It isn't fair to me or the kids. And the burden of handling their confusion about this will fall on *me*, and I can hardly understand it myself."

Understandably, this is a difficult revelation for spouses to hear. It upsets their lives enormously, and like parents, they may go through stages of grief. A wife may have had a great relationship with her husband and would never have expected anything other than the death of one of them to end the marriage. Yet the person who was her husband is alive but no longer her husband.

Some wives show compassion, but others, in their rage, demand an immediate divorce and, out of fear, vindictiveness, or lack of understanding about transsexualism, banish the transsexual from family functions, withhold visitation rights with the children, and poison the minds of the children against the transsexual parent.

Sometimes husbands are accused of being evil, insane, and depraved, as in this excerpt from a letter from one MTF's ex-wife:

Do you think you are strong enough to endure the whispers, the jokes, the closed doors? Do you think you will be safe from rape? Are you not afraid of some homophobic bastard beating you till you are dead? What have you done? Where is your future? What legacy have you left your family and generations to come?

You are an immoral freak who will inherit misery as a companion. I will never forgive you and will pray that your insanity has not invaded further on our family's gene line. You will grow old without anyone who cares if you live or die.

Conversely, other wives don't experience any anger or vindictiveness. Instead they feel pain and confusion. Some initially blame themselves for the situation: if only they had been prettier, slimmer, sexier, or more loving, maybe this wouldn't have happened. Some want to stay in the marriage and make it work. Others want to stay but are concerned about what family and friends will say if they stay married to a spouse who has transitioned.

In many ways, as married transsexuals move out of the closet, their spouses move in, especially when husbands ask that their wives not tell anyone. The transsexual has been freed by coming out, and now the burden of keeping the secret, the bad feelings, the solitude, the fear of exposure, the ridicule, the stigmatization, and the rejection often shifts to the wives. One wife expressed her feelings this way:

I feel very isolated. I can't talk to any of my friends about this. They'll lose respect for me. They'll think that something is wrong with me. In fact, I feel so tainted that I was in therapy for two years and never told my therapist about my husband's gender issues. I worried about what she would think; I worry about what everyone will think of me. Will I be the focus of gossip? My parents were here for a one-month visit and because of my shame I waited until the day they were leaving to tell them. I was sure they would think I created this.

Sometimes before a wife learns about her husband's transsexualism, distancing in the marriage makes her suspect that the husband may be involved with another woman. As the wife of one patient said during a family session, "I thought my husband was having an affair. We were fighting all the time. There was no sex at all. Then I found a bra and so I *knew* it was an affair. I confronted him, and he told me about his transsexualism. I felt so stupid that I had never realized this before. He used to tell me how to dress and bought me clothes. I thought he didn't think I looked feminine enough. Now he tells me that he was trying to make me look the way *he* wanted to look."

A wife may experience considerable confusion about the way her husband's transsexualism affects her own feminine image and her own sexuality and sexual orientation. As one wife said, "After he came out, the last time we tried to have sex I went to put on my sexiest nightgown, and when I walked into the bedroom, there 'she' was in an even sexier one. I was completely turned off. So now I don't have a male sex partner, and I'm not a lesbian, so where does that leave me? What do I do?"

## Making Adjustments

It is important to note that these are *initial* reactions. Whereas some wives are never able to move much beyond this point, others, with time, discussion, learning, and possibly therapy and support groups, are able to work through their issues. They may choose to continue in the marriage with the transsexual through transition and sex reassignment surgery (if the transsexual goes that route), or they may separate but remain friends, even "best friends." Others seek an immediate divorce.

When wives do stay in the marriage, they need time to adjust to the many changes that their husbands undergo. For example, wives have to get used to their husbands' shaving their legs or chest, cross-dressing in front of them, growing breasts as a result of hormone treatments, speaking in a more feminine voice, and if completing SRS, having genitalia similar to their own and thus requiring new and different forms of sexual relating.

For the many wives who have remained in the marriage through it all, the key factors that made it "workable" were the mutual respect, understanding, affection, and love that existed between the two spouses. In addition, the husbands introduced the changes slowly, explained the necessity for each new step, and then allowed their wives time to adjust.

There was also continuing acknowledgment and appreciation by the husbands of their wives' sacrifices, compromises, loyalty, and support during the transition period. As one wife said, "I ran the gamut from sad to glad, but Jim was loving and patient with me and understanding of my need for time to adjust to some of the more dramatic changes. I went through a grieving process for what was lost but also euphoria about finding this part of him. Now he could be real and I could truly know him. As for what other people think—I wrestled for a long time worrying about that, but now it's 'bring 'em on!'"

Some wives have little or no struggles and are immediately understanding and accepting. They love a person, not an image; they are close friends and share mutual interests, histories, and kids with their spouses. They get involved in their husbands' transition, attend support meetings with their husbands, accompany them on their early public outings, and shop with them and for them. One wife explained:

I love him and want to remain married to him. It means tearing down the walls that his secret built between us and sharing openly. If we can do that, I see a potential for a really good relationship that would carry us through the future—one in which we could enjoy each other as people.

I married for life. I didn't just marry his body. I love him. He's a fabulous person. I want to stay and deal with whatever happens. I want to protect him and take care of him. And after his sex change, I'll still be his partner and lover; I just won't be his wife anymore.

This loving wife, in staying with her spouse, gave up her heterosexual relationship. Other wives or partners, though extremely supportive of their transsexual partner, understandably mourn the loss of their former relationship. This is so regardless of the sexual orientation of the persons involved, and is beautifully illustrated in the following letter a lesbian woman wrote regarding her transsexual partner:

My partner and I have been together about three years. About a year into our relationship, my partner's long-standing gender issues arose again, and she realized that they had to be dealt with. At first, when we actually began discussing it, the whole situation was like a dream—a seemingly overwhelming situation full of "what ifs." What if this happens? What if people are cruel and unaccepting of him and of us? What if our friends reject us? What if we have to move? What if, what if? Then I wondered, what if I'm not a lesbian anymore? What if the testosterone changes my partner as a person?

I have always felt that people have to do whatever they have to do to be happy and complete persons. Sometimes, however, there were days when I just wanted life to be the same as it was before, to be smooth. . . . Does anyone ever wonder how *I* am feeling? . . .

When he had the mastectomy, it was hard for me to imagine that anyone would want to lose her breasts, but I took care of him, watched over him, bathed him, made him eat, and generally hounded him until he was up and about, and I will again be there for him for the hysterectomy and the "bottom surgery."

Now the world sees us as a straight couple, and I'm still getting used to it. I have realized that it is OK to mourn the lesbian connectedness I once felt. Now my partner is no longer welcome at certain women's festivals or lesbian events, and I don't want to go by myself if my partner is no longer welcome.

On the other hand, a whole new world is opening up to us. New experiences await!

## Children

Until around fifteen years ago, therapists used to suggest that transsexual parents disappear forever from their young children's lives. The plan was to tell the children that the parent had died or gone far away for a new job. Ostensibly, this was done to prevent the child from being psychologically traumatized or confused. Some spouses, out of anger or revenge, might insist on this even today.

However, banishment of the transsexual parent is no longer advocated by most gender therapists. If the child is told that the parent is far away and that parent never visits or calls, the child feels abandoned, unloved, and unlovable. This tactic (or saying the parent is dead) is unnecessarily painful for both the child and the transsexual parent. It deprives the child of the love and involvement of that parent, and it deprives the parent of the pleasure of watching and participating in the development, growth, and rearing of the child. This is unreasonable and unfair. As one of my female-to-male patients wrote:

> My feelings of love for my daughter overwhelm me. My ex-husband has taken her from me, saying that as a transsexual, I should never be given the right to raise my own daughter or even see her—the daughter I carried, gave birth to, and nursed.
>
> The emptiness and pain inside from being separated from her has left me cut and bleeding from inside out, and frantically trying to patch and plug the feeling of emptiness and pain. At times, I have nothing inside, no feeling, no soul. It's as if my spirit has left me.

I have heard sentiments such as these all too often over the years. Although many losses are inherent in transition, loss of or separation from one's children is the one that causes transsexuals who are parents the greatest pain.

There is no logical reason why someone living in the opposite gender role should be separated from his or her offspring. A sex change does not in any way diminish the parent's love for the child, nor does it affect the ability to be a good parent.

Approximately a dozen of my transsexual patients have had sole custody of their children, and these children have grown up to be happy, well-adjusted, non-gender-conflicted, sexually confident adults.

In fact, a study conducted by Richard Green in 1978 found that children raised in transsexual households developed a nonconflicted gender identity and a heterosexual orientation and did not differ from children raised in more conventional households.

## The Revelation

Most transsexual parents disclose their condition to their children face to face. Sometimes, when parent and child live long distances apart or are estranged, the disclosure is made by letter. In both cases, if the child is young, the transsexual may enlist the aid of the other parent or other family members to give the child further information and continuing emotional support.

Two letters are presented here. The first was written by an FTM to her estranged grown son, the second by a divorced MTF to a young daughter who lives with her mother in a distant city.

Dear Son,

Some letters are harder to write than others. This one is really tough. What I have to tell you is that I am a transsexual.

What does that mean? It means that ever since childhood, I thought I should have been born male. It also means that for over fifty years I have been resisting and fighting my inner nature. On the advice and counsel of other people, I tried to become a woman, to grow up and face my responsibilities as a female, and be like everyone expected me to be. To some extent I succeeded. Yet I always had the notion that someday I could take action to be true to myself. The agony I lived with was knowing that no matter what I did, I was going to hurt someone.

If I continued as a female, I was hurting myself and also those around me because of my own frustration. If I discontinued living as a female, I would hurt those close to me by not being what they wanted me to be. It seemed like a no-win situation until the issues got down to live or die, and self-preservation took over. I could at least salvage myself from the mess.

Why am I telling you now? I intend to live the rest of my life as a man. No more female appearances. You need to know this despite your father's wishes over the years that I not tell you. This declaration may explain a lot of my behavior since I left ten years ago.

What are you supposed to do with this information? I can't tell you. You have to decide. You can be hurt, angry, confused, disappointed—or you might even be glad for me. You have probably guessed for some years that something weird has been going on with me. So now you know. It's up to you how you react.

What happens next? That, too, is up to you. We can be friendly or not. You may have questions to ask me. If so, I will answer all questions you care to ask as fully and as honestly as I can.

What would I like? I would like to see you, talk with you, and explain myself to your satisfaction. I have felt that I have been a disappointment to you and failed you as a mother. Maybe there is a chance for us as friends. I hope so.

I await your answer.

*Your loving mother,*
Mary/Max

*Dear Melissa:*

I have a few things to tell you, but I am not sure how to do it. There have been many changes in my life, most of which you may not understand. Perhaps your mother can help explain what I am about to tell you.

When I was very young, younger than you are now, I wished that I was a girl like you. The wish grew inside me for many years until one day I had to do something so that I could be happy and not have this feeling that was growing inside me burst and cause me or anyone else pain. So in October, I went to the hospital, where the doctors performed an operation and made that wish come true.

Because I am now a girl, I had to change my name, and so I chose Angela. It's not as pretty as Melissa, but I like it. What do you think?

Melissa, I will always be your daddy. No one can ever take that away from you or me. But now that I am a girl like you and your mother, I find it hard to sign my name as John or Daddy. I can never be your mother because you already have the best mother in the world. But I can be your very special friend—a friend who loves you very much and wants only the best for a very special little lady named Melissa.

If you have any questions and would like to talk about what has happened, please write, and I will try to explain everything the best I can. If you would like a photo of your new special friend—*me*—please let me know, and I will send you one.

I hope you understand and you know that I still love you and always will.

## Children's Reactions

The impact of the telling on the children is largely dependent on their parents and possibly the immediate family. If adults in their environment are bitter or hostile about the situation, angry at the transsexual, and secretive, as if shielding others from some despicable or criminal act, children are without a doubt negatively affected. They can become depressed, anxious, and conflicted. And if asked to guard a family secret, they can become ashamed and isolated. However, if the adults deal with their own feelings rationally and resolve issues properly, the children can experience a parent's transsexualism as a source of enlightenment and a gift of perspective and challenge that can empower them.

As a rule, prepubescent kids can handle the transition well as long as the other parent and family members don't undermine the transsexual parent. It helps to recognize that children grow up with fairy tales and cartoons in which transformation occurs all the time. In *Beauty and the Beast*, one of the most popular recent animated films, the beast and all the utensils are enchanted—they were all human beings until a spell was cast on them.

In *The Frog Prince*, the prince was bewitched and turned into a frog. In the case of both beast and frog, unconditional love and acceptance turned the spell around, and the man who was trapped inside emerged. Children usually understand this concept and are comfortable with it; it's not really such a reach for them to understand the transformation of a man into a woman or a woman into a man.

In cartoons, figures change form constantly, animals speak, flowers sing, Superman flies. Children accept transformation as normal, everyday fare. And if explained to them lovingly and rationally, they can deal with their parent's situation and with having two parents of the same sex. Most kids want loving parents and would rather deal with the realities of transsexualism than lose the involvement and love of their transsexual parent.

If the relationship between parent and child was good before transition, it can remain good after transition. What is important is that lines of communication be kept open, that the child's questions and concerns be dealt with honestly, and that the transsexual parent move slowly and respect the child's boundaries.

One ten-year-old boy whose father still works as a male but spends most of his leisure time as female explained:

When I found out, I was amazed. I always thought I just had a dad, and then I found out about Gina. Now I have a dad that's part mom. What helped me was that my dad brought it on slowly. First, he told me and let me get used to it and then he showed me pictures of Gina. That's why I wasn't shocked when I met the real person. Then he didn't push that person on me all the time, just now and then until I got used to it. Now I spend a lot of time with both of them. When she's around, I have two moms.

I have a friend like me who has two moms. He lives with one and then goes to live with the other. There's all kinds of different families. Mine is not really so strange. I have a lot of fun with both Gina and John. Gina does things better than John, and I can do different things with each of them. As long as I know that dad is still inside too and that he still loves me and always will, I don't think I will have any trouble when he changes over permanently.

If kids are adolescents or teens at the time of a parent's transition, it can be more difficult to deal with. Some teens experience fear that they will lose their friends or will be a laughingstock in school and the focus of gossip. Teens of the same sex as the transsexual parents may fear that their parent's transsexualism may "rub off" on them or that they may have inherited the problem.

Others experience shame and embarrassment. Image is important to adolescent children, and they are easily embarrassed by anything that does not conform—the wrong brand of tennis shoes or jeans, the wrong make of car, parents with accents—and these things are trivial compared to having a parent who is changing sex. These teens may become depressed, distant, surly, or rebellious at having to face the shame or embarrassment of their parent's transsexualism. Some get so angry that they say they wish their transsexual parent was dead. Sheila, a fifteen-year-old girl said:

I felt dirty when I first found out. I felt like it was my doing. My brother knew, and when he told me, I couldn't believe it. First

I laughed, and then I cried. Why was dad doing this to our family? It's dysfunctional enough. At the beginning, I was so angry that sometimes I wished he was somebody else's father or even that he was dead. Then I got sad because all I could think about was how he wouldn't be there as my father to walk me down the aisle when I get married. I remember that I "closed down" for three months. And then on my fifteenth birthday, I broke down in class and couldn't stop crying. I was sent to the school's social worker, who arranged for me to get regular counseling. The counselor explained to me that it's not my fault, that people have all kinds of problems in life, and that I should learn to accept it and move on because there's nothing I can do to change Dad's condition. I understand that intellectually, but emotionally it still hits me hard at times.

Children of transsexuals often need individual or family counseling to help them understand and deal with their parents' transsexualism. Confiding in close friends who are fairly accepting about transsexualism also makes it a lot easier for the adolescent to accept. One teenager expressed it well:

I was in eighth grade when I first found out and was really afraid of how my close friends would handle it. I worried that they would think that the situation was so weird that they would give up on me as a friend rather than deal with this. At first, I fell into a depression while I tried to figure all this out. But my friends were great about it. They offered immediate support. They didn't judge it; they didn't say it was strange. If they had cut out on me, I would have gone insane. Instead they think it's interesting. Now, if I'm not home when they come by, they'll hang out with Wendy. I have a steady boyfriend, and he's totally fine with it too. He just wants to know what pronouns to use so as not to offend her. I would tell other kids in my situation that they are only losing the societal symbol of a father, but they are *not* losing their parent. I would also tell them that their parent will probably be happier and more loving, and so the relationship between them and their parent will probably get better, just like mine did with Wendy.

Some teens, especially girls, accept their transsexual parent unconditionally and love them as always—or even more, now that they know how much the parent has suffered. An eighteen-year-old female said:

I'm fine with all this. My relationship with Tonya has never been better. Tonya is vastly different from the male, Tim. The wall of anger is gone. A lot of negative attitudes have disappeared. Tonya is more positive and cheerful. She doesn't get those big testosterone rushes. He would always come home from work angry. Everything was bad. He'd drink twelve beers and roar. Now we have a good, stable, loving relationship. We've become more like equals. I respect her, and I'm proud of her for her courage.

Adult children's reactions vary. Some are rejecting, some are tolerating, and some are very loving. Some invite their transsexual parent to all major family events, even including them in their wedding party, and after they have children of their own, they include the transsexual grandmother or grandfather in the lives of their kids.

Jonathan, age thirty, in spite of some initial apprehensions was supportive of his transitioning father:

I think my father is happier than he's ever been and more open than ever before. There was always a distance between us when I was a kid. I didn't know why. When I found out the news, it was difficult but not relationship-ending. I had to go back and put it in its place.

My father was always the smartest person I knew. If he's improving himself, it would be my loss if I threw him away. But I haven't seen him cross-dressed yet. I told him early on "give me some idea of what to go on, because all I can do is imagine you in this awful polka-dot yellow dress, and the image scares me to death." On the other hand, this is my father, and I love him. If he wants to be a woman, it's OK with me—as long as she continues to love me the way he always has. The bottom line is how she treats me. I just want her to show me that I'm loved.

The initial reactions of parents, spouses, and children of transsexuals discussed in this chapter by no means cover the entire range of possible reactions—but they are typical of the families that I've worked with over the years.

Similarly, the reactions of other relatives such as siblings, aunts, uncles, and cousins can be equally diverse. The only exception I've found in my practice has been grandmothers. In almost every case, grandmothers have been supportive of their transsexual grandchild.

As we have illustrated, although some family members are immediately able to offer love, support, and understanding to the transsexual in their lives, others require more time. Sometimes it takes weeks or months. Other times, it takes years for certain family members to overcome their negativity, anger, pain, and resentment. Fortunately, however, most are eventually able to open their hearts and minds.

Up until now we've shown the psychological, social, and interpersonal aspects of transition for transsexuals who have come out to family and coworkers. The next chapter discusses the physical changes and the various medical and surgical options open to transsexuals.

# 9

## Medical and Surgical Options

Transsexuals living full-time in the opposite gender role want to look authentic and believable. Toward that end, they often undergo hormone therapy, various facial and scalp surgeries, breast and chest surgeries, and in many cases genital sex reassignment surgery. This chapter discusses the most common medical interventions and how they contribute to the transsexual patient's sense of rightness, completion, and wholeness.

### Hormones

The purpose of hormone treatment for transsexuals is twofold. First, physically, hormones reduce the secondary sex characteristics of the original sex and enhance the development of the secondary sex characteristics of the desired sex. Estrogens are given to males to feminize their bodies, and androgens are administered to females to masculinize their bodies. Second, psychologically, hormone treatments result in feelings such as calmness, peacefulness, and a sense of fulfillment and well-being. This could be an effect of the hormones or due to the uplifting feeling that arises from knowing that they are taking a definitive step toward becoming more like the sex that they self-identify as.

According to the Standards of Care (SOC) guidelines, to begin hormone treatment, patients are required to present their physician with a letter from a therapist confirming that they have been diagnosed as transsexual and have undergone a minimum of three months of therapy. Beginning hormone treatment is an eagerly awaited "rite of passage" for transsexuals. As they develop the secondary sex characteristics of the opposite sex, each new bodily change that occurs is a sign of progress and a cause for celebration.

## Female-to-Male Transsexuals

Testosterone, the male hormone, is administered by injection every two to four weeks for FTMs, and generally causes the following changes:

- Growth of facial and body hair
- Thickening of vocal cords so that voice pitch becomes lower
- Increased muscle mass, which results in increased physical strength
- Redistribution of body fat, such as loss of waistline and slimming of hips, although breast size does not decrease
- Coarsening of the skin and possible flare-ups of acne because the skin often becomes oilier
- Thinning of the hair on the head; development, with age, of male-pattern baldness (if part of the person's heredity)
- Cessation of menstruation and reproductive functioning
- Increased libido
- Enlargement of the clitoris

## Male-to-Female Transsexuals

Female hormones, such as estrogen, are administered to MTFs by pill, injection, or skin patches, and generally cause the following changes:

- Growth of breasts
- Softening of the skin
- Redistribution of body fat (typically, waistline becomes smaller, and hips and buttocks become rounder)
- Diminished ability to achieve erections and to ejaculate
- Loss of muscle mass, resulting in less physical strength
- Thinning of body hair
- Cessation of scalp hair loss

## Reactions to Hormone Treatments

Both FTMs and MTFs generally find themselves more emotionally stable and less angry and depressed than before hormone treatment. In addition, many (but not all) MTFs are less stoic and more sentimental and emotional; they may cry easily for the first time in their lives since childhood.

One MTF patient, expressing a typical sentiment, said: "I'm amazed that things that would have driven me out of my mind a few months ago don't faze me anymore. People say that I'm calmer and more open."

An FTM patient made similar comments: "Before I began taking testosterone, I had so many mood swings. Frequently, I would wake up exhausted in the morning and find it difficult to get out of bed. Depression and a 'sucked-down' feeling were more typical than not. Intellectually, I could detach from the physical aspects of menstrual cramps and PMS, but emotionally, I could not. I used to cry or go into rages for no reason—anything could trigger it. Now it's dramatically different. I'm calm, happy, and full of energy."

"Over the past year, I have been delighted at the changes that have occurred," another FTM said. "I now have facial and body hair, a deep masculine voice, a strong jawline, and a renewed libido. My deep depressions completely stopped within one week of the first testosterone injection. Simple things, such as the joy of shaving, have become part of a routine that I look forward to each day.

I have changed my name to Donald and have a new driver's license with a picture that I am proud to show off."

Transsexuals who undergo hormone treatment frequently state that the experience is like going through puberty again. And indeed, even though they are adults and have adult bodies, the hormone regimen that transsexuals follow triggers some of the same secondary sex characteristics and mood fluctuations that teens experience.

"I'm experiencing an incredible rejuvenation from the hormones," said an MTF patient. "I'm forty-three years old and feel like I'm in my twenties. It's remarkable. I now have my long-awaited breasts, and my skin gets softer every day. I was pretty clearly on the road to the blahs—but not so now. The hormones provide me with different insights, emotionally and ego-wise."

## A Spectrum of Changes

Although hormones allow transsexuals to achieve some of the desired physical changes and to become more masculine or more feminine, some areas of the body will not be affected. Basic bone structure (the skeleton) does not change, so height, the width of the pelvis, and the size of the hands and feet cannot be modified with hormones.

The effects of hormone treatment may appear slowly. Some changes occur after six to eight weeks, whereas others may take six to twenty-four months or even longer. In fact, FTMs may not have facial hair growth until they have had four or five years of hormone treatment. And full breast development for MTFs may require ten or even fifteen years.

Because every individual's genetic makeup and metabolism are different, the same hormone in the same dosage can have vastly different effects, much as in puberty. For example, whereas some MTFs will experience hardly any breast growth, others will show substantial development. And for FTMs, facial hair growth ranges from "peach fuzz" to a heavy beard. Since there is no way to predict the precise outcome, patients are cautioned against unrealistic expectations; hormones do not produce rapid or "magical" results.

As with all drugs, there are risks involved in taking hormones. Some possible side effects are increased blood pressure, liver disease, heart disease, and blood clots in the legs. Regular visits to the prescribing physician or endocrinologist are essential in order to check general health; monitor hormone levels, blood chemistry, and blood pressure; and check for any adverse side effects.

Patients need to be forewarned of the potential side effects. They must be made aware that they will have to continue hormone treatments for the rest of their lives and that the long-term risk factors are still unknown. So patients are generally requested to sign an informed-consent release with their physician before they begin treatment. If the patient is married at the time, some physicians will request that the spouse sign a release as well.

Not all transsexuals take hormones. Some, usually for health reasons, cross-live and proceed with the real-life test without hormone treatment and may or may not go on to have SRS.

## Surgical Options

While hormones can help to bring transsexuals' bodies more in line with their gender identity, some patients seek out nongenital cosmetic surgeries to further enhance their masculinization or feminization.

### Cosmetic (Nongenital) Surgery

Transsexuals who undergo cosmetic surgeries report an enhanced self-image, greater self-confidence, and a sense of "congruity" or "rightness" when they look in the mirror and see an image that conforms with their gender identity.

"I had long felt," one patient said, "that my unattractive, large, and rather masculine 'Italian nose' was very much of a problem for me in terms of being able to look like and be socially accepted as a woman, so I spent a lot of time isolated, locked away in my room.

Ever since I had my nose and jawline recontoured, though, I love going out in public. My friends say I've become a social butterfly."

A wide variety of nongenital cosmetic surgeries are available, and the list of surgical specialties is constantly expanding. The following are the most common surgeries that transsexuals may choose to undergo in order to look more attractive and more convincing:

- Tracheal shave—a reduction procedure performed on the cartilage of the trachea that MTFs undergo because most believe that a noticeable or prominent Adam's apple is a "dead giveaway" of maleness.
- Rhinoplasty (nose job).
- Baldness corrective procedures—hair plugs or scalp reduction to decrease areas of baldness.
- Face-lift.
- Acid peel (for younger-looking, less blemished, smoother skin).
- Liposuction of fat deposits on various parts of the body.
- Changing the shape of the forehead, especially the brow and mid-forehead (males tend to have fullness over the brow area, whereas female skulls appear smoother).
- Changing or contouring the shape of the chin (females tend to have a narrower, more pointed chin, while males' chins tend to be broader).
- Modifying the angle and sides of the lower jaw.
- Cheek implants—for augmentation or contouring.
- Voice surgery—a procedure that some MTFs undergo to tighten the vocal cords for greater tension. The results can vary depending on the patient's voice pitch, the technique used, and the skill of the surgeon.

Patients who choose to undergo one or more of these surgeries generally do so when they begin full-time cross-living so that they will look more passable.

## Sex Reassignment Surgery

Sex reassignment surgery (SRS) is surgery on the genitalia or breasts performed for the purpose of altering them to approximate the physical appearance of the genetically other sex.

Although there are no SOC prerequisites for patients seeking nongenital cosmetic surgeries, patients must meet the following requirements before breast and genital surgeries can be performed:

- They must have been under the care of a therapist for at least one year (six months for breast augmentation or mastectomy).
- They must have been diagnosed as gender dysphoric.
- They must have completed the real-life test by living in the opposite gender role for at least one year.
- They must receive a written referral from their primary therapist and a second referral from a clinician other than the therapist. At least one of the two therapists must hold a Ph.D. or M.D. degree.
- They must be in good physical health.

It should be noted that transsexuals must discontinue hormones at least three weeks prior to SRS (and abstain for two weeks afterward) to prevent potentially life-threatening blood clots.

## Male-to-Female Surgeries

The SOC lists two surgeries under the category of genital surgeries—breast augmentation surgery and vaginoplasty.

### Breast Augmentation Surgery

Breasts are an external cultural symbol of femininity and female sexuality and are also associated with the female sustenance and nurturing role. For these reasons, most MTFs look forward to breast development more than any other changes in their body. Breast augmentation is generally sought when hormone treatment does not produce sufficient breast development.

Breast augmentation surgery (also called *augmentation mammoplasty*) is done by inserting saline-filled implants below the breast tissue in order to simulate natural breasts.

As one patient said, "After my breast augmentation surgery, I ran over to the mirror to look at my profile and saw the chest contour that I had always seen in my mind's eye. For the first time in my life, I could look in the mirror and see the woman I always knew I was."

Another patient said, "Why do I feel these feelings, like memories I never had before, that echo through my soul? How could I possibly miss the feeling of lying on my side, one breast laying atop the other, when I never had breasts before? But I did miss that, and now things are right, like they've never been before."

Because breast implants can impair the reading of mammograms, breast augmentation should be carefully considered before surgery is performed.

## Vaginoplasty

*Vaginoplasty* is the construction of the vulva and vagina.

There are two standard methods for creating a vagina. The most common method, *penile inversion*, uses the inverted skin of the penis to create the lining of the vagina. A space is made between the rectum and the urethra. The erectile tissue is removed from the penis and the penile skin is then turned inside out and placed into the new vagina as the lining. When there is not ample penile skin to create adequate depth, a skin graft is taken from the stomach, buttocks, or thigh for that purpose.

The second method, *rectal sigmoid transfer*, uses a segment of the large intestine to create a vaginal lining. The main advantage of this method is that it provides natural lubrication and unlimited vaginal length. Some disadvantages, when compared to the inversion method, are that the rectal sigmoid transfer is more invasive

surgery, costs more, requires a longer hospitalization stay and recu-
peration period, and sometimes results in prolonged mucoid leak-
age through the vagina.

In both methods, the scrotum is removed and the leftover scro-
tal skin is used to create the labia, and part of the glans (head of the
penis) is used to create a clitoris. Most MTF patients have a capac-
ity to be orgasmic postsurgically with either method, and when performed by skilled surgeons, both methods produce female genitalia
that are indistinguishable from that of a genetic female.

## Labiaplasty

The purpose of *labiaplasty* is to form a junction between the inner
and outer labia in order to create a vulva that closely resembles the
vulva of a genetic female. With certain surgical techniques, the
labiaplasty is done at the same time as SRS and is simply an adjunct
to the vaginoplasty procedure. With other techniques, a minimum
of a three-month wait is required after SRS before labiaplasty can
be performed, and it is done on an outpatient basis under local
anesthesia.

## Reactions

Genital sex reassignment gives MTF transsexuals the body and contours they have always dreamed of having. At long last, they can
stand naked in front of a full-length mirror and not be repulsed.
They are free to wear bathing suits or form-fitting slacks or jeans
without embarrassment. Finally, they have the right genitalia with
which to be sexual (if they choose to do so).

Many patients describe SRS as lifesaving or sanity-saving.
"Choosing to undergo SRS for me," one patient said, "involved the
same kind of lifesaving logic as choosing to *not* jump off a cliff. To
choose differently in either case would be a completely irrational
act. When transsexualism is viewed from this context, one sees that
SRS is no more of a lifestyle decision than elective heart surgery, for

instance. SRS is as important to me as water is to someone dying of thirst."

Another patient expressed sentiments about SRS like this: "Being rid of my penis made such a difference in my life! I didn't know how much longer I could go on with that ugly growth dangling there. I would have flown anywhere in the world or given up my career in order to have SRS. I got to the point where even death seemed more palatable than keeping my male genitals. Now I no longer have to worry about telltale bulges and protrusions in places where they don't belong on my body. My genitals fit, my body fits, my clothes fit—*I fit.*"

## Female-to-Male Surgeries

Whereas most MTFs need only vaginoplasty surgery to create the appearance of a complete female genital anatomy, FTMs need at least three surgeries to create a complete male genital anatomy: mastectomy, hysterectomy, and penis construction. Sometimes all three sites are operated on at once, but for most patients, because of cost factors, they are done separately over a period of time.

### Mastectomy

This operation is the first and most common FTM surgery performed. There are two procedures for *mastectomy*, depending on the amount of breast tissue to be removed. For patients with a lot of breast tissue, the breasts are surgically removed and the nipple and areola are repositioned to create a chest that is masculine in appearance. This procedure leaves a rather large scar. For FTMs with small and medium-sized breasts, a small incision is made around the areola, and the excess tissue is removed by liposuction or by a combination of liposuction and surgical removal.

Breasts are visible symbols of femininity and are perceived by FTMs as indisputable evidence of their gender incongruity. Most are repulsed by their breasts and bind them or wear many layers of clothing to conceal them. After their mastectomy, however, they can for the first time publicly wear T-shirts and tank tops and go shirtless on the beach. It is a freeing and exciting experience.

"I am now very comfortable walking around in the world," one patient said. "I am no longer wearing multiple layers of clothing or sitting in a way that would hide the outline of my breasts. I now make big arm movements and am louder and more boisterous because I am not afraid to call attention to myself. I can flirt in public and even walk with my chest out."

One patient used metaphor to express her feelings about her chest and genital surgeries: "Before my surgeries, my life was like a television set that had only the sound but no picture. I could understand what was going on, but I never experienced it as it was intended to be experienced—I only had a glimpse of what life was like. Now everything's there, picture and sound. It is a spiritual and physical awakening for me."

## Internal Reproductive and Sex Organ Surgeries

Most FTMs have all of their internal reproductive organs—the uterus (*hysterectomy*), ovaries (*oophorectomy*), fallopian tubes (*salpingectomy*), and vagina (*vaginectomy*)—removed because for them these are unwanted, unnecessary organs that don't belong in a male body. Furthermore, these organs are possible sites for cancer and, if not surgically removed, would necessitate regular gynecological exams and pap smears. FTMs do not want this reminder of their former lives. They are relieved to be rid of these organs.

*Penis Construction.* There are two surgical methods used to construct a penis—genitoplasty and phalloplasty. *Genitoplasty* (also known as *clitoral release surgery*) is the simplest. In this procedure, the surgeon frees the skin surrounding the hormonally enlarged clitoris and wraps it around the clitoris to form a very small penis (usually thumb-sized or slightly larger) that maintains sensitivity and orgasmic capability but is not generally large enough for intercourse.

In *phalloplasty*, a penis is created from skin transferred from some area of the body, usually the abdomen, groin, thigh, or forearm. This tissue transfer, called a *flap*, requires from two to eight stages of surgery and leaves large scars at the graft sites.

There are two common phalloplasty methods for creating a full-sized penis for the FTM patient—the pedicle flap and the radial forearm flap.

*Pedicle flap.* In this procedure, a tube of skin is raised up out of the groin or the mid-abdominal area and attached to the pubis, with the end result resembling a suitcase handle. Then, in the course of two to four months, secondary procedures are done to augment the blood supply to this flap, cut it free from its origin, and sculpt it so that it resembles a penis. Although the neophallus may look quite realistic, it is highly risky to attempt to create a urethra with this procedure that would allow the FTM to stand up to urinate. Moreover, it lacks sexual feeling and no orgasm or erection is possible. However, temporary stiffeners (silicone rods that can be placed in the phallus at time of use and then removed) or inflatable penile prostheses can be used for penetration. In the latter method, a manual pump is placed in the scrotum and a fluid reservoir in the abdomen and an erection is obtained by squeezing the scrotum.

*Radial forearm flap.* During an extensive operation of up to thirteen hours, skin is taken from a significant area of the forearm along with the blood vessels and nerves that supply it and is fashioned into the shape of a penis. Then, using microsurgery, the arteries, veins, and nerves are hooked up to the arteries, veins, and nerves in the pubis.

The principal advantage of this operation is that the penis appears natural, has sensation, and can have the urethra extended and attached so that one can stand to urinate. Because the nerves are intact, orgasm is possible, but ejaculation is not. As with the pedicle flap procedure, stiffening devices or inflatable prostheses can be used to create erections.

**Scrotum Construction.** The scrotum is formed from the labia majora (outer lips of the vulva). Following the removal of the labia minora (inner lips of the vulva), the labia majora are sewn together on the midline. Inflatable implants are placed under the skin and slowly inflated by injecting saline. Once the expansion is complete, testicular prostheses may be implanted immediately or at some later time. Scrotum construction is generally done at the same time as the genitoplasty or phalloplasty.

**Urethroplasty.** *Urethroplasty*—urethral extension to the end of the glans—is an optional surgical procedure that allows patients to urinate standing up and can be done in conjunction with both genitoplasty and radial forearm flap phalloplasty.

From a psychosocial point of view, the ability to stand while urinating is significant to most FTMs. However, this is a costly surgery with a high complication and failure rate. Patients who desire this surgery should explore it carefully with the surgeon before proceeding.

Though most female-to-male patients would prefer to have a full-sized penis; the vast majority find the invasiveness and scarring of phalloplasty overwhelming (not to mention the cost, which can be as high as $100,000 for the radial forearm flap) and elect not to proceed with it. They may decide to have no genital surgery at all or may postpone the decision in the hope that phalloplasty will be improved in the future. What they are seeking is a technique that is less expensive and causes less scarring, yet provides an organ that is sensitive and aesthetically pleasing as well as functional for both urination and sexual intercourse. For now, the majority of FTMs who do have genital sex reassignment opt for clitoral release and the creation of a scrotum and testicles.

Patients who are planning to have surgery are urged to talk to postoperative transsexuals about their procedures and, if possible, to see the results for themselves. While people don't normally bare their genitals to others, in some cases, postoperative patients are willing to share the benefit of their SRS experiences in order to help others make a responsible, informed decision about proceeding with surgery. Although surgeons have photographs to enable patients to see the results of past operations, it helps to see results firsthand.

## Cost of Sex Reassignment Surgery

Prices for SRS vary enormously, depending on the number of procedures, the length of the hospital stay required, the part of the country where the surgery is performed, and the fee the particular surgeon charges. In the United States today, SRS can cost from $10,000 to $45,000 for MTFs and from $25,000 to $100,000 for FTMs who have a phalloplasty, hysterectomy, vaginectomy, and mastectomy.

In general, costs are higher in major medical centers in the larger cities in the United States. In many European countries, parts of Asia, and Canada, the cost of SRS is approximately one-third to one-half the cost in the United States.

Most insurance companies have exclusion clauses for SRS and related "sex change" procedures and will not pay for them. They consider such procedures "cosmetic, experimental, or elective surgeries." Therefore, transsexuals must usually assume the burden of the medical and surgical fees themselves.

## Surgery Is a Personal Choice

One of the first things people think when they hear the word *transsexual* is "sex change operation," and this phrase often evokes a strong emotional reaction. Although SRS is something that many transsexuals eventually undergo, not all do. It is an individual choice.

For some transsexuals, as long as they can cross-dress and cross-live as their true gender, they do not feel the need to change their physical body surgically. But for most, SRS is an important and positive event that enhances their body image and self-image and frees them to enjoy a better quality of life. Surgery allows MTFs (and some FTMs) to be sexual with sex organs that look and function like "the real thing."

Genital sex reassignment is only one of several choices open to transsexuals. Most transsexuals opt for hormone treatment and full genital SRS; others pursue a variety of options. For example, some transsexuals may be content to cross-live in the opposite gender role with no hormones and no surgery, some may be content with hormonal treatment only, and some FTMs may choose only to have a mastectomy or a hysterectomy and forgo any genital surgeries. Any of these are valid options and can be ends in themselves.

Individual patients must decide which surgical procedures are appropriate for them and how far they want to go. The deciding factor is usually what is affordable and at what point they can stop and still be comfortable with their bodies and themselves.

Because the cost of full SRS can be prohibitively high, some patients have to wait many years between procedures until they save up the money. Some postpone SRS for other reasons, reconsidering it only when they arrive at a different stage or mind-set in their lives and surgery becomes a more viable choice for them.

Whether or not to have sex reassignment surgery is a personal choice. The transsexual journey is unpredictable as to timetable, path, and destination. Like a highway, there are many off-ramps, rest stops, and turnabout points along the way. Transsexuals can always stop, start again, or turn around at any point in the journey. Therapists don't assume that any one step will necessarily lead to the other or that SRS is the end goal of gender therapy. If SRS does occur, most patients no longer consider themselves transsexual because they are hormonally, anatomically, and psychologically the correct sex.

## Life After Sex Reassignment Surgery

For most transsexuals, sex reassignment surgery is psychologically uplifting. They experience an enormous sense of pleasure and well-being in finally having the body they have yearned for ever since they first became aware of their gender dysphoria. After SRS, they are generally happier and much more self-confident.

For some, however, these good feelings are not immediate. For a period after SRS, some transsexuals fall into a depression, not unlike a new mother's postpartum blues. This type of depression usually arises from the letdown that occurs when transsexuals are no longer in the limelight, as is the case for many during transition. It also may be related to unrealistic expectations about life after SRS, which is why it is so important that this be addressed in therapy in advance and that the entire real-life test be completed. For others, the emotional lows after SRS may be attributed to postsurgical complications or poor surgical results—either aesthetic or functional.

Most of those who suffer some post-SRS depression state that they nevertheless feel better than when they were living in the wrong body and gender role. "I may not be ecstatic as Joanne, but I was miserable as Joe," one patient said. "I'd never want to go back to being male." In fact, according to a recent study, very few patients—fewer than 1 percent of FTMs and 1.5 percent of MTFs—regret having had SRS.

Even though patients may not end up with the perfect body, most are realistic and philosophical about their surgical outcome. One patient explains: "I knew going into surgery that the doctor wouldn't be giving me the body of my dreams. He was going to do one thing only—make it impossible for me to ever live as a normal male again. And I wanted that—I wanted it badly. But I couldn't help noticing that the doctor didn't have a magic wand in his medicine kit. And even a magic wand couldn't make anyone into a genetic girl, or rewrite the past."

Life after sex reassignment surgery is seldom idyllic. SRS does not guarantee happiness, nor does it cause gender-related problems to disappear magically. Some postoperative transsexuals still retain anger and shame. Many continue to be frequently "read" and to face harassment and discrimination. In addition, they also, like everyone else, have day-to-day problems. Postoperative transsexuals still have to earn a living; deal with family, relationship, and health concerns; clean the house; pay taxes; and pay their bills. What is different is that now they can do all this without gender dysphoria and with a body and gender identity that are congruent.

# 10

## Guidelines for Support

Even the most supportive coworkers and loving family members and friends can, as we have discussed, have strong responses to discovering that a person they thought they knew is transsexual. They often experience some concern, fear, and discomfort (if not outright negativity) when they first find out. Although these feelings can vary significantly from individual to individual, certain initial reactions and misconceptions are quite common. This chapter presents some of these reactions and their underlying notions, and gives some advice on how you can help yourself and the transsexual person you care about.

## Common Reactions to the News

### "But I Never Saw Any Signs. . . ."

This is a frequent statement of individuals who are close to the transsexual (whether family, friend, or coworker). It's hard for them to believe that someone they thought they knew so well is transsexual because, as far as they were concerned, there were never any signs or evidence. And in some cases, there may truly have been no signs to see. The transsexual may have done such a good job of covering up his or her gender dysphoria that nothing seemed amiss.

In other cases, however, the signs were there. Parents may have noticed that their transsexual child had trouble adjusting to his or her gender role, hated to wear gender-appropriate clothing, or was often depressed. But they may have denied or ignored these signs, hoping that the behaviors would disappear with time. Or a spouse may have noticed anger or distancing on the part of the transsexual or experienced problems with their sex life, but didn't know what to make of those observations. Coworkers may have observed some changes in the transsexual's appearance, but wrote it off as nonconformity or eccentricity.

Frequently people will dismiss the signs they see by saying things such as, "But she dated a lot of boys," "But he married three times," "But he always loved sports," "But she gave birth to two children," or "But he seemed so macho." These statements may well be true, but they don't have anything to do with whether or not a person is transsexual. Just because someone dates, gets married, has children, and seems to fit into a gender role doesn't mean that person can't be transsexual. Just because you didn't see the signs doesn't mean that a person isn't transsexual. Some transsexuals are so skilled at playing a role that no one ever sees signs that would arouse suspicions that something might be wrong.

### "It's Just a Whim. . . ."

Family members may respond to transsexualism by dismissing it as just a whim, a phase, a stage, something that's "here today and gone tomorrow." It's their way of denying the information. Some tend to view it as a revelation that was just arrived at on the day that it was made—sudden, impulsive, and therefore irresponsible and ill-considered.

They may reach these erroneous conclusions because they are caught off-guard. The disclosure is so totally unexpected, the cover-up so superb, that it may seem impulsive.

However, rather than being anything remotely like a whim or a passing fancy, gender dysphoria is a serious lifelong condition that transsexuals spend years struggling to repress, deny, or come to terms with before disclosing to others. As one patient said, "Right. If this is just a phase, it's one that's lasted twenty-five years!"

## "You Must Be Crazy"

Some family members, because they don't understand what is happening, assume that the only possible explanation is that the transsexual is delusional or mentally ill. These individuals may consider a sex change a sick or crazy thing to do, something contemplated only by someone who is out of his or her mind. *But on the contrary, transsexuals are in their right mind—it is their body that is wrong.*

Gender dysphoria is not caused by mental illness, nor is it a mental illness itself. Psychiatric conditions such as clinical depression, however, may be the result of the stress associated with being transgendered.

On the whole, transsexuals are not any "crazier" than the nontransgendered population. Psychiatric clinics and therapists' offices are *not*, after all, filled with transsexual patients but rather with non-gender-conflicted people with a wide range of problems.

## "But You'll Never Be Real. . . ."

The reaction of many who know the transsexual is, "How can you even consider doing this? You will never be real." But the question is, "real" by whose standards? This is a judgment call and one that transsexuals must make for themselves.

When people tell a transsexual male that he'll never be real, they are implying that the transsexual's physical appearance does not match cultural stereotypes of masculinity and femininity. They are focusing on external appearances, rather than on what the transsexual feels inside. The assumption is that a transsexual's future depends on physical characteristics, and if the person can't pass, he or she should not transition.

Accusations such as "you're too tall," "you're too short," "you're too broad and muscular," "you're not muscular enough," "your voice is too deep," and "your walk is too inappropriate" are the kinds of things family members say in response to the transsexual's transition plans. In the interest of discouraging the transsexual from proceeding, they feel compelled to point out "flaws": "You'll never be a real woman because you can't experience menstruation, childbirth, or nursing" or "No matter what you do, you will always look like a man in a dress."

Some family members who say "But you'll never be real" are coming more from a position of concern and apprehension about their loved one's ability to integrate into society and be accepted by others. Patients need to reassure them that although passing is important, it is not the only thing. Being real encompasses so much more than what is going on externally; it especially involves how the transsexual identifies inside.

Transitioning means no more faking or pretending to be someone that one is not. From a transsexual's perspective, transitioning means being *more real* than ever before or being real for the first time.

### "The Person I Knew and Loved Is Gone Forever. . . ."

If transsexuals do eventually decide to transition, they will begin to take steps to change the way they look, act, and dress, but that doesn't mean that they are different from the individuals you've known and loved for many years. If they were kind or funny or intelligent before transition, they will continue to be so after they transition.

The concept of a book jacket illustrates this point nicely. If you take a favorite book of poetry, for example, and put the jacket from a detective novel on it, when you open up the book, all the beautiful words that made you feel good are still inside just as before; only the outside has changed. So it is with the transsexual, only in the case of your transsexual loved one, who no longer has to guard a profound secret, you are likely to find an "improved version" of the person you previously knew.

### "How Could You Choose to Do This . . . ?"

After working with many families over the years, it has become clear that one of the most important things for loved ones to recognize about transsexualism is that it is not a choice. People have no more control over gender dysphoria than they do over their height, bone structure, or skin color. The only choice they have with regard to their gender conflict is whether to take actions to ease it and, if so, which actions.

When people realize that transsexuals are well aware that they may conceivably lose their family, their friends, their jobs, and their savings, they are less likely to think that transsexuals have any choice about the matter.

Why would anyone voluntarily do something that would turn his or her life upside down and inside out? Who, after all, would *choose* transsexualism knowing full well how costly it is going to be emotionally, physically, socially, and financially?

A sentiment every one of my transsexual patients has expressed at one time or another is, "No one would ever choose to be born this way" or "I wouldn't wish this on anyone."

Although transsexuals don't have a choice about their condition, the important thing to remember is that family members, friends, and coworkers *do have a choice* about how they react and respond to transsexualism (or any other shocking news, for that matter). There is no one way to respond to an emotional blow. Remaining angry, ashamed, hurt, and depressed and banishing the transsexual is a choice *you* may make for yourself, but others may choose to deal with transsexualism in different and healthier ways (as demonstrated in Chapter Eight).

Remember, transsexualism doesn't have to ruin or destroy relationships or break up families. Some aspects of the transsexual and the relationship may change, but that doesn't mean that they have to change for the worse.

## Help for Family, Friends, and Coworkers

Changing basic perceptions and attitudes about transsexualism is difficult, and altering expectations, hopes, dreams, and ways of interrelating with a transsexual friend or loved one is even harder.

Everyone involved with a transsexual faces the challenge of adjusting not only to the revelation but also to the transsexual's new gender and gender presentation.

As you look toward creating a better relationship with the transsexual in your life, you might find the following ideas helpful.

## Keep an Open Heart

Even though changes, both good and bad, are an inherent part of life, change is often hard to accept. This is particularly true in the case of the profound changes that occur when a loved one transitions from one gender to the other. It is easy to love and accept people who live up to our expectations. The challenge is to love them even when they don't.

But if you are able to keep an open heart, both for the transsexual in your life and for your own struggles in coming to terms with transsexualism, the changes don't have to devastate you or adversely alter how you feel about the transsexual.

People are resilient and adaptable, especially when given the right tools and support. The fact that you are reading this book means you have a desire to learn and understand more about transsexualism and about the struggle of your transsexual family member or friend. And knowledge is often the first step toward compassion, acceptance, and support.

## Be Patient with Yourself

You may not be a person who adjusts quickly to new situations. Some people simply need more time than others. You may initially be immobilized or move at a snail's pace, and your progress may be filled with starts and stops. You may take two steps forward and then one step back.

Don't be surprised if you become frustrated or impatient at times. The transsexual in your life has had many years to struggle with and get used to a whole spectrum of feelings, doubts, fears, and uncertainties. However, for you, the fact that your friend or loved one is transsexual is new information, and there is a lot to learn and process. You may find that it takes time to absorb all of the changes and all that you need to know about this complex phenomenon, and it may be difficult or even overwhelming at times. So be patient with yourself and give yourself a chance to get used to the situation and to be at peace with it. There is no correct time frame for accomplishing this. Go at your own pace as you learn to adjust and to deal with your feelings.

## Take Time to Grieve

It may be appropriate and necessary to grieve the loss of your son or daughter, sister or brother, father or mother, or friend. It's all right; it's natural and healthy. You probably had particular dreams, expectations, or perceptions of your transsexual loved one that died when you found out about his or her transsexualism. When your dreams die, there is often a great sense of loss, and you may have to go through various grief or mourning stages for that broken dream and its unfulfilled potential. But remember that the death that you are mourning is a symbolic one. Your loved one is still alive. The image presented to the world has changed, but the person's endearing and attractive qualities are the same. So after grieving for your loss, celebrate your gain, the birth of an enriched relationship with unlimited potential that you are going to have in the future with your "new and improved" family member or friend.

## Try Not to Assign Blame

It's human nature to assign blame, or to find reasons, individuals, and circumstances on which to place blame. Try to avoid this urge; it serves no useful purpose. Your loved one is transsexual, and science, as yet, has not provided definitive answers as to what causes transsexualism. Even if we knew the etiology, it wouldn't change the fact that there are transsexuals in the world and one of them happens to be your loved one.

Transsexualism is not the transsexual's fault, nor is it your fault. There is nothing that you or anyone else could have done to prevent this condition. No one is to blame. Life is an obstacle course, and we all face many challenges and hurdles. Transsexualism is one of the hardest ones. Understanding makes it easier.

One of the purposes of this book is to expand your ability to understand the complexities of transsexualism. And understanding is the antidote to blame because it creates compassion and empathy.

## Talk to People

Often when people first hear that a loved one is transsexual, they have a tendency to withdraw from friends and relatives and silently guard their feelings and what appears to be a shameful occurrence in the family. Keeping inner turmoil locked away, however, can lead to stress-induced illnesses. Talking is an excellent way to work through your issues in a less solitary way and create healing.

People find solace and release in talking to others, so vent your emotions. If someone turns away from you or doesn't understand, find others to talk to. And don't let one or two bad experiences discourage you. Keep talking. It helps.

It is especially important to also talk to the transsexual and keep an open dialogue going. Express your concerns and explain how he or she can make things easier for you while you are learning to adjust. If both you and the transsexual in your life are able to communicate openly and honestly about your emotions and to respect each other's feelings along the way, you may find that in time your relationship will blossom and become even stronger than it was before.

## Don't Worry About What Others Will Say

It is difficult for most people not to care about what others think or say. It's natural to be concerned about what relatives, neighbors, and coworkers think, but it's not natural to make their opinions count more than yours. People talk—and sometimes without the best of motives and intentions. They always have, they always will, and nothing is going to change that. But what we can change is our perception of that and move through to a new stage of awareness. It is, after all, just idle talk from people who don't really know the person or understand transsexualism. What they say doesn't matter. What really matters is what *you* (who know and care for the transsexual) think, say, and do.

## Learn

Whenever you must face new or difficult challenges, a good place to start is to obtain all of the relevant facts that will help you become knowledgeable. Make a concerted effort to learn as much as you can about all aspects of transsexualism. It is a subject that may require you to develop a new way of thinking. As one patient put it, "I think a lot of people don't understand that the possibilities are unlimited. The fact that a person can have a gender identity that is entirely different from the one that is visible to the outside world simply does not occur to them." But there is information out there.

Buy books and watch videos on the subject; schedule an information-and-education session with a gender specialist; log on to a transsexual Web site on the Internet and "chat" with transsexuals and their family members; ask questions of them and of the transsexual in your life. The value of learning is that it is one of the most powerful ways to move beyond your fears and misconceptions to a place of understanding and acceptance.

## Get Counseling

Sometimes people find themselves stuck in a state of blame, guilt, and rejection and can't seem to break through these barriers. Therapy provides a forum for addressing and resolving issues. Even those who have not sought therapy in the past may find that the help of a professional, especially a gender therapist, can make a big difference in assisting the whole family to come to terms with transsexualism. Therapy sessions provide a safe place to vent feelings, examine choices, and learn how to cope with life's blows without becoming victimized or paralyzed by them. Counseling from a supportive member of the clergy is often helpful as well.

## Join Support Groups

There's a good reason why support groups of all types are so popular and benefit so many people. No matter what the problem is, it helps to know that there are others struggling with the same issues, and it is beneficial to find out how they are handling the situation.

There are support groups for family and friends of transsexuals in some cities. If there are none in your part of the country, consider forming your own. Also, if you prefer to be anonymous, there are dozens of gender-related resources on the Internet that provide an opportunity for learning about transsexualism and sharing your feelings, getting support, and increasing understanding and empathy.

## Keep Things in Perspective

Sometimes when people receive difficult news, they freeze up and develop tunnel vision. Things may appear bleak and hopeless; they don't see any way to change things for the better. It's important to keep things in perspective and realize that although transsexualism can be a challenge and difficult to accept, there are worse things for families to deal with. Your loved one is not dying a slow, painful death from a horrible disease. Nor has he or she committed some heinous crime. It's not as if you have received news that your family member or friend is a serial killer, a rapist, or a child molester. Instead the transsexual is simply a human being with an emotionally distressing medical condition that he or she is trying to correct. And yet I have seen some families give more support to loved ones who are in prison for committing horrible crimes than to those who simply admit to having been born with gender dysphoria. It is important to remember that you are dealing with a human being who has spent many years in emotional pain and turmoil. Respond to the transsexual as you would to anyone you love who is in pain or conflict.

## Suspend Your Prejudices

The word *prejudice* means to prejudge and reflects an unfortunate and all-too-human tendency. Too often our prejudices are based not on reality but on preconceived notions so that labels such as *homosexual, transvestite*, and *handicapped* immediately bring to mind certain images (usually negative or fear-inducing ones) even if we have never met a person to whom the label applies.

If you grew up in the American culture, the word *transsexual* no doubt evokes similar preconceived, negative images. Demeaning portrayals of transsexuals are pervasive in our society, and it's difficult not to be influenced by them.

Much as we'd like to ask you from this moment on to throw away all prejudice about transsexualism (or anything else, for that matter), it would be an unrealistic request. We know that it is difficult for anyone simply to jettison a lifetime of conditioned responses and beliefs. We are asking instead that you *suspend* your prejudices and old viewpoints and make room for a new vantage point from which to view transsexualism.

If you have always viewed the transsexual in your life as a good and worthwhile human being, yet society says that all transsexuals are strange and sick, can you continue to define transsexuals by society's definition instead of your own? Restructuring is practical and necessary. Start with the love, affection, and respect you already have for the transsexual in your life, and then augment that with the new understanding you have gained from reading this book. Your new point of view will be centered on the knowledge that your transsexual friend or family member, whom you found loving and admirable before, does not fit into society's negative or distorted view of transsexualism. We hope that in time this viewpoint will become firmly entrenched and replace your former one.

## How You Can Help the Transsexual

In times of personal crisis, we all look to important people in our lives for support. During the emotional upheaval that can occur after coming out, transsexuals need the help of family and friends. They look to the people closest to them to understand the changes that are going on and ultimately to accept and love the new emerging opposite-gender person. The friendly acceptance of coworkers makes the transition smoother too.

It's not always easy, but friends, family members, and coworkers can make the journey upon which the transsexual has embarked immeasurably more comfortable with their empathy and support. If you can reach out to the transsexual in some of the following ways, there is a good chance that you will maintain and strengthen an important relationship.

- *Recognize* how important your love, acceptance, and support are to the transsexual.

- *Listen* and be willing to hear what the transsexual has to say without judgment, anger, argument, or confrontation.

- *Learn* more about the person's condition and struggles. Show that you care enough to make an effort to read, ask questions, and educate yourself.

- *Communicate*. Don't shut the transsexual out or give him or her the silent treatment. Keep the lines of communication open between the two of you, even if at first your communication is about your fears and pain.

- *Respect* the person as a human being. Transsexuals don't want to be treated like freaks or oddities. They are not sick or perverted. They have a medical condition. Offer the same respect, courtesy, and compassion that you would like to have in return if you were to announce that you have a medical condition that requires radical treatment.

- *Remember* that being transsexual involves perpetual inner conflict and that you are dealing with someone who is constantly struggling and facing challenges (and probably will continue to do so throughout life). There are few welcome places for transsexuals in this world. Try to create one for them with you.

- *Trust* that what the transsexual is doing is right for that particular person and that he or she has not made this decision frivolously but rather after years of struggle and soul searching. Remain warm and affectionate even if you experience discomfort with the situation at present.

- *Admire* the courage and determination of the transsexual to do what must be done to survive, and let the person know this.

- *Understand* that the basic character, temperament, and personality of the transsexual remain the same as before, with all admirable qualities intact.

- *Empathize*. Try to put yourself in the transsexual's shoes. Envision what it would be like to have to go through the lifetime of emotional pain that the transsexual has experienced. Consider how hard it would be to tell people, "I've switched my gender, my name, everything. You've been an important part of my life, and I'd like you to continue to be." If that were you, wouldn't you want them to continue to care about you?

- *Anticipate* the pleasure of a more positive relationship. If the transsexual in your life seemed troubled and unhappy in the past, with the source of the unhappiness now finally known and addressed, you can look forward to a more satisfying relationship.

Finally, it is often in small but important kindnesses that your empathy and love can be demonstrated. Wordsworth called them "the little unremembered acts of kindness and love."

For example, you can invite your transsexual friend or loved one to your home and include the person in your activities and celebrations. Give gender-appropriate gifts and cards on the person's birthday and other special occasions. Compliment the person's appearance or courage. Always treat the person as the gender with which he or she self-identifies, and use the preferred name and gender-appropriate pronouns. If the transsexual is your own child, fill in the gaps in his or her socialization—teach MTFs what you would have taught a daughter and FTMs what you would have taught a son. Most important for everyone in the transsexual's life, listen to the person's hopes and fears and maintain a warm, loving, friendly attitude and manner.

Your grateful transsexual relative or friend will appreciate your sensitivity and support.

# 11

## In Their Own Words

The journey that transsexuals make from one sex to the other can be long and treacherous. They must listen to the inner voice of their true selves and re-create themselves as they emerge anew, integrating all that they value from their old selves. And because of what they must go through—things that most of us will never have to face ourselves—transsexuals have a truly unique perspective. They've seen life from both sides.

In this chapter, transsexuals speak in their own voices to express themselves—the emotional pain they experience, the highs and lows of transition, and the exhilaration of being free at last.

These are the words of eloquent people caught in extraordinary circumstances. Their words and thoughts capture the essence of what it means to move through the fear and pain of isolation, then social trauma, and finally the joy of personal growth and change. The beauty of these thoughts is the unfolding of the human spirit, the validation of "being" for one's own sake.

### This Moment

I have lived my life for this moment
Every road taken, every poem written
every game won, or lost

every joy, sorrow, anger, or acceptance
has brought me here today

I've traveled far to be here
seen ten thousand sunsets
and ten million drops of rain

I've known love and loss
and birth, and death
I've learned the secret tricks of survival
that nobody could ever teach
all so I could come to this place

## Remarkable Journey

This is a remarkable journey. I'm like Alice
through the looking glass seeing the world
turned inside out and upside down.

I haven't changed my intrinsic outlook on life,
and yet my perspective has shifted almost completely.
The scene is the same, but the watcher's eyes
have somehow changed. The map of my soul remains
  unaltered,
only the context is completely new.

## Is There a Place for Me?

Is there a place for me
Among the beings of light?
Or must I grow like a fungus
Alone in the musty dark?

Am I like a wildflower
Providing beauty in the wilderness?
Or am I like a weed
That needs to be removed from a lawn?

Can I find someone
Who will love me as I am?
Or am I to be doomed
To a life of loneliness?

Is there a place for me
Where I can thrive and provide beauty?
Or am I forever condemned
To the dark ugliness of society's cellar?

## The Girl Beyond the Glass

I always felt when I looked into the mirror
There was someone looking back from there
Somewhere beyond where I could see
Awaited the one who was the real me
She's the girl beyond the glass

And as I'd look into her eyes
I'd see the soul past the disguise
But still I tried to live a lie
And keep her locked away inside
She's the girl beyond the glass

And there within the mirror she waited
Softly calling out to me
With a desire that never faded
She longed to be free
She's the girl beyond the glass

Now so many years have passed
And still she waits beyond the glass
But at last she's breaking through the fear and doubt
And the girl inside the mirror is coming out
She's the girl beyond the glass

*Loneliness and Isolation*

The mind—yearning, seeking, questing, emerging—
   female
The body—betraying the mind—male.
Can one express what it feels like to be transsexual?
Before I was a man and was treated like man.
After I will be woman. Now I am both/neither.
Neither generally wins, excluded from both.

Is it too difficult for others to comprehend
Or is it too difficult for me to explain?
Is there anyone who will accept me as I am
Or will I only be accepted/rejected
For who I was/will be?
Loneliness and isolation nip at the edges of my being.

*Images*

I stand before the mirror, often for minutes at a time,
gazing at my reflection; at the woman I see there
partially hidden by my perception of my still-as-yet
   male body.
My body has started to soften; curves and bumps,
shapes and angles, dissolving slowly (too slowly
   it seems),
under a chemical influence.

By sheer force of will, I draw the female image
out of my reflection, I literally pull it out of the mirror,
inch by inch.

Slowly, as retrieving a stone from quicksand, I close
   my eyes
and slip into the image as if a suit.

Little by little, progress measured hair by hair,
I slide into the image.
I comfort in it, I revel in it. I rejoice in it.
I have met the image, and it is me!

## Hidden Within

She lies half hidden, submerged,
in an ocean of overwhelming frustration.
Waiting and wanting to be herself.
Shame holding her back
Society's shame, but she feels it all the same.

Programmed since childhood to a strict code,
a code that strength of will and determination
alone cannot break.
She tries to be the same, inside she is different,
tears turned bitter with the passage of time
and the futile efforts of others to be understanding.
A pretense. How can they?

To be trapped inside without release, no escape,
suicidal emotions roller coasting and escalating
in a collision course with humanity.
Isolated and outcast.
Deserted on an island of inner turmoil
to feel that there's no hope. Frightened.
Sheer terror once realization is accepted.
Prejudice and humiliation becoming a part of everyday
    existence.

The need to hide away her very presence, as though
    tainted.
The degradation turning to self-pity, then to anger.
A searing red ball lodged in her chest, visible to those
    who know.

Meek sympathy offered but rejected. After all unless
   you're there you will never know. Will you . . .

## Partings

Putting my old heart back on the shelf,
like cracked and ancient pottery,
a sentimental tear slips down my cheek,
and in the place of my old dead heart
now beats something new and strong,
wild and yearning

I place my hand on the hand
of the woman I have spent two decades with,
I can't seem to find the dance,
the love is there,
but we can't connect anymore,
she's sleeping with the ghost,
the ghost of a man who doesn't live in my skin
   anymore
I despair at the infidelity

I am at once lost in melancholy
and touched by promise,
the nostalgia is palpable,
so much lost, so much gained,
tearing away from the past,
set adrift in the sea of possibility,
with only my courage, my woman's heart,
to guide the way, but I am free,
I am free

## A Future Time

I wish I lived in a future time
Where it was accepted that each individual

could choose their own sex.
Till then, it is much easier to change a body
than to change one's heart or soul.

### Freedom!

Free from the prison of my mind
Free from the fear that bound me
Free from denial and guilt and pain
Free of the sorrows of the past

Free to experience passion and joy
Free to grow, free to feel, free to love, free to laugh
Free to cry, free to sing, free to live rather than merely
   exist

Free to walk my own path
Free to follow my dreams
Free to embrace the splendor and the beauty
Free to explore; free to be me

### Hello Out There

I may be your friend, lover, or colleague.
I may be your physician, lawyer, minister, or anyone.
You see me but have never seen me.
You know me but you really don't know me.
In fact, I don't really know myself, but I'm trying.

I am a transgendered person; you know, one of those
   odd people
you've read about or have seen on a talk show.
My brothers and sisters are more numerous than you
   think.
Why don't you see us? Because we are afraid of you,
of what you will say and how you will treat us when
   you know.

So we hide.
That is, we hide until we can stand the shadows
   no longer.
Then, for a number of us it means a terrifying
   beginning,
for others it means the end of life.

You are lucky. Your genetic gender, your gender identity
and your sexual preference are aligned with society's
   "norm."
Everyone questions who they are, but imagine that
   question
repeated a thousand times each day, even invading
   your dreams.
But really try to imagine *not knowing the answer!*
That is the "norm" for us.

So why am I telling you all of this?
Because you may be there when one of us finally
   attempts
the transition from one gender role to the other.
This is the most difficult time for a transgendered
   person.
Try to envision what it would be like to have to live
through your teenage years but as an adult.
We will make mistakes and dress funny,
but we do not wish to harm anyone.

We are also very lonely because people tend to avoid us.
So I am asking you to be patient and try to understand
even if you don't wish to help.
If you do wish to help, you may find a rewarding
   experience;
we will learn and grow together.

# Resource Guide

This list has been compiled to help transsexuals and other transgendered individuals, their families and loved ones, friends, coworkers, and the helping professionals who serve the transgender community find support and resources for their personal and professional needs. We have tried to provide up-to-date information; however, phone numbers, addresses, and Web sites frequently change.

The list has more resources on the West Coast because that is the area we are most familiar with. Local resources for other areas of the United States and other countries can be located by contacting any of the organizations found on this list, by contacting a gender clinic or mental health services agency in your area, by obtaining a copy of a transgender publication or newsletter (which will include resource lists), or by logging on to transgender resources available on the Internet.

## Resources for Professionals Serving the Transgender Community

Harry Benjamin International Gender Dysphoria Association
(HBIGDA)
3790 El Camino Real, #251
Palo Alto, CA 94306
(415) 322-2335

HBIGDA is a professional membership organization of gender-specializing counselors, psychotherapists, psychiatrists, surgeons, and researchers. They hold professional-level conferences at international locations and publish *HBIGDA: Standards of Care* for transsexual medical and psychological treatment. They also publish a newsletter, an international membership directory, and periodic bulletins.

## Resources for Youth and Young Adults

Gender Minority Youth Project
1609 Church Street
San Francisco, CA 94131
(415) 641–8890
Counseling for gender-questioning youth between fourteen and twenty-three without the ability to pay who are referred by an agency.

Lavender Youth Recreation and Information Center (LYRIC)
127 Collingwood Street
San Francisco, CA 94114
(415) 703–6150
(415) 863–3636   Youth talk line
(800) 246-PRIDE Youth talk line (for out of the area)
(415) 431–8812   TDD
E-mail: LYRIC.talkline.info@TLG.net
Social interaction and activities for transgendered, gay, lesbian, bisexual, and questioning youth. Sponsors monthly discussion groups and other gender-oriented events.

Teenage Kids of Ts
1740 S. Buckley Road, #6-178
Aurora, CO 80017
Support group for children of T-persons.

## National and International Organizations

American Educational Gender Information Service (AEGIS)
P.O. Box 33724
Decatur, GA 30033–0724
(770) 939–2128 Business
(770) 939–0244 Information and referrals
(770) 939–1770 Fax
E-mail: aegis@mindspring.com
AEGIS is a nonprofit clearinghouse for information about transgender and transsexual issues. It publishes *Chrysalis: The Journal of Transgressive Gender Identities* and *AEGIS News*, a newsletter, and maintains the National Transgender Library & Archive, a large collection of material that is available to the public.

FTM International
5337 College Avenue, #142
Oakland, CA 94618
(510) 287–2646
Internet: http://www.ftm-intl.org/
FTM is a not-for-profit educational and networking group providing specialized information on FTM issues. This organization publishes a quarterly *FTM Newsletter* and sponsors local support groups in San Francisco and Oakland and an annual FTM conference for professionals and transgendered individuals.

Gender Identity Center of Colorado (GIC)
1455 Ammons Street, Suite 100
Lakewood, CO 80215
(303) 202–6466
Internet: http://www.transgender.org/tg/gic/index.html
GIC provides information and education on the issues of crossdressing and gender conflict through a library of books and articles, workshops, seminars, and a speaker's bureau.

International Conference on Transgender Law and Employment Policy (ICTLEP)
P.O. Drawer 35477
Houston, TX 77235–5477
(713) 777–8452 Voice
(713) 777–0909 Fax
E-mail: ictlep@aol.com
ICTLEP is a nonprofit organization that organizes an annual international law conference dealing with a wide range of legal, employment, and medical policies affecting transgendered persons.

International Foundation for Gender Education (IFGE)
P.O. Box 229
Waltham, MA 02154–0229
(617) 894–8340
E-mail: IFGE@world.std.com
Internet: http://www.transgender.org/tg/ifge/index.html
IFGE is a nonprofit membership organization providing information and educational resources for the transsexual/transvestite (TS/TV) community, family members, and professionals. It holds a convention in a different city each year, publishes *TS/TV Tapestry Journal*, a quarterly newsletter, and pamphlets and books. IFGE's publications include a directory of organizations and services, which lists nonprofit support organizations and helping services.

Intersex Society of North America (ISNA)
P.O. Box 31791
San Francisco, CA 94131
E-mail: info@isna.org
Internet: http://www.isna.org
ISNA is a peer support, educational, and advocacy group founded and operated by and for intersexuals, or persons born with mixed sexual anatomy. Their goals are to provide a safe space and community support for intersexuals to share their experience and heal together. They advocate a new paradigm for the management of intersexed infants and children, based on qualified mental health

care for the child and his/her family, complete disclosure, and avoidance of harmful and unnecessary genital surgeries.

Outreach Institute of Gender Studies
126 Western Avenue, Suite 246
Augusta, ME 04330
(207) 621–0858
This institute sponsors a service for helping professionals (GAIN), seminars and workshops, books, publications, and hard-to-find videos on cross-gender behavior. It also provides Theseus Counseling Services (617/868–3157), which specializes in gender issues.

Renaissance Education Association, Inc.
987 Old Eagle School Road, Suite 719
Wayne, PA 19087
(610) 975–9119
E-mail: bensalem@cpcn.com
Renaissance is a national nonprofit organization that sponsors local support groups. It publishes a monthly newsletter, *Renaissance News and Views*, that provides an open forum for the discussion of gender-related social, political, and legal issues and provides information about events in the transgender community. It also operates a speakers' bureau. There are four chapters and thirteen affiliates in nine states.

TransParent
P.O. Box 2122
Harrisburg, PA 17105
This organization is for parents of transgendered individuals. Please contact by mail.

## West Coast Gender Support Groups, Centers, Organizations, and Health Clinics

Asian AIDS Project (AAP)
785 Market Street, Suite 420

San Francisco, CA 94103
(415) 227–0946
AAP provides HIV/AIDS information and prevention education
to the Asian/Pacific Islander. It sponsors a transgender support (rap)
group targeting Asian and Pacific Islander transsexuals but open to
all transgendered people.

The Billy deFrank Lesbian and Gay Community Center
175 Stockton Avenue
San Jose, CA 95126
(408) 293–2429
E-mail: bdfcpres@aol.com
Internet: http://www.rahul.net/rhollis/bdf
This nonprofit organization (home to over 60 groups) offers support
groups, activities, referrals, and a large lending library and archives
for the lesbian and gay, bisexual, and transgendered community.

Diablo Valley Girls (DVG)
P.O. Box 272885
Concord, CA 94527
(510) 849–4112
Diablo Valley Girls is an informal social club and support group in
the Concord–Walnut Creek area, just east of San Francisco, and is
an affiliate of ETVC. DVG publishes a monthly newsletter.

Education TV Channel (ETVC)
P.O. Box 426486
San Francisco, CA 94142
(415) 564–3246 Hotline
(415) 334–3439 Voice mail
(415) 239–8467 BBS (2400 baud)
(415) 664–1499 Information on significant-other support groups
Internet: http://www.zoom.com/personal/cindym/indextg.html
ETVC is an active support organization serving the educational,
social, and recreational needs of "gender-challenged" people; their

spouses, significant others, family members, and friends; and help-ing professionals. This group publishes the *ETVC Newsletter*, offers various support groups for transgendered individuals and their sig-nificant others, sponsors monthly social activities, and maintains a lending library.

Gender Dysphoria Program of Orange County, Inc.
32158 Camino Capistrano, Suite 203
San Juan Capistrano, CA 92675
(714) 240–7020
This program for gender dysphoric persons offers evaluative and treatment techniques (with extensive screening and interaction with patients) but at minimum cost and geared to integration into the mainstream of society. It permits patients to explore alterna-tives to sex reassignment while providing an effective support mechanism during transistion. The four-block procedure consists of intake, transition/support, surgery approval/disapproval, and follow up.

Ingersoll Gender Center
1812 East Madison, #106
Seattle, WA 98122
(206) 329–6651
Internet: http://www.halcyon.com/ingersol/iiihome.html
Ingersoll provides MTF and FTM support groups and publishes *Information for the Female-to-Male Cross-Dresser and Transsexual* by Lou Sullivan, as well as a local newsletter.

Los Angeles Gender Center
3331 Ocean Park Boulevard, Suite 100
Santa Monica, CA 90405
(310) 475–8880
This center is a collaborative of mental health professionals who pro-vide counseling for individuals and their families dealing with gender-related issues. Services include individual, family, group therapy, and

education related to cross-dressing/transsexual/lesbian/gay/bisexual issues. A screening session with psychotherapist is required.

Loved Ones of Transsexuals
Irvine, CA 92715
(714) 786–6891
This organization, facilitated by the mother of a transsexual, is a self-help support group for transsexuals, their loved ones, and interested medical professionals. Please contact by phone.

Pacific Center for Human Growth
2712 Telegraph Avenue
Berkeley, CA 94705
(510) 841–6224
This center has various gender support groups for members of the bisexual, gay/lesbian, transvestite, and transsexual community.

Rainbow Gender Association (RGA)
P.O. Box 700730
San Jose, CA 95170
(408) 984–4044
(408) 248–4162 BBS
RGA publishes a newsletter every other month and is a social club for individuals interested in gender issues.

Sacramento Gender Association (SGA)
P.O. Box 215456
Sacramento, CA 95821
(916) 482–7742
SGA serves the educational, social, and recreational needs of the gender-challenged community.

Silicon Valley Gender Association (SVGA)
c/o Billy deFrank Lesbian and Gay Community Center
175 Stockton Avenue

San Jose, CA 95126
(408) 293–2429
SVGA is dedicated to providing advocacy, education, and support to the transgendered community. It has twice-monthly support groups and political action committees.

Tenderloin AIDS Resource Center
187 Golden Gate Avenue
San Francisco, CA 94102
(415) 431–7476
Transgender support groups meet regularly (including peer support and substance abuse recovery).

The Transgender Counseling and Research Center
4545 Park Boulevard, Suite 207
San Diego, CA 92116
(619) 542–0088, ext. 1
The center provides counseling, support groups, and education from pre-transition to post-op and beyond. It follows Benjamin SOC.

Transgender Nation
584 Castro Street #288
San Francisco, CA 94114
(415) 586–6409
Transgender Nation works specifically for transgender rights regardless of sexual orientation or attraction.

Transgender Tuesday (TGT)
Tom Waddell Clinic
50 Ivy Street
San Francisco, CA 94102
(415) 554–2950
This transgender clinic provides comprehensive medical care and a support group. Open every Tuesday evening. Appointments are preferred.

Transsexuals Support Group
Community Counseling Center
1120 Almond Tree Lane
Las Vegas, NV 89104
(702) 594–7884
The group holds twice-monthly meetings. They will consider hormones, doctors, surgery, name changes, passing problems, relationships, careers and job problems, and educational issues and provide a non-threatening environment for spouses, significant others, and family members.

## Hotlines

These hotlines are run by nonprofit organizations and may not be answered live at all times. Listings are primarily transsexual-oriented groups (rather than groups for both transvestites and transsexuals).

### New England and North Atlantic

| | | |
|---|---|---|
| East Coast F2M Group | Cambridge, MA | (413) 584–7616 |
| Gender Identity Program | New York, NY | (212) 969–0888 |
| XX (Twenty) Club | Hartford, CT | (203) 646–8651 |

### South

| | | |
|---|---|---|
| Atlanta Gender Explorations | Atlanta, GA | (404) 962–3118 |
| Fantasia | Orlando, FL | (407) 425–4527 |
| Montgomery Institute | Augusta, GA | (404) 603–9426 |
| Montgomery Institute | Gainesville, FL | (352) 462–4826 |

### Midwest

| | | |
|---|---|---|
| Gender Dysphoria | Shawnee Mission, KS | (913) 371–0658 |
| NGDO | Detroit, MI | (313) 842–5258 |

### Southwest and Mountain Region

| | | |
|---|---|---|
| ReCast | Dallas, TX | (214) 641–4842 |
| TS Peer Support | Houston, TX | (713) 333–2278 |
| Texas Association of Transsexuals | Houston, TX | (713) 435–7293 |

### Pacific Northwest

| | | |
|---|---|---|
| Transsexual Lesbians and Friends | Seattle, WA | (206) 292–1037 |

### California

| | | |
|---|---|---|
| American Transsexual Educational Center | Hollywood, CA | (213) 389–6938 |
| ETVC | San Francisco, CA | (415) 564–3246 |

### Canada

| | | |
|---|---|---|
| Entre Femme | Quebec, Ont. | (418) 529–1132 |

## Internet Resources

### Transgender Newsgroups

alt.transgendered

soc.support.transgendered

alt.personals.transgendered

### Discussion Lists

| List name | Address | Subscription request |
|---|---|---|
| AEGIS-List | majordomo@lists.mindspring.com | subscribe aegis-list (your e-mail address) |

| | | |
|---|---|---|
| TGS-PFLAG | tgs-pflag@mtcc.com | subscribe tgs-pflag (your e-mail address) |
| Tg-Spirit | listserv@listserv.aol.com | subscribe tg-spirit (your name) |
| Transactive-l | listserv@netcom.com | subscribe transactive-l (your e-mail address) |
| Transgen | listserv@brownvm.brown.edu | subscribe transgen (your name) |
| Tsmenace | majordomo@zoom.com | subscribe tsmenace (your e-mail address) |
| Bisexu-l | listserv@brownvm.brown.edu | subscribe bisexu-l (your name) |
| GLB-News | listserv@listserv.aol.com | subscribe glb-news (your name) |

## IRC Sites

#Transgen

#Crossdress

America Online (AOL) Transgender Community Forum (Type "Go TCF")

## Anonymous ftp

ftp://ftp.mindspring.com/users/aegis (user ID: anonymous; password: your e-mail address)

ftp.netcom.com/pub/os/osprey

## Gopher

gopher.casti.com/70/11/gaystuff/QRD/trans

## World Wide Web

Numerous personal and community-related resources are included here. Julie Pond and Transgender Forum are especially recommended. Be aware that Web sites vary in quality and frequently change or disappear.

| | |
|---|---|
| Above and Beyond | http://www.abmall.com |
| And Justice for All | http://www.qrd.org/qrd/ www/orgs/aja/home.htm |
| Blur Your Gender | http://drycas.club.cc.cmu. edu/~julie/ |
| Community United Against Violence | http://www.xq.com/cuav/index.html |
| Creative Design Services (CDS) | http://www.cdspub.com/index2.html |
| Gender and Sexuality | http://english-server.hss.cmu.edu/ Gender.html |
| Gender Issues Directory | http://www.cpsr.org/dox/program/ gender/index.html |
| Julie Pond | http://www.pond.com/julie |
| Nu-Woman Transgender Cabaret | http://www.nu-woman.com |
| Parents and Friends of Lesbians and Gays (P-FLAG) | http://www.critpath.org/pflag-talk/ |
| Phoenix Project | http://www.abmall.com/tss/tss.html |
| Pooh's Page | http://members.gnn.com/pooh/index.htm |
| Scandinavian Tg-Page | http://www.oslonett.no/home/jane/ index.html |
| Tennessee Vals | http://www.transgender.org/tg/ |
| Transgender Forum | http://www.tgforum.com/ |
| T-Star | http://travesti.geophys.mcgill.ca/tstar |

# Notes

## Introduction

P. 2, *transsexuals make up less than 1 percent of the population:* American Psychiatric Association, *Diagnostic and Statistical Manual of Mental Disorders,* 4th ed. (Washington, D.C.: American Psychiatric Association, 1994).

## Chapter One

P. 9, *1 per 30,000 adult males and 1 per 100,000 adult females:* American Psychiatric Association, *Diagnostic and Statistical Manual of Mental Disorders,* 4th ed. (Washington, D.C.: American Psychiatric Association, 1994), p. 635.

P. 9, *an estimated 6,000 to 10,000 transsexuals had undergone SRS:* Richard F. Docter, *Transvestites and Transsexuals: Toward a Theory of Cross-Gender Behavior* (New York: Plenum, 1988), p. 26.

P. 9, *U.S. population in 1988:* Mark S. Hoffman (ed.), *The World Almanac, 1989* (New York: Pharos Books, 1989), p. 217.

P. 9, *scores of unoperated cases:* Wardell Pomeroy, "The Diagnosis and Treatment of Transvestites and Transsexuals," *Journal of Sex & Marital Therapy,* 1975, *1*(3), 217.

P. 9, *an MTF-to-FTM ratio as high as 50 to 1:* Pomeroy, "The Diagnosis and Treatment of Transvestites and Transsexuals," p. 217.

P. 9, *MTF-to-FTM ratio to be 3 to 2:* Docter, *Transvestites and Transsexuals,* p. 36.

P. 9, *equal number of male and female transsexuals:* Leslie M. Lothstein, *Female-to-Male Transsexualism: Historical, Clinical, and Theoretical Issues* (New York: Routledge, 1983), p. 76; Lou Sullivan, *Information for the Female-to-Male Crossdresser and Transsexual,* 3rd ed. (Seattle: Ingersoll Press, 1990).

P. 9, *even more FTMs than MTFs:* Lothstein, *Female-to-Male Transsexualism,* p. 310.

P. 11, *Estimates of attempted suicide:* Anne Bolin, *In Search of Eve: Transsexual Rites of Passage* (New York: Bergin & Garvey, 1988), p. 57.

P. 12, *Typically, transvestites are . . . :* Virginia Prince, *The Transvestite and His Wife* (Los Angeles: Chevalier Publications, 1967), p. 35; Kim Elizabeth Stuart, *The Uninvited Dilemma: A Question of Gender. A Researched Look into the Myths and Real-Life Experience of Transsexuality* (Lake Oswego, Oreg.: Metamorphous Press, 1983).

P. 14, *women almost never have fetishistic tendencies:* Pomeroy, "The Diagnosis and Treatment of Transvestites and Transsexuals," p. 217.

P. 15, *5 percent of the total gay population:* Deborah Feinbloom, *Transvestites and Transsexuals* (New York: Delacorte Press, 1976), p. 124.

P. 16, *She-males are men:* Ray Blanchard, "The She-Male Phenomenon and the Concept of Partial Autogynephilia," *Journal of Sex & Marital Therapy,* 1993, 19(1), 69.

P. 16, *distinguished by flamboyant feminine attire:* Docter, *Transvestites and Transsexuals,* p. 35.

P. 16, *These men are less likely to pursue surgical sex reassignment:* Blanchard,

"The She-Male Phenomenon and the Concept of Partial Autogy-nephilia," p. 75.

P. 18, *a form of denial:* Lothstein, *Female-to-Male Transsexualism*, p. 69; Pomeroy, "The Diagnosis and Treatment of Transvestites and Transsexuals," p. 217; R. J. Stoller, *Sex and Gender* (Northvale, N.J.: Aronson, 1975).

P. 21, *by the time we are five:* Bolin, *In Search of Eve*, p. 45.

P. 22, *disturbed interaction:* D. F. Swaab and M. A. Hofman, "Sexual Differentiation of the Human Hypothalamus in Relation to Gender and Sexual Orientation," *Trends in Neuroscience*, 1995, *18*(6), 269.

P. 23, *key area of the hypothalamus:* "Study: Male Transsexuals' Brains Resemble Women's," *The Washington Post*, Nov. 2, 1995.

P. 24, *home environment and patterns of rearing have a powerful impact:* Docter, *Transvestites and Transsexuals*, pp. 84–87.

P. 24, *parents are physically or emotionally absent:* Robert J. Stoller, "Etiological Factors in Female Transsexualism," *Archives of Sexual Behavior*, 1972, *2*, 47; Robert J. Stoller, *Sex and Gender*.

P. 24, *smothering, overbearing mother:* Bolin, *In Search of Eve*, p. 57.

P. 25, *genetic predisposition:* John Money, "The Concept of Gender Identity Disorder in Childhood and Adolescence After Thirty-Nine Years," *Journal of Sex & Marital Therapy*, 1994, *20*(3), 163–167.

P. 26, *François Timoléon de Choisy:* Peter Ackroyd, *Dressing Up: Transvestism and Drag: The History of an Obsession* (New York: Simon & Schuster, 1979), p. 84.

P. 26, *Chevalier d'Éon:* Ackroyd, *Dressing Up: Transvestism and Drag*, p. 78.

P. 26, *Edward Hyde:* Ackroyd, *Dressing Up: Transvestism and Drag*, p. 84.

P. 27, *female pirates:* Ackroyd, *Dressing Up: Transvestism and Drag*, p. 76.

P. 28, *the word* transsexualism: D. Cauldwell, "Psychopathic Transexualis," *Sexology, 16,* 274–280.

## Chapter Two

P. 32, *By age five, most children are fully aware:* John Archer and Barbara Lloyd, *Sex and Gender* (Harmondsworth, England: Penguin Books, 1982) pp. 206–207.

P. 33, *Robert Fulghum's story "Giants, Wizards, and Dwarfs":* Robert Fulghum, *All I Really Need to Know I Learned in Kindergarten: Uncommon Thoughts on Common Things* (New York: Random House, 1986), pp. 81–82.

## Chapter Five

P. 108, *psychiatric disorders . . . not considered contraindications:* Highlights of the Harry Benjamin International Gender Dysphoria Association meeting, Kloster Irsee, Germany, Sept. 7–10, 1995, p. 1.

P. 113, *anger alienates us from others:* Theodore I. Rubin, *The Angry Book* (New York: Macmillan, 1969), p. 157.

P. 115, *self-condemnation and the self-loathing that shame precipitates:* Carl Goldberg, *Understanding Shame* (Northvale, N.J.: Aronson, 1991), p. 8.

## Chapter Six

P. 144, *one transsexual who was involved in a car accident: In Your Face* newsletter, Fall 1995, pp. 2–3.

## Chapter Eight

P. 188, *children raised in transsexual households:* Richard Green, "Sexual Identity of Thirty-Seven Children Raised by Homosexual or Transsexual Parents," *American Journal of Psychiatry,* 1978, *135*(6), 693.

# Chapter Nine

P. 211, *fewer than 1 percent of FTMs and 1.5 percent of MTFs:* Friedemann Pfafflin, "Regrets After Sex Reassignment Surgery," *Gender Dysphoria: Interdisciplinary Approaches in Clinical Management,* Walter Bockting and Eli Coleman, eds. (Binghamton, N.Y.: Haworth Press, 1992), p. 78.

# Selected Bibliography

Ackroyd, P. *Dressing Up: Transvestism and Drag: The History of an Obsession.* New York: Simon & Schuster, 1979.

American Psychiatric Association. *Diagnostic and Statistical Manual of Mental Disorders. (4th ed.)* Washington, D.C.: American Psychiatric Association, 1994.

Archer, J., and Lloyd, B. *Sex and Gender.* Harmondsworth, England: Penguin Books, 1982.

Benjamin, H. *The Transsexual Phenomenon.* New York: Julian Press, 1966.

Benjamin, H. "Should Surgery Be Performed on Transsexuals?" *American Journal of Psychotherapy,* 1971, 35(1), 74–82.

Blanchard, R. "The She-Male Phenomenon and the Concept of Partial Autogynephilia." *Journal of Sex & Marital Therapy,* 1993, 19(1), 69–76.

Blanchard, R., and Steiner, B. *Clinical Management of Gender Identity Disorders in Children and Adults.* Washington, D.C.: American Psychiatric Press, 1990.

Bockting, W. O., and Coleman, E. (eds.). *Gender Dysphoria: Interdisciplinary Approaches in Clinical Management.* Binghamton, N.Y.: Haworth Press, 1992.

Bolin, A. *In Search of Eve: Transsexual Rites of Passage.* New York: Bergin & Garvey, 1988.

Bornstein, K. *Gender Outlaw: On Men, Women and the Rest of Us.* New York: Routledge, 1994.

Docter, R. F. *Transvestites and Transsexuals: Toward a Theory of Cross-Gender Behavior.* New York: Plenum, 1988.

Eaton, T. "Japan's FTM Performers Achieve Cult Status." Synopsis of article from *Baltimore Morning Sun*, Nov. 21, 1994. *FTM Newsletter*, Apr. 1995.

Feinbloom, D. *Transvestites and Transsexuals: Mixed Views*. New York: Delacorte Press, 1976.

Friedl, E. *Women and Men: An Anthropologist's View*. Austin, Tex.: Holt, Rinehart and Winston, 1975.

Green, J. "Investigation into Discrimination Against Transgendered People." A report by the Human Rights Commission, City and County of San Francisco, Sept. 1994.

Griffin, C. W., Wirth, M. J., and Wirth, A. G. *Beyond Acceptance: Parents of Lesbians and Gays Talk About Their Experiences*. New York: St. Martin's Press, 1986.

Katz, J. L. "Biological and Psychological Roots of Psychosexual Identity." *Medical Aspects of Human Sexuality*, June 1972, 6(6), 103–116.

Lothstein, L. M. *Female-to-Male Transsexualism: Historical, Clinical, and Theoretical Issues*. New York: Routledge, 1983.

Money, J. *Sex Errors of the Body: Dilemmas, Education, Counseling*. Baltimore, Md.: Johns Hopkins University Press, 1968.

Money, J. "The Concept of Gender Identity Disorder in Childhood and Adolescence After Thirty-Nine Years." *Journal of Sex & Marital Therapy*, 1994, 20(3), 163–178.

Money, J. and Walker, P. A. "Counseling the Transsexual." In J. Money and N. Musaph (eds.), *Handbook of Sexology*. New York: Elsevier/North Holland Biomedical Press, 1977.

Pomeroy, W. "The Diagnosis and Treatment of Transvestites and Transsexuals." *Journal of Sex & Marital Therapy*, 1975, 1(3), 215–224.

Saltzman, J. *Masculine/Feminine or Human? An Overview of the Sociology of Sex Roles*. Itasca, Ill.: Peacock, 1974.

Steiner, B. W. (ed.). *Gender Dysphoria: Development, Research, Management*. New York: Plenum, 1985.

Stoller, R. J. *Sex and Gender*. Northvale, N.J.: Aronson, 1975.

Stuart, K. E. *The Uninvited Dilemma: A Question of Gender. A Researched Look into the Myths and Real-Life Experience of Transsexuality*. Lake Oswego, Oreg.: Metamorphous Press, 1983.

Sullivan, L. *Information for the Female-to-Male Crossdresser and Transsexual*. (3rd ed.) Seattle: Ingersoll Press, 1990.

# The Authors

Mildred L. Brown is a clinical sexologist and therapist in private practice in Los Gatos, California. She holds a Ph.D. degree in Human Sexuality from the Institute for Advanced Study of Human Sexuality in San Francisco, where she has been a professor of clinical sexology since 1980.

Brown is certified as a sex therapist by the American Association of Sex Educators, Counselors, and Therapists (AASECT) and as a clinical sexologist and clinical supervisor by the American Board of Sexology (ABS). For the last twelve years, she has been a member of the Harry Benjamin International Gender Dysphoria Association (HBIGDA), the organization that sets the Standards of Care for professionals who treat transsexuals.

An internationally recognized sexologist, Brown has participated in panel discussions on transsexualism, been interviewed for numerous newspaper articles and radio shows, and appeared on the television show *People Are Talking* and the HBO special *What Sex Am I?* Her articles covering the physical, psychological, and cultural components of human sexuality and related aspects of family life have been published in *Medical Aspects of Human Sexuality*, a journal for physicians, and in the *Journal of Sex Research*, a publication of the Society for the Scientific Study of Sex.

Although Brown treats couples and individuals for traditional sex problems, since 1979 she has specialized in helping transsexuals, transvestites, and other transgendered individuals resolve their gender identity problems. She conducts group therapy for transsexuals; leads workshops and support groups for their spouses, children, and family members; and consults with various corporations on gender issues.

*Chloe Ann Rounsley* is a San Francisco–based writer, journalist, and marketing consultant with her own firm, Rounsley Associates. In addition to more than fifteen years of work in corporate communications, she has conducted extensive research on the topic of transsexualism.

# Index